THE
SECOND
COMING

p. 33-55

p. 161-188

"Presupposition of a
Wesleyan Eschatology"

THE
SECOND
COMING

A WESLEYAN APPROACH
TO THE
DOCTRINE OF LAST THINGS

H. RAY DUNNING, EDITOR

Beacon Hill Press of Kansas City
Kansas City, Missouri

CONTENTS

INTRODUCTION

Wesleyan scholars have been noticeably silent for several decades on the subject of last things, known as *eschatology*. Several reasons for this may be given, but because of it there have been some unfortunate consequences. Thus, this book is an effort on the part of biblical, theological, and historical scholars in the Wesleyan tradition to both address this void and seek to impact the serious theological problems that have emerged around the subject of eschatology during this "silent period."

Wesleyan theology has been primarily preoccupied throughout its American history with its distinguishing emphasis, the doctrine of Holiness. Efforts to address some of the knotty problems biblically, theologically, psychologically, and practically have consumed the time and energy of most of those in the tradition who write on religious topics.

The outcome of this silence by competent scholars has resulted in what William Barclay said about Rev. 20: Eschatology has become the "playground of the eccentrics." While we have been busy with other themes, foreign ideas have virtually stolen the store in this area of theology, with the odd phenomenon that eschatological teachings that are contrary to both good biblical scholarship and Wesleyan theology have virtually assumed the status of orthodoxy among Wesleyans, as well as among other evangelical Christians.

This fact has created a climate in which it is professionally risky to speak the truth and any who venture to speak out are precipitously criticized and maligned. Thus, to our discredit, we have simply been prudently silent. The idea of this anthology is an attempt to hear several voices from a broad perspective so that the interested and open-minded student can see that Wesleyan scholars present a solid phalanx on this topic. Without collaboration, it is amazing how the scholars contributing to this symposium concur in basic perspective and biblical interpretation.

J. B. Chapman once sagely observed that if we were silent on any subject for a generation, it would be lost from the church. While he was speaking specifically about the doctrine of entire sanctification, his prediction has all but come true with regard to biblical eschatology. This contribution is an effort to reverse the effect of the recent silence. I say "recent" because early scholars of the Holiness Movement spoke out vigorously against the views that have become so popular in Wesleyan circles today.[1]

The essays that comprise this volume are not direct attacks upon the prevailing nonbiblical views, although several of the essays point out the divergence of a sound position from the dominant pop prophecy that goes under the general rubric of dispensationalism. Rather, they explore certain issues relevant to eschatology to demonstrate indirectly that historically, theologically, and biblically, the prevailing popular concepts diverge from the classical Christian faith.

In doing this, we are merely perpetuating a position stated many years ago in *Exploring Our Christian Faith*, by W. T. Purkiser, or one of his writing team: "It is odd that these men [dispensationalists], who as Calvinists have so ardently opposed the doctrine of entire sanctification, should have had such influence in the holiness movement. . . . The whole system of dispensationalism rests upon a reading into the Bible *(eisegesis)* the ideas of men, rather than *a leading out* of the Word *(exegesis)* of the truths of revelation."[2]

For the Wesleyan, the Bible is the primary source of authority, but not used in isolation from tradition, reason, and experience. Reflecting this commitment to the centrality of Scripture, our anthology is organized so that we will hear first from some issues relating to Scripture, then look at tradition, and finally explore some theological matters.

One of the major issues in the contemporary context relates to the meaning of biblical prophecy. Numerous books have been published proposing to give guidance on how to read and interpret prophecy. The recent flurries that have surrounded ill-fated predictions of the time of the Second Coming ("88 reasons in '88," predictions by Hal Lindsey in relation to the state of Israel; two major catastrophes of setting dates in Korea, etc.),

---

1. Daniel Steele, *A Substitute for Holiness* (1887; reprint, New York: Garland Publishing, 1984). This work was subtitled *Antinomianism Revived, or The Theology of the So-called Plymouth Brethren Examined and Refuted*. The Calvinism of the Darbyites, with its devastating antinomian implications from the doctrine of eternal security, occupies most of Steele's attention, but he devotes one entire chapter to refuting the Brethren eschatology, especially the theory of a "secret rapture." Steele was an avowed postmillennialist.

2. W. T. Purkiser et al., *Exploring Our Christian Faith* (Kansas City: Beacon Hill Press of Kansas City, 1978), 425.

most precipitated by laypersons in biblical studies, highlight the necessity for understanding the nature of prophecy in Scripture. Thus, Frank Carver has given us a careful analysis of the proper meaning of biblical prophecy. He has taken a unique approach, using the Book of Revelation, a self-professed prophecy, as an entrée into the broader meaning of prophecy. If the reader will follow his line of argument through to the end, it will be a rewarding venture. It should become apparent that the way much so-called prophecy is used today is an abortion of its own self-understanding.

Two buzzwords of today's popular literature are "last days" and "signs of the times." Roger Hahn carries us through a careful analysis of the proper meaning of these terms when they are looked at in their context. Likewise, one of the most often appealed-to passages of prophetic Scripture is Jesus' Olivet Discourse, found in all three Synoptic Gospels. Jirair Tashjian analyzes these sayings in terms of the setting in which they were recorded and gives us a sound perspective on these much-controverted passages.

The purpose of the historical section that is the centerpiece of this book is to help the reader become aware of several things: (1) there is no ecumenically orthodox position on eschatology, (2) there has been a diversity of views throughout history, and (3) recent popular views on last things are just that—recent, and would have been considered heretical by the Early Church fathers because of their theological presuppositions.

George Lyons has done a massive piece of research and made available to the student a well-organized and brilliantly done history of eschatological speculation during the early Christian centuries. Those who work through this material will find some extremely interesting ideas that will support the conclusions to which Dr. Lyons arrives in his conclusion. Apart from the sheer fascination of the ideas, they have practical implications for our own situation.

The Wesleyan Movement stems from John Wesley, and thus we have asked a well-known specialist on Wesley to provide us with a survey of Wesley's views on last things. William M. Greathouse is widely recognized and respected and has done a superb job in ferreting out Wesley's few comments on the topic, as well as putting them in the theological context of Wesley's total perspective. Harold Raser has surveyed the issue of last things as thought and written about among Wesley's successors in the American situation. The result may be illuminating to those who have preconceptions about what Holiness people have believed about end-time matters.

The final section of this anthology explores some theological topics that bear on the theme of eschatology. I have written a relatively brief essay, attempting to delineate certain theological presuppositions from a Wesleyan perspective that are germane to eschatology. Its purpose is, in part, to provide a benchmark by which to evaluate the hodgepodge of teachings confronting us in print, through the media, and via a multitude of other sources.

There is a significant difference between prophetic theology and that of the Apocalyptic Movement that flourished during the few centuries surrounding the time of Jesus, chiefly in non-canonical literature. Since most modern popular prophetic teachers are more apocalyptic than prophetic in their view of things, it seems important to help the reader justify this accusation. To that end, Harvey Finley has given us an overview of the distinctive theological perspectives of this movement. The most popular theology of last things among evangelical Christians today is actually a modern version of apocalyptic theology, so we have asked William Miller to provide us with a theological history of this "new apocalypticism," better known as dispensationalism. A careful study of this movement will demonstrate its shallowness and lack of biblical soundness. Dr. Miller's research also shows how people in this movement, as they explore it with scholarly rigor, are moving away from it.

Finally, Rob Staples has written an essay that to some degree pulls together theologically all the implications of the other contributions in this book. In a scintillating analysis, he truly gives us a "last word" that should help the sensitive student avoid the pitfalls of much of the present-day popular apocalypticism and maintain a balanced, biblical point of view.

It is hoped that after reading these essays, the readers will be able to see the issues more clearly and draw their own conclusions regarding the position that is consistent with Scripture and Wesleyan theological commitments.

—H. Ray Dunning

part I

BIBLICAL STUDIES

■ **FRANK G. CARVER**

The Nature of Biblical Prophecy

*B*IBLICAL PROPHECY has both a broad and a narrow meaning. In the narrow sense, it refers to a succession of men such as Amos, Isaiah, and Jeremiah who had significant influence upon both the religion of Israel and the Old Testament canon, where the books of the prophets occupy a central position between the Law and the Writings.[1] The distinctive characteristic of the preaching of these men is presupposed in the broader meaning of prophecy, which refers to "that understanding of history which accepts meaning in terms of divine concern, divine purpose, divine participation."[2]

One may conclude from this definition that "the vast bulk of [the] biblical record is produced by prophets or at least reflects an unmistakably prophetic understanding of history."[3] This implies that the Bible as a whole is basically prophetic in character, since it is concerned with the impingement of the divine—Yahweh in the Old Testament and Jesus Christ in the New Testament—upon the history of His people and through them upon the whole of humanity. This is an important consid-

---

1. The Hebrew canon is divided into three divisions known as the Law, the Prophets, and the Writings. The typical structure of the English Bible has four, designating a group of writings as "historical books," which the Hebrew canon refers to as the "Former Prophets" and includes in the section known as "the Prophets."

2. B. D. Napier, "Prophet, Prophetism," in *The Interpreter's Dictionary of the Bible* (hereafter cited as IDB), ed. George Buttrick et al., 4 vols. (Nashville: Abingdon Press, 1962), 3:896.

3. Ibid.

■ *Frank G. Carver is professor of biblical literature at Point Loma Nazarene College in San Diego.*

eration for our contemporary use of the biblical material and how we understand its function in the life of the Church. The issue here concerns how Scripture functions as the Church's rule of faith.

The broader definition of biblical prophecy includes the entire literature of the Old and New Testaments as prophetic in nature. Consequently, in attempting to identify the nature of biblical prophecy, we propose to focus this study on the prophetic character of the canonical literature. Our central question will be "What is the prophetic nature of the Christian canon?" Or "How does biblical literature function as prophecy?"

The phenomenon of "prophecy" occurred in cultures other than Israel's and manifested a significantly different characteristic. Also, there are various types of early "prophecy" referred to in the Old Testament historical records that predate the classical form of prophecy referred to above. However, we will not here concern ourselves in this study with those problematic and complex matters of either the ancient Near Eastern precedents of the biblical phenomenon, the origins of the biblical prophetic movement, or even the life and ministry of the particular prophets of Old and New Testament history.[4] We cannot ignore completely, however, the nature of the prophetic experience as reflected in the canonical literature or bypass the function of the prophet in Israel and in early Christianity. So these will be

---

4. Most recent summary updates are found in the articles titled "Apocalyptic Literature," "Eschatology," "Prophet, Prophecy," in *The International Standard Bible Encyclopedia* (hereafter cited as ISBE), ed. Geoffrey W. Bromley (Grand Rapids: William B. Eerdmans Publishing Co., 1986), vol. 3; "Prophet," in *The New International Dictionary of New Testament Theology* (hereafter cited as NIDNTT), ed. Colin Brown (Grand Rapids: Zondervan Publishing House, 1978), vol. 3; "Prophet in the NT" and "Prophet, Prophetism," in IDB; and "Apocalypticism," "Eschatology of the NT," "Prophecy in Ancient Israel," "Prophecy in the Ancient Near East," and "Prophecy in the Early Church" in *The Interpreter's Dictionary of the Bible, Supplementary Volume* (hereafter cited as IDBS), ed. Keith Crim (Nashville: Abingdon Press, 1976). See also David E. Aune, *Prophecy in Early Christianity and the Ancient Mediterranean World* (Grand Rapids: William B. Eerdmans Publishing Co., 1983); David Hill, *New Testament Prophecy* (Atlanta: John Knox Press, 1979); J. Lindbloom, *Prophecy in Ancient Israel* (Philadelphia: Fortress Press, 1962); John F. A. Sawyer, *Prophecy and the Prophets of the Old Testament* (Oxford: Oxford University Press, 1987); Gerhard von Rad, *The Message of the Prophets* (London: SCM Press, 1968); and Robert R. Wilson, *Prophecy and Society in Ancient Israel* (Philadelphia: Fortress Press, 1980). The amount of literature is enormous.

touched on as they bear on our primary task, which is to identify the prophetic character and function of the canonical record.[5]

We propose to approach this task by way of an examination
of the one book in the New Testament that explicitly claims to
be a prophecy, the Book of Revelation (see 1:3). This will provide us with a self-conscious understanding of the nature of
prophecy. This will in turn lead us to a summary look at the
biblical prophet, after which we return to the question of how
Revelation functions as prophecy. In a word, the claim of Revelation to be a prophecy is the window through which we will
look at the prophetic character of the biblical record. Throughout this exercise, we want to keep in view the question of how
the modern reader is to relate the Bible as prophecy to the life of
faith in the contemporary world.

The Revelation to John: A Prophecy?

The final book in the Christian canon, the Revelation to
John, is described from the start by its author as prophecy:
"Blessed is the one who reads aloud the words of the prophecy,
and blessed are those who hear and who keep what is written
in it; for the time is near" (1:3).[6]

John refers to his book as a "prophecy" four times in the
last chapter (22:7, 10, 18, 19). B. D. Napier declares, "The entire
book of Revelation is a classic example of Christian prophecy.
Though cast in an apocalyptic form, it is the proclamation of a
man 'in the Spirit' who expounds from the imagery of the OT
the new revelation of God's victory in Christ and in those who
belong to Christ."[7] Because of this apocalyptic literary form,
Wall speaks of it as "an apocalyptic-prophetic epistle."[8] The

---

5. We will not therefore limit our touchstone perspective to the reconstructive results of the excellent attempt of Aune to reconstruct "the history and character of early
Christian prophecy," but we will reference his perspectives when pertinent to our purposes. The stated purpose of Aune's study is to "understand prophets and prophecy *as
historical phenomena* in the history of early Christianity," *Prophecy*, 15 (emphasis added).

6. *The Holy Bible: New Revised Standard Version* (Grand Rapids: Zondervan Bible
Publishers, 1989). All scripture citations in this chapter are from this version unless otherwise indicated.

7. "Prophecy," IDB 3:919-20. See also Aune, *Prophecy*, 274, n. 149. The evidence is
furnished by Hill, *New Testament Prophecy*, 70-76.

8. Robert W. Wall, *Revelation, New International Biblical Commentary*, ed. W. Ward
Gasque (Peabody, Mass.: Hendrickson Publishers, 1991), 39. Hill, *New Testament Prophe-*

prophetic aspect, however, appears to be basic. It is therefore appropriate to begin our study of biblical prophecy where the canon completes itself, with the characterization of Revelation as a prophetic document.

A. Feuillet has observed that the profound originality of Revelation "lies in the fact that, whilst making use of the style, imagery, and methods of Jewish apocalyptic, it remains faithful to that which creates the greatness of ancient prophecy."[9]

Wall reinforces this understanding when he states that John's designation, "words of the prophecy," should be understood as indicating "the overarching purpose of his composition: to transmit a word from God that is constitutive for faith and life."[10] So there is good reason to characterize Revelation as prophetic proclamation, a book in continuity with and in fulfillment of the prophetic impulse that permeates the Old Testament and flows forward into the New. It is a rereading of the Old Testament in light of the central Christian event.[11]

It follows from the prophetic character of Revelation that John was an early Christian prophet, itself evidence for the preceding judgment. He had received a revelation from the exalted Lord as to the meaning of events then taking place (1:3) and was writing it to "the seven churches that are in Asia" (v. 4) as a "prophecy" (v. 3; 22:7, 10, 18, 19).[12] What he sent was an ecumenical letter (1:11, 19; 22:16), "not esoteric knowledge or secret wisdom, but an unsealed, open, clear, eschatological message and exhortation which is related to the present and immediate future."[13] His work was done "in the Spirit" (1:10; 4:2) and thus carried the authority of the exalted Christ: "For the testimony of

cy, points out that although the book is apocalyptic in form, it lacks many of that genre's most characteristic features and can "justifiably, and probably correctly, be regarded as prophetic in intention and character, especially in its concern with and interpretation of history," 75. For him, "it is in terms of its attitude toward history that the character of Revelation as a whole may be discerned," 74.

9. L'Apocalypse. Etat de la Question (1963), quoted in Hill, New Testament Prophecy, 75-76.

10. Wall, Revelation, 22.

11. Brown, "Prophet," NIDNTT, 89, citing Feuillet, 65.

12. Hill, New Testament Prophecy, 72-73.

13. Ibid. Hill notes that there are similarities in his opening sentences to the first words of the prophetic books (Isa. 1:1; Amos 1:1; 3:7).

Jesus is the spirit of prophecy" (19:10).[14] Thus "we have in Revelation a literary deposit of such Spirit-inspired prophecy as is referred to elsewhere in early Christian writings."[15]

John's account of his prophetic call in 10:1-11 is reminiscent of Ezekiel's call in its symbolism (2:8—3:3) and of Jeremiah's (1:10) in its charge to prophesy concerning the nations. Finally, he appears to identify himself as among the prophets: "I am a fellow servant with you and your comrades the prophets" (22:9). It will be helpful now to briefly relate John as prophet to the Christian prophetic movement and its background in the Old Testament prophetic experience.

The Character of the Biblical Prophet

In Revelation the term "apostle" is used only of false apostles (2:2) and the apostolic Twelve (18:20; 21:14). On the other hand, the term "prophet" (found eight times: 10:7; 11:10, 18; 16:6; 18:20, 24; 22:6, 9) seems to be used for those who have received an authentic word from God, and John numbers himself among them (22:9). Although the book never directly designates John as a prophet, the implication of 1:3 as explored above makes it obvious that he viewed himself as a prophet and can thus be considered among the Christian prophets of New Testament times. Now briefly, who were they, and how does John relate to them?

The roots of the New Testament prophetic phenomenon go back to the Old Testament to "Israel's experience of God's mind to his people through divinely chosen individuals."[16] The Old Testament word for these individuals was *nabi*. It is significant that this word was translated by the earliest translators of the Old Testament, not by *mantis*, "soothsayer,"[17] but by *prophetes*,

---

14. Ibid. Hill interprets these and other references (17:3; 21:10) not as "the ecstatic trance-like rapture characteristic of advanced apocalypticism, but action in the sphere of and under the inspiration of the Spirit (of God) . . . understood, at least partly, in terms of the spirit of prophecy."

15. D. Moody Smith, *John, Proclamation Commentaries*, ed. Gerhard Krodel (Philadelphia: Fortress Press, 1976), 83.

16. E. Earle Ellis, "Prophecy in the Early Church," IDBS, ed. Keith Crim (Nashville: Abingdon Press, 1976), 700.

17. In Greek religion these figures "employed incantations and practiced divination by material signs (e.g., the interpretation of omens, stars, etc.)" (Hill, *New Testament Prophecy*, 9).

meaning "interpreter," implying both "prediction (foretelling) and proclamation (forthtelling)."[18]

The Old Testament prophets based their credentials on the direct call of God. Their authority to speak the word of the Lord came from a personal and immediate encounter with God, an intuitive consciousness of Yahweh. They "drew upon, modified and added to the religious traditions of Israel, sometimes rejecting them, sometimes affirming them."[19] They did not "prophesy the deceit of their own heart" (Jer. 23:26) but spoke as ones who have stood in the council of the Lord with a "Thus says the Lord," often in the "I"-form or messenger-formula. Their ministry was not separate from the rest of Israelite life, culture, and religion but was carried out in relation to the priestly tradition and to wisdom.[20]

The classical form of Old Testament prophecy (which reached its highest point in the eighth century B.C.) was modified somewhat in the later writings of the Old Testament and especially in the intertestamental literature. This took the form of apocalyptic literature. In the apocalyptic writings, "wisdom" exerted a prominent influence on the form of prophetic thought (see note 20). Ellis summarizes this development: "The apocalyptic seers combine, within the content of a revelation of final and cosmic dimension, the prophetic vision and the word of

---

18. Sawyer, *Prophecy*, 1. See Aune, *Prophecy*, 195-96, for his brief yet comprehensive and well-documented summary of the linguistic data.

19. Hill, *New Testament Prophecy*, 14. The description in this paragraph is distilled from Hill's detailed discussion of Old Testament prophecy, 11-21. This can be compared with the general description by Lindbloom, *Prophecy in Ancient Israel*, 6, of the prophetic type in the world of religion: "They are entirely devoted, soul and body, to the divinity. They are inspired personalities who have the power to receive divine revelations. They act as speakers and preachers who publicly announce what they have to say. They are compelled by higher powers and kept under divine constraint. The inspiration which they experience has a tendency to pass over into real ecstasy. . . . A prophet knows that he has never chosen his way himself: he has been chosen by the deity. He points to a particular experience in his life through which it has become clear to him that the deity has a special purpose with him and has designated him to perform a special mission." See also Aune, *Prophecy*, 81-88.

20. The wise man was a third force in Israel, along with the prophet and priest. The product of this class of persons, known as Wisdom Literature, is embodied in the Old Testament in Proverbs, Job, Ecclesiastes, the Song of Songs, and some psalms. Scholars have only recently recognized the pervasive influence of this school of theology on the Old Testament, some (notably Gerhard von Rad) suggesting that it has made significant impact upon the apocalyptic literature that appeared in the closing years of the Old Testament period. This position is assumed in this essay.

knowledge with the wise discernment of its meaning. As forerunners of Christian prophecy such apocalyptic writers are best
represented in the book of Daniel and in the Qumran scrolls."[21]

The affinity between wisdom and prophecy was growing
in part because of the increasing identification of both with Israel's Scriptures.[22] From this perspective, prophecy can be understood "not only as a word or vision or discernment from
God, but also as the inspired exposition and application to the
current scene of earlier prophecies."[23] This is what we have, not
only in Daniel and the Qumran teachers, but also in the prophecies cited in the infancy narratives of Matthew (1:23; 2:6, 18) and
Luke (1:5—2:52) and in the witness of John the Baptist to Jesus
(Matt. 3:3; Mark 1:2-3; John 1:23).[24]

In addition, the use of Old Testament Scripture as evidence
of a new outbreak of the prophetic Spirit permeates the infancy
narratives as men and angels herald the birth of Jesus (Matt.
1:20-21; Luke 1:30-33, 67; 2:25-27, 36-38). John the Baptist as "the
prophet of the Most High" (Luke 1:76) gave full expression to
the Spirit of prophecy in his testimony to Jesus (Matt. 3:11-12;
Mark 1:7-8; Luke 3:7-17; John 1:29-34). Both the Jews (Matt. 14:5;
21:26; Mark 6:15; 11:32; Luke 9:8; 20:6) and Jesus (Matt. 11:9-15;
Luke 7:24-28) held the Baptist to be a prophet.[25]

Jesus' baptism by John (Matt. 3:13-17; Mark 1:9-11; Luke
3:21-22; John 1:29-34) involved the endowment with authority
and the Spirit of prophecy to carry out His ministry. In the Judaism of His time, this would indicate that He was a prophet,
and He no doubt understood himself as such. The Gospels witness to the fact that in Him the era of the expectation and hope
of the Kingdom, climaxing in the ministry of John, has become

---

21. Ellis, "Prophecy," 700. See also Hill, *New Testament Prophecy*, 21-43, and Aune, *Prophecy*, 112-14.

22. The Pentateuch was the first of the three segments of the Old Testament canon to be acknowledged as authoritative Scripture. The other two segments came into this status later.

23. Ellis, "Prophecy," 701.

24. Aune, *Prophecy*, 217, although not denying a teaching function to apostles and prophets, believes that those identified as teachers in the New Testament were "regard-ed as specialists in the transmission and inculcation of Christian norms and values."

25. See the discussion of Hill, *New Testament Prophecy*, 43-47.

the era of inauguration and fulfillment; in His ministry the Kingdom is a present reality in history.[26]

Some of Jesus' contemporaries concluded from His manifest inspiration and authority that He was a prophet (Matt. 21:11, 46; Mark 6:15; 8:27), at times a particular prophet (Mark 6:14-16; 8:28; Luke 9:8, 19). Even apart from His baptism there is evidence that Jesus probably understood himself in that role.[27] And examination of the characteristics of His ministry—His speech-forms, His teaching with wisdom and authority, His gift of human insight and prophetic foresight, His symbolic acts— all point to "prophet" as "the working concept which guided Jesus in the task of his ministry."[28] But in relation to the Old Testament prophets as well as the charismatics of Jesus' day, Hill concludes that "this 'prophet' was unique in the sense that his proclamation and activity were confronting men and women with the present saving action of God in the midst of history, and that his commitment and obedience to God made him the channel of that gracious and saving action."[29]

Thus Jesus appears as the New Testament prophet par excellence, the character of whose ministry sets the stage for all future prophetic activity in the New Testament Church. Jesus' exemplification in speech and action of many of the characteristics of the Old Testament prophets may have mediated them to the earliest Christian prophets. The inspiration and chief concern of Christian prophecy was "the testimony of Jesus" (Rev. 19:10; cf. 1:2, 9), the witness He bore to the word and purpose of God as prophet and more-than-prophet.[30]

Early Christian prophecy appears as a gift from the exalted Lord that follows the model of Jesus. One of the tests of its gen-

---

26. Ibid., 49-50.

27. Ibid., 57. Hill observes from Matt. 13:57; Mark 6:4; Luke 4:24; 13:33; and John 4:44 that "Jesus is not describing himself as a prophet but quoting a common view. Nevertheless, by not merely adopting the view but also preparing to exemplify it, Jesus numbers himself among the prophets." On the basis of Mark 6:4 (Matt. 13:57) and Luke 13:31-33, Aune, *Prophecy*, suggests that "the conclusion that Jesus closely identified his own mission with that of the prophets of ancient Israel is very probable."

28. Ibid., 68. See also Ellis, "Prophecy," 701, and especially Aune, *Prophecy*, 157-69.

29. Hill, *New Testament Prophecy*, 48-68.

30. Ibid., 68-69. "The Greek genitive 'of Jesus' here has three senses which are inseparable: (1) Prophecy is bound indissolubly to the testimony the earthly Jesus gave as he faced the Roman authorities (subjective genitive), (2) to the testimony from the risen

uineness is its witness to Him (1 Cor. 12:3; Rev. 19:10). The forms of prophetic utterance that characterized Jesus' earthly ministry are reflected in oracle, inspired teaching and discernment, and the exposition of Scripture. Prophecy appears both as the occasional utterance of any Christian[31] and as a continuing ministry by some in one or several congregations. Prophets functioned singly or in groups either within or apart from Christian worship.[32] The working definition of Hill completes our brief sketch of this phenomenon in the New Testament Church: *"A Christian prophet is a Christian who functions within the Church, occasionally or regularly, as a divinely called and divinely inspired speaker who receives intelligible and authoritative revelations or messages which he is impelled to deliver publicly, in oral or written form, to Christian individuals and/or the Christian community."*[33]

To this class of Christians John belonged and probably was one who possessed a continual calling as a prophet, possibly as an itinerant prophet who traveled with some regularity from one congregation to another in western Asia Minor.[34] And among the latter he may have held a unique position. He appears to stand closer to Old Testament prophecy than to what is known elsewhere about New Testament prophecy, and in at least two respects he seems to claim a distinctive authority for

---

Jesus identified as the Word of God (1:2, 9, 19:9) (genitive of origin), and (3) to the message of the church centered on the crucified earthly Jesus (objective genitive)" (M. Eugene Boring, *Revelation*, in *Interpretation: A Bible Commentary for Teaching and Preaching*, ed. Paul J. Achtemeier [Louisville: John Knox Press, 1989], 194).

31. Aune, *Prophecy*, 200-201, asks, "WERE ALL CHRISTIANS POTENTIAL PROPHETS?" and concludes, "Some, but not all, early Christians acted as inspired mediums of divine revelation and that these individuals alone received the label 'prophet.'"

32. Ellis, "Prophecy," 701. See also Napier, "Prophet," 919-20, and Aune, *Prophecy*, 195-98.

33. Hill, *New Testament Prophecy*, 8-9. The italics are his. Hill's entire work is given to the examination of this phenomenon as reflected in all the literature of the New Testament. See Aune, *Prophecy*, 10, who criticizes Hill from his strict phenomenological/historical perspective. Aune suggests that Hill is caught up in a methodological muddle, not having decided "if he is presenting a history of early prophetism or a theologically normative study in which the NT evidence is regarded prescriptively." He concludes that Hill, for reasons of his theological orientation "insists on staying within the canonical framework in treating NT prophecy" rather than "trying to use history-of-religions categories to describe the role of the NT prophet."

34. Aune, *Prophecy*, 215.

himself in relation to his fellow prophets. First, he wrote a book, which none of the rest did, and second, he had a special task of mediation; through him the other prophets in the Church would become sharers in the knowledge and ministry of the divine revelation. In other words, he was a leader of a prophetic group, different from them not in kind but in authority.[35] As one who can be defended as having a representative status as an early Christian prophet, however, the characteristics John "holds in common with his colleagues appear more decisive than the differences."[36]

Hill concludes his chapter on Revelation with eight characteristics of John's relation as a Christian prophet to his community that will serve as a transition to our consideration of how the Book of Revelation functions as prophecy. We list these without explanation. The Christian prophet is one who (1) speaks with assumed authority within the congregation(s) he addresses, (2) addresses a community that itself has a prophet character, (3) exercises his function primarily in the setting of congregational worship, (4) is a man controlled by the Spirit, (5) functions as an interpreter of events in history, (6) reinterprets the Old Testament in light of the Christ event, (7) is not directly associated with miracles and signs, and (8) differentiates between himself and false prophets.[37]

The Prophetic Function of Revelation

We have characterized the nature of the Book of Revelation as a prophetic document and have identified its author as a member of and probably a leader among the early Christian prophets. Now we look carefully at the document itself as prophecy, how as a part of the Christian canon it functions prophetically in the Christian community.[38] This will be our

---

35. Ibid., 87-88. See Brown, "Prophet," NIDNTT, 89.
36. Aune, *Prophecy*, 207-8, 231.
37. Hill, *New Testament Prophecy*, 87-93.
38. Wall, *Revelation*, 36-37, for example, defines his interpretative approach to Revelation as "canonical critical." He writes, "The distinctive contribution of canonical criticism is its efforts to recover the *idea of canon* as a guide to biblical interpretation—to guide the interpreter to locate meaning in biblical texts that will allow Scripture to function as the church's rule of faith." For his application of this principle to Revelation, see 37-39. For a recent summary of approaches to the interpretation of Revelation for con-

touchstone as we look at the literature, first of the New Testament, and second of the Old Testament, in an attempt to define the Scripture's canonical function as prophetic in character.

We take our clue from an examination of the first chapter of the book. This chapter contains John's greeting to his readers, using what scholars call an "epistolary format."[39] This "creates the proper context for reading his composition as the word of God" and is therefore "of considerable theological and rhetorical significance for how one interprets the rest of the book."[40]

This literary judgment, along with a careful look at the chapter's contents and perspective in light of John's complete work, convincingly suggests that it contains in essence the purpose and message of the book. As such we can examine it for guidance as to what Revelation is designed to do as prophecy: "Blessed is the one who reads aloud the words of the prophecy, and blessed are those who hear and who keep what is written in it; for the time is near" (1:3).

First, "the words of the prophecy" are designated in the title as "the revelation of Jesus Christ" (1:1). Whether the genitive is subjective, "given by Christ," as most interpreters take it, or objective, "about Christ," the book claims the authority of Jesus Christ, which in turn "God gave him" (v. 1). Second, and significant for our purpose, is what was made known through the angel to John "who testified to the word of God and to the testimony of Jesus Christ" (v. 2; cf. v. 9; 19:10). "The testimony of Jesus Christ," witnessed to by John, is the witness of all that Christ was and what He accomplished through His incarnation, death, and exaltation (1:5). This is the content of what John saw (vv. 2, 19; 22:8). In a word, the substance of his written (1:3-4, 11, 19; 22:18-19) "prophecy" is Jesus Christ, a revelation from and

---

temporary culture, see Elisabeth Schuessler Fiorenza, *Revelation: Vision of a Just World*, in *Proclamation Commentaries*, ed. Gerhard Krodel (Minneapolis: Fortress Press, 1991), 6-20. For her own literary-rhetorical and sociopolitical approach, see 20-37.

39. Fiorenza, *Revelation*, 23. Revelation is written within an epistolary frame, its opening and its closing. See 23-24 and Wall, *Revelation*, 23-25, for the characteristics of Revelation as an early Christian letter.

40. Wall, *Revelation*, 56. His outline, 41-43, indicates the epistolary character of both the beginning (1:1-29) and the ending (22:6-21) of the document. Note how the Gospel of John 1:1-18 (51), the First Epistle of John 1:1-4, as well as Heb. 1:1-4, fulfill a similar role. Cf. Isa. 1:1-31 and Jer. 1:1-19.

of Christ "that discloses the full measure of what God has done in Christ and its consequences for human existence in the midst of history."[41]

This basic stance of the book is quite fully developed as the chapter moves into John's greeting to the seven churches (1:4-8). The "grace . . . and peace" of the greeting is not alone from God and "the seven spirits who are before his throne" (symbolically referring to the Holy Spirit) but particularly "from Jesus Christ, the faithful witness, the firstborn of the dead, and the ruler of the kings of the earth" (1:4-5a). These words describe Jesus' relationship to God in the three decisive stages of His messianic work as understood in the Johannine tradition. His entire messianic career is included, climaxing with His death, His resurrection, and His present reign over the powers of the earth as glorified Lord.[42] The doxology that follows adds its weight to the same reality as it elucidates the continuing love of the risen and reigning Christ for the Church: "To him who loves us and freed us from our sins by his blood, and made us to be a kingdom, priests serving his God and Father, to him be glory and dominion forever and ever, Amen" (1:5b-6).[43]

John emphasizes Christ as victoriously alive in the full power of His past redemptive work, active in the world and in the Church, making "us to be a kingdom, priests serving . . ." This description implies that a new Exodus has taken place as a delivered people become a new covenant people (Exod. 19:6) now living under God's reign as His witnessing and worshiping servants.[44]

John's focus on the present reigning Christ, however, reaches out implicitly to include the future as well. That there is to "be glory and dominion forever and ever" to Him finds its full meaning in the hope of Christ's second coming, His consumma-

---

41. M. Robert Mulholland, Jr., *Revelation: Holy Living in an Unholy World* (Grand Rapids: Francis Asbury Press, 1990), 60. See note 30 above for Boring's comment on the similar phrase in 19:9, which may well apply here.

42. Wall, *Revelation*, 58.

43. The shift from the present participle "loves" to two aorists, a participle and the first active, "freed . . . made," suggests that the current benefits of Jesus' past messianic work are rooted in His continuing love for the covenant community. So Wall, *Revelation*, 58.

44. Ibid., 58-59.

tion of all things. Both truths are embodied in 1:7, which con-
joins quotations from Dan. 7:13 and Zech. 12:10:

> Look! He is coming with the
>   clouds;
> every eye will see him,
> even those who pierced him;
> and on his account all the tribes
> of the earth will wail.
> So it is to be. Amen.[45]

The concern of the author of Revelation, however, is not
primarily to work from the present to the future, from the experience of Christ to the hope of His return, but from the certainty
and nature of His end-time consummation to its meaning for
the Church in the present: "The time is near" (1:3). This order of
emphasis is suggested first in the oracle from God that follows
(v. 8), which repeats the language descriptive of the first Source
of "grace . . . and peace" (v. 4): "'I am the Alpha and the
Omega,' says the Lord God, who is and who was and who is to
come, the Almighty." The unexpected placing of "who is" before the past and the future indicates that John is stressing the
"who is," that is, the One through whom the total work of
Christ "is," is the One who first "was" and who, second, "is to
come."

John's concern to work from the future to the present is further confirmed by his indescribable vision of the risen Christ
(1:12-18) that he "in the spirit on the Lord's day" (v. 10; cf. 4:2;
17:3; 21:10) saw as present in the midst of the churches (1:13).
He saw "one like the Son of Man" (1:13), the same one who in
1:7 "is coming with the clouds." When John fell as though dead
at the feet of this Christ who stood "in the midst of the lamp-

---

45. Note the similarity with Matt. 24:30, where "the dramatic return of the Son of
Man vindicates Christian faith before a cosmic courtroom" (Wall, *Revelation*, 59).
Whether the mourning referred to here by the term "wail" is penitential grief resulting
in salvation, as in the Zechariah passage, or a wailing because of judgment and calamity, John does not discuss. Although many commentators take the latter sense here, the
former notion "is not inappropriate to John (cf. Rev. 15:3-4; John 12:30-33)" (Wall, *Revelation*, 59). See also G. B. Caird, *A Commentary on the Revelation of St. John the Divine*, in
Harper New Testament Commentaries (New York: Harper and Row, 1966), 18-19; and Boring, *Revelation*, 80, who concludes that "perhaps John leaves the matter dialectically ambiguous, so that these words can be taken as either promise or threat."

stands" (1:13),[46] He placed His right hand on John and said, "Do not be afraid; I am the first and the last, and the living one. I was dead, and see, I am alive forever and ever; and I have the keys of Death and of Hades. Now write what you have seen, what is, and what is to take place after this" (vv. 17b-19). The message of the prophecy encompasses the full meaning of the Christ who is "the first and the last," the One who is "alive forever and ever" reigning in the Church with "the keys of Death and of Hades" in His hands. The purpose of the prophecy, the written "revelation of Jesus Christ" (1:1), is to bear witness to this fact of Christian faith. This, in substance, is "the testimony of Jesus" (1:2, 9; 19:10). Fiorenza correctly concludes on this basis that "the inaugural vision's main theological interest . . . lies in the present relationship of Christ to the Christian community."[47]

If the vision of Christ in the midst of the Church is the focus of chapter 1, and chapters 2 and 3 interpret the meaning of that presence in the seven churches of Asia (representing the whole Church), then it is quite probable that chapters 4 to 22 are likewise similarly motivated. This implies that John, with a pastoral concern, is working out the implications of the presence of the Christ of the Cross and the consummation for the faith of a church in crisis. In other words, "what is, and what is to take place after this" qualifies the whole of what John has been commanded to write, which in turn is immediately relevant for John's audience.[48] A careful consideration of the book as a

---

46. Mulholland, *Revelation*, 87, suggests that "John's falling in 1:17 and 19:10/22:8 may very well be the same single response of a unified, holistic visionary experience" (cf. 36-37).

47. Fiorenza, *Revelation*, 52. See 51-53 for her interpretation of 1:10-20 in support of this point.

48. So Wall, *Revelation*, 63-64, although he insists that "this conclusion does not vitiate our contention that the main body of the composition envisions a sequence of past-present-future 'moments' within salvation's history which can be observed at a microscopic level." The central point is that 1:19 does not organize Revelation "into discrete visions of the past, present, and future of salvation's history." Caird, *Revelation*, 26, concurs in writing that the words "what you have seen" mean "the whole of John's vision, which in all its parts is equally concerned with the interpretation of past and present and the anticipation of the future." But see Robert H. Mounce, *The Book of Revelation*, New International Commentary on the New Testament (Grand Rapids: William B. Eerdmans Publishing Co., 1977), 82, who sees a twofold division with the first "and" as epexegetical.

whole and its use of apocalyptic language bears this out. The frame of the book is epistolary, its substance is prophetic, and its literary form is apocalyptic.[49]

Then what about "what is to take place after this" (1:19; cf. vv. 1, 3, 7) and similar expressions throughout the work? Is the crisis John has in mind simply the persecution of the Church,[50] or the end (v. 7)? The first chapter (vv. 4, 7, 8) seems to indicate with Mounce that "the most satisfying solution is to take the word in a straightforward sense, remembering that in the prophetic outlook the end is always imminent," a perspective "common to the entire NT."[51] Mulholland, commenting on "the time is near" (v. 3), notes that the Greek word *eggus*, translated "near," "simply means 'proximity,' with no inherent indication of whether it is temporal, spatial, or relational."[52] He sees it here as qualified by the word used for time (*kairos*, cf. 22:10), the special or decisive time of the kingdom of God that "has broken into human history in the person of Jesus" (see Mark 1:15) and at any moment may become the time (*chronos*, "period of time") "of its final consummation in Christ."[53] The "present" Kingdom looks to its "future," and the nature of its future impacts the quality of the present. The question is "How?"

The beatitude (Rev. 1:3) with which we began our discussion of the meaning of Scripture as prophetic pronounces "blessed . . . the one who reads aloud" and "those who hear and who keep what is written in" the words of John's prophetic book. Revelation as prophecy functions then as "the authorita-

---

49. See Fiorenza's discussion of "The Generic Tenor of Revelation" in *Revelation*, 23-26. See also Wall, *Revelation*, 12-25.

50. Caird, *Revelation*, 12.

51. Mounce, *Revelation*, 65. George Eldon Ladd, *A Commentary on the Book of Revelation* (Grand Rapids: William B. Eerdmans Publishing Co., 1972), 22, reminds us here that "biblical prophecy is not primarily three-dimensional but two; it has height and breadth but is little concerned about depth, i.e., the chronology of future events. There is in biblical prophecy a tension between the immediate and distant future." See also Philip Edgecumbe Hughes, *The Book of Revelation: A Commentary* (Grand Rapids: William B. Eerdmans Publishing Co., 1990), 16.

52. Mulholland, *Revelation*, 68.

53. Ibid., 68-69. But see Boring's discussion, *Revelation*, 68-74, on the "'Near' in Revelation" who sees chronological discrepancy between what John meant and what actually happened: "Without sharing their chronology, we can share their sense of urgency, the sense that our generation is the only generation *we* have in which to fulfill our calling."

tive medium by which the believing community is nurtured and corrected by the word of God."[54] Its intent is thoroughly pastoral for the Church in its real life in the world of its day, in the "Babylon" that is already fallen through the messianic career of "Jesus Christ, the faithful witness, the firstborn of the dead, and the ruler of the kings of the earth" (v. 5).[55]

Implicit in John's affirmation of identity with his readers is the essence of his pastoral message: "I, John, your brother who share with you in Jesus the persecution and the kingdom and the patient endurance" (1:9). John is expressing his solidarity as a "brother" with his readers not only in their "persecution," their religious and political situations, but also in "the Kingdom." With them he "both participates in the eschatological power of God's and Christ's royal reign and shares as a partner in God's empire even in the present."[56] Inherent in their mutual suffering is the reign of Christ from the Cross, which is the final victory of Christ, although yet hidden from the world. Christ even now reigns in their world from the Cross.[57] This is the witness (v. 2) he seeks to communicate (v. 1) to their faith as he appeals to their imagination in this unusual prophetic document.[58] This, then, is the context, the eschatological reality within which He can exhort them to "patient endurance" with Him as togeth-

---

54. Wall, *Revelation*, 54.

55. "Fallen, fallen is Babylon the great!" (Rev. 14:8; 18:2; cf. 16:19; 17:5; 18:10, 21). See Mulholland, *Revelation*, 247; 46-53. This perspective is in line with Luke 10:18; John 12:31; 14:30; 16:11; Rev. 12:9. For the pastoral function of Revelation, see also Boring, *Revelation*, 5-8.

56. Fiorenza, *Revelation*, 50.

57. Caird, *Revelation*, 19-20, writes that John "does not think of the suffering of Christ as the prelude to kingly glory; Christ reigns from the Cross (v. 6). So too for his followers the coming **ordeal** is not a qualifying test through which they must pass in order to enter upon their promised reign with Christ. **Ordeal** and **sovereignty** are obverse and reverse of the one calling; for those who endure with Christ also reign with him, and reign in the midst of their **ordeal**."

58. See the work of Eugene H. Peterson, *Reverse Thunder: The Revelation of John and the Praying Imagination* (San Francisco: Harper and Row, 1988), xii-xiii: "That St. John was a pastor, and wrote his Apocalypse as a pastor is too little taken into account by his interpreters. . . . My primary question before the text is 'How does this work in the community of believers in which I am a pastor?' I have taken the position that this book does not primarily call for decipherment, as if it were written in code, but that it evokes wonder, releasing metaphors that resonate meanings and refract insights in the praying imagination." His introduction and first chapter (vii-10), where he first defines his approach and then discusses John as theologian, poet, and pastor, illuminate what we are doing with Revelation.

er they constitute the Church in the world; for the final victory of the cross in the world is certain: "the time is near" (v. 3).

Revelation as "prophecy" (1:3; 22:7, 10, 18, 19) is designed to bring the real presence of the God "who is and who was and who is to come" (1:4, 8) to bear on the human situation in judgment and in salvation. The canonizing church "included it as a part of the Christian biblical canon because of its normative character for subsequent generations of believers. . . . The proper hermeneutical judgment, consistent with its author, is that Revelation is useful informing Christian faith for today."[59] We read it and hear it in order to live and grow in the faith, in the knowledge of our Lord and Savior Jesus Christ.

Is this general prophetic perspective characteristic of the whole canon of Scripture, the New and the Old Testaments? We turn now to that final question.

The Prophetic Function of the Biblical Canon

The general function of prophecy in Scripture is to proclaim the theological quality of the present life of the people of God and His chronological purposes for them. Although prediction is present, the primary purpose is to ask such questions as "What sort of persons ought you to be in leading lives of holiness and godliness" (2 Pet. 3:11). The judgment and salvation of God are always in view whether it is the Day of the Lord in the prophets of the Old Testament or our Lord's prediction of His coming in the Gospels of the New Testament. It follows, then, that from the standpoint of its prophetic character, the function of the whole of the biblical canon is likewise to bear a transforming witness to the life of the individual and to the faith community and to the world. This we have seen in our examination of "the words of the prophecy" (1:3) in relation to the contents and canonical function of the Revelation to John.

There is then a theology of hope that permeates the biblical traditions and the shape of their final expression. As we have seen, the New Testament bears witness both to the certainty and to the nature of God's future in Christ. In the Synoptic Gospels we saw it in the incarnation of Jesus, inherent in His proclama-

59. Wall, *Revelation*, 55.

tion of the Kingdom, made fully effective in the final events of
His crucifixion and resurrection-exaltation, an already-but-not-
yet that furnishes the motivation and content of the life of faith
in the Christian community. Acts, with its emphasis on the Holy
Spirit of Pentecost, translates the Christ crucified-consummated
event into the witness life of the expanding Church. The Johannine literature—the Fourth Gospel in particular—in simple
terms, yet with theological profoundness, gives expression to
the nature of belief, life, and love in the divine Son of God
through the indwelling Paraclete. The New Testament Epistles
of Paul, Peter, James, Jude, and Hebrews, each with their chosen
terminology, bear their witness to the future of God in Christ for
the present life of the Church in "the present evil age" (Gal. 1:4).

Illustrative of the canonical function of the New Testament
could be the Beatitudes (Matt. 5:3-10), which introduce the Sermon on the Mount (5:1—7:28), with their poetic description of
Christian discipleship. The Beatitudes uniquely bring together
the future and present aspects of the Kingdom in their true relation. Each beatitude shifts from the present tense in the first line
to the future tense in the second line, usually both by verb tense
and concept. Typical of them all is "Blessed are the peacemakers, for they will be called children of God" (5:9). The following
analysis demonstrates how Christian discipleship is eschatolog-
ically defined:

The blessings are *promises* that are
   first *future* in nature—"they will be called,"
   then *present* in life—"Blessed are."
The promises are *blessings* that are
   now *present* in experience—"the peacemakers,"
   yet *future* in quality—"children of God."[60]

Revealed in the Beatitudes is the Jesus kind of life, a way of living open to the Christian in which the values and joys of God's
final future are transformingly turned loose into the everyday
reality of human existence, Jesus' "gospel of the Kingdom," the
good news of God's grace and righteousness.[61]

---

60. It should be noted that the expression "children of God" is literally the eschatological expression "sons of God" as in Rom. 8:18-25.

61. The paragraph is taken in part from Frank Carver, *Matthew, Part One: To Be a
Disciple* (Kansas City: Beacon Hill Press of Kansas City, 1984), 26-27.

The Old Testament as well is permeated with the motif of hope; its God is a God of promise. The Law is foundational. It contains the promise to the patriarchs whose descendants were constituted a covenant people through the Exodus deliverance and the revelation at Mount Sinai. The narratives fascinatingly reveal the impact of the future blessing on the lives of Abraham, Isaac, Jacob, and Jacob's descendants, the Israelites, as they awaited in the wilderness of Sinai the fulfillment of the promise. The prophets—former and latter—continue the thread of hope for the covenant people of God. The former prophets tell the story of success and failure, both militarily and in covenant obedience, until all hope of the fulfillment of the promise appears to be lost:

> Has a nation changed its gods,
>> even though they are no gods? . . .
> for my people have committed two evils:
>> they have forsaken me,
> the fountain of living water,
>> and dug out cisterns for themselves,
> cracked cisterns
>> that can hold no water *(Jer. 2:11, 13)*.

Into this deteriorating scene the latter prophets bear their pungent witness. The dominant theme is judgment for covenant failure, but never without the call to repentance and the offer of forgiveness:

> "Come, let us return to the LORD;
> for it is he who has torn, and he will heal us;
> he has struck down, and he will bind us up"
>> *(Hos. 6:1; cf. 4:1—6:6).*

When the divine judgment of national destruction is inevitable, the hope of a new future, dependent solely on the grace of a sovereign Holy God, the Holy One of Israel (Isa. 41:14 et al.), is promised to a faithful remnant:

> Comfort, O comfort my people; . . .
> that she has received from the LORD's hand
> double for all her sins . . .
> "Then the glory of the LORD shall be revealed,
> and all people shall see it together,
> for the mouth of the LORD has spoken. . . .

The grass withers, the flower fades;
but the word of our God will stand forever"
       (Isa. 40:1-2, 5, 8).

The Writings in their vastly differing ways come to terms with the reality of life in the covenant community of hope, whether through the calm of wisdom: "The fear of the LORD is the beginning of knowledge" (Prov. 1:7), or, in the urgency of more apocalyptic times, "But if not, be it known to you, O king, that we will not serve your gods and we will not worship the golden statue you have set up" (Dan. 3:18). As in the Law and the Prophets, the certainty and quality of God's future for His people is determinative of their behavior in the present.

Conclusion

We have left a lot unsaid about the particulars of prophecy in both the Old and the New Testaments. Excellent studies of these issues are plentiful. We have attempted rather to focus on the question of the nature and function of the biblical canon as prophetic. That is, how do the Scriptures function as prophecy in the life of the Christian and in the witness of the Christian community?

Our hermeneutical conclusions are threefold. First, the Bible is eschatological; it does promise a future for the people of God in history, a future that is ultimately defined in terms of the Christ of the Incarnation into the world and of the consummation of God's purposes for the world. God's final victory over all evil is certain. Second, the quality of that end, that future, is evident throughout the biblical canon as it progresses to its full revelation in the Christ of the Cross and the consummation. Third, the primary task of the Christian and the Church in relation to the prophetic character of the Scriptures is to search them intelligently to hear their multicolored witness to the "kingdom [that] has come and is yet to come"—meaning the kingdom of Christ. Then in fellowship with the Spirit of the risen Christ, the Holy Spirit, let this meaning become transforming of life and proclamation. "Surely the Lord GOD does nothing, without revealing his secret to his servants the prophets" (Amos 3:7).

■ **ROGER HAHN**

The "Last Days" and "Signs of the Times"

THE RISE OF THE "Biblical Prophecy" Movement in the past century has led to the widespread and popular use of many words and phrases related to the Second Coming. However, phrases like "rapture," "premillennial," and "midtribulational" are not found in the Bible at all. They are terms developed by theologians to summarize ways of interpreting certain aspects of the end time. "The mark of the beast," "great tribulation," and "antichrist" are biblical terms though they are often connected to passages of Scripture in which they are not found. The phrases "last days" and "signs of the times" also appear in the Bible, but the way they are most often used with reference to biblical prophecy is rather different from the way they are used in the Scripture itself. A biblical understanding of eschatology should incorporate the way the Bible actually uses the terms "last days" and "signs of the times." The New Testament use of the phrase "last days" requires discussion of the New Testament understanding of eschatology.

The Last Days

The exact phrase "last days" (*eschatai hēmerai*) appears only rarely in the New Testament (and never in the nominative [subject] case). Acts 2:17; 2 Tim. 3:1; James 5:3; and 2 Pet. 3:3 are the only places the exact phrase appears. Heb. 1:2 uses a quite similar expression, the "last of these days" (*eschatou tōn hēmeron*

■ *Roger Hahn is professor of New Testament at Nazarene Theological Seminary in Kansas City.*

toutōn). Related phrases include the singular "last day," "last hour," and "last time(s)."

These five references to the last days are noteworthy in that all appear to be referring to the time frame of the biblical author rather than the future.[1] Acts 2:17 begins, "And it will be in the last days, says God, I will pour out from my Spirit on all flesh . . ."[2] This verse begins an extended quotation from Joel 2:28-32. The words "in the last days, says God" are not part of the quotation but were inserted by the author of Acts to replace the general expression "after these things," found in the Greek version of Joel 2:28.[3] While it is true that Joel was speaking of a time future to himself, the use of this passage in Acts 2:17-20 has a different function. Peter states in Acts 2:16 that the events of the first Christian Pentecost had already been described by the words of Joel's prophecy.[4] Thus, the author of Acts (or Peter) uses the expression "the last days" to describe the time in which the first Christian Pentecost occurred.

Second Tim. 3:1 states: "But know this, that in the last days difficult times will come." The future tense of the verb would suggest that this passage looks to last days that are yet to come. However, in the verses immediately following, the author of 2 Timothy catalogs the evil persons who characterize such difficult times. In verse 5 he commands Timothy, "Avoid these people." The command to avoid is in the present tense, indicating that Timothy should keep on avoiding these evil people and their practices. Verses 6-8 then further describe the practices of these evil people as taking place in Timothy's own time. The in-

---

1. Adrio König, *The Eclipse of Christ in Eschatology: Toward a Christ-Centered Approach* (Grand Rapids: William B. Eerdmans Publishing Co., 1989), 5, states: "The phrase 'last days' is never used in the New Testament for some future period."

2. Unless otherwise noted, Scripture quotations in this chapter are translations of the author.

3. The LXX (standard abbreviation for the Septuagint—Greek translation of the Hebrew OT) has different chapter-and-verse numbering, so the citation may be found in Joel 3:1 of the LXX.

4. F. F. Bruce, "The Book of Acts," in *The New International Commentary on the Old Testament*, rev. ed. (Grand Rapids: William B. Eerdmans Publishing Co., 1988), 61, comments, "Luke, matching the prediction to the fulfillment uses the more precise phrase, 'in the last days.' For Luke the sign of the age to come is the presence of the Spirit."

evitable conclusion is that 2 Tim. 3:1 envisions the last days as being the time in which the letter itself was written.[5]

The view that the "last days" refers to a present reality is most clear in Heb. 1:2. Verses 1-2 read, "After God had spoken long ago in many and various ways to our fathers by the prophets, he has spoken to us in the last of these days by the Son." The contrast is between divine revelation via the prophets in the ancient past and divine revelation via Christ in the "last days." The "last days" are clearly the time of Christ's life and ministry, and they extend to the time of the writer of Hebrews.

James 5:3 reads, "Your gold and silver have corroded and their rust will be a witness against you and it will eat your flesh like fire. You have stored up treasure in the last days." The punctuation and translation of this verse are difficult.[6] One of the issues is the question of whether "last days" refers to the time present to the author or to the future. In order for the meaning to be "future," the word "in" (en) must be stretched to mean "for," which is not a natural meaning of the word. James' point is that his rich readers have stored up their wealth for security, but that wealth has become worthless. One of the reasons it is worthless is that the "last days" are present. Saving silver and gold at the end of time makes no sense.[7] Davids states that the rich readers "had treasured up as if they would live and the world would go on forever, but the end times, in which they have a last chance to repent and put their goods to righteous uses, are already upon them."[8]

---

5. The same conclusion follows regardless of whether one regards Paul as the author of 2 Timothy. See George W. Knight III, "The Pastoral Epistles: A Commentary on the Greek Text," in the *New International Greek Testament Commentary* (Grand Rapids: William B. Eerdmans Publishing Co., 1992), 428-29, assuming Paul to be the author; and A. T. Hanson, *The Pastoral Epistles*, in *The New Century Bible Commentary* (Grand Rapids: William B. Eerdmans Publishing Co., 1982), 143-44, assuming that Paul did not write 2 Timothy.

6. See Sophie Laws, "A Commentary on the Epistle of James," in *Harper's New Testament Commentaries* (San Francisco: Harper and Row, 1980), 198-200, for some of the options.

7. Laws, "James," 200-201; Peter H. Davids, *The Epistle of James: A Commentary on the Greek Text*, in *The New International Greek Testament Commentary* (Grand Rapids: William B. Eerdmans Publishing Co., 1982), 177; and Ralph P. Martin, *James*, vol. 48 of *Word Biblical Commentary* (Waco, Tex.: Word Books, 1988), 178, all take the "last days" to be present to the time of the author of James.

8. Davids, *James*, 177.

Second Pet. 3:3 is the final New Testament reference to use the exact phrase "the last days." The verse reads, "First, know this, that in the last days mockers will come with their mocking following their own desires." The immediate impression is that the author is describing "mockers" as one of the signs of the future when the end of time will come. However, mocking false teachers were one of the present dangers against which the author was warning his readers. It is possible that 2 Peter envisioned the last days as still future and that the problem of mocking false teachers would increase. However, the text makes complete sense with the understanding that the last days were the very days in which this letter was written.[9]

Based on this study of all the texts of the New Testament that refer specifically to "the last days," the most natural understanding of that phrase is that it refers to the time of the New Testament rather than to some future end of time. However, the New Testament concept of the end of time is more complex than can be understood by simply investigating the passages that speak of the last days. The singular form of the phrase—"the last day"—appears at least six times in the Gospel of John. First Pet. 1:5, 20, and Jude 18 speak of the last times or time, and 1 John 2:18 speaks of the last hour. A study of these texts indicates that the New Testament did not dismiss a future understanding of the end of time.

Four times in the Bread of Life discourse, Jesus states, "I will raise him up on the last day" (John 6:39, 40, 44, and 54). End-time language in John very frequently reveals the view that the end of time was present in the ministry of Jesus. In fact, Brown states that John is the "best example in the New Testament of realized eschatology."[10] However, it is impossible to avoid the conclusion that the four references to Jesus' raising of believers in the last day spoke of a future resurrection.[11] It is true

---

9. Richard J. Bauckham, *Jude, 2 Peter*, vol. 50 of *Word Biblical Commentary* (Waco, Tex.: Word Books, 1983), 288.

10. Raymond E. Brown, *The Gospel According to John (1-xii): Introduction, Translation, and Notes*, vol. 29 of *The Anchor Bible* (Garden City, N.Y.: Doubleday and Co., 1966), CXVII.

11. Rudolf Bultmann, *The Gospel of John: A Commentary*, trans. G. R. Beasley-Murray (Philadelphia: Westminster Press, 1971), 219-20, attributes the words "I will raise him up on the last day" to an "ecclesiastical editor."

that in each of the four verses the first part of the sentence speaks of the present relationship of the believer and Jesus. However, the contrast between the present and future does not represent a contradiction, as Haenchen states.[12] C. K. Barrett's comment is much more to the point: "John exactly balances the two aspects of the Christian life, in present possession and future hope; and there is nothing to indicate that he thought one more important than the other."[13]

John 12:48 also refers to the last day as a future event. In a final discourse before Jesus' final night with His disciples, He declared, "The one who rejects me and does not receive my words has the one who is judging him. That word which I have spoken will judge him on the last day." Like the verses in John 6, this passage balances both the present and future aspects of Jesus' understanding of the Christian life. The one who rejects Jesus and does not accept His words is in the present state of condemnation. However, future judgment also awaits, as the final sentence of verse 48 shows. Brown points out that the future judgment on the last day explains the reality of the present condemnation of the one who rejects Christ.[14]

John does not always use the phrase "the last day" to refer to the future, however. John 11:23-25 contains an interesting interchange between Jesus and Martha regarding her hope for Lazarus' resurrection. In verse 23 Jesus told her, "Your brother will be raised." Martha responded in verse 24, "I know that he will be raised in the resurrection on the last day." The language of resurrection is future tense thus far. Then in verse 25 Jesus responded to Martha, "I am the resurrection and the life." Martha had expressed the Jewish faith in a future resurrection at the end of time. Had Jesus been content with her understanding, He would not have responded as He did in verse 25. Though the statements in chapter 6 had connected resurrection and life in the future, Jesus here connects resurrection and life in the

---

12. Ernst Haenchen, *A Commentary on the Gospel of John, Chapters 1—6*, trans. Robert W. Funk, in *Hermeneia—A Critical and Historical Commentary on the Bible* (Philadelphia: Fortress Press, 1984), 291.

13. C. K. Barrett, *The Gospel According to St. John*, 2d ed. (Philadelphia: Westminster Press, 1978), 294.

14. Brown, *Gospel According to John*, 491.

present.[15] The last day has a present rather than a future meaning in John 11:25.

The singular expression "the last day" appears six[16] times
in the Gospel of John. Five of those references speak of a future
end time, while one appears to have a present meaning. Were it
not for the present emphasis of John 11:25, one might conclude
that the New Testament writers used the plural form, "the last
days," to refer to the time of Christ and the Church and the singular form, "the last day," to refer to the future end of time.
Hoekema has suggested such a distinction and illustrated it
with the following diagram:[17]

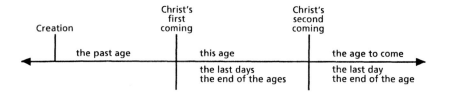

Creation	Christ's first coming	Christ's second coming
the past age	this age	the age to come
	the last days the end of the ages	the last day the end of the age

While such a distinction between "last days" and "last day"
may be a helpful way to describe the fact that the New Testament speaks of the end of time as both present and future, it is
not the way the New Testament uses the phrases. The singular
is limited to the Gospel of John and has both present and future
meanings.

The Johannine attraction to the singular also appears in 1
John 2:18, where the phrase "the last hour" (*eschatē hōra*) appears twice. The verse reads, "Little children, it is the last hour,
and just as you heard that anti-christ was coming, even now
many anti-christs have come. By this we know that it is the last
hour." The word "hour" can refer to either a general period of
time or a moment of time. The length of time involved in the
last hour could vary according to John.[18] However, it is clear

---

15. Ibid., 434.

16. The phrase "the last day" also appears in John 7:37 in reference to the final day
of the Jewish festival. There is no eschatological significance to its usage there.

17. Anthony A. Hoekema, *The Bible and the Future* (Grand Rapids: William B. Eerdmans Publishing Co., 1979), 20.

18. Stephen S. Smalley, *1, 2, 3 John*, vol. 51 of *Word Biblical Commentary* (Waco, Tex.:
Word Books, 1984), 95-97.

that this "last hour" is present already in the mind of John as he writes 1 John 2:18. John may prefer the singular "last day" or "last hour" to the plural, but the singular does not consistently refer to the future end of time in his writings.

The matter is not made clearer by the New Testament expressions for "the last time" or "last times." First Pet. 1:5 speaks of those, "who are being kept by the power of God through faith for a salvation ready to be revealed in the last time." The expression "ready to be revealed" and the fact that the concept of salvation in 1 Peter is generally future make it clear that this verse is speaking of a future end of time.[19]

The Greek word frequently translated as "time," found in 1 Pet. 1:5, is *kairos*. This word is often contrasted to another Greek word normally translated as time: *chronos*. *Chronos* is the word used in 1 Pet. 1:20 that describes Christ as "known before the foundation of the world, but manifested at the last of times for your sake." Though Davids[20] takes this reference to the "last of times" to mean the future end of time, it is more likely that Peter is referring to the time in which he lived and wrote. The other uses of *chronos* in 1 Pet. 1:17 and 4:2 suggest that he understood the word to mean a period of time. The contrast of verse 20 is then between the period of time before the beginning of the world and the last of the time periods that comes at the end of the world. This final period of time had begun with the appearance of Christ and thus was present at the time of the writing of 1 Peter.[21]

One might conclude that Peter used the singular of the last *kairos* to refer to the future and the plural of the last of *chronos* to refer to the present. However, a single example of each usage is simply an inadequate sample upon which to base any conclusions about patterns in 1 Peter. Jude 18 provides an example of the singular use of *chronos*. This verse is quite similar to 2 Pet.

19. J. Ramsey Michaels, *1 Peter*, vol. 49 of *Word Biblical Commentary* (Waco, Tex.: Word Books, 1984), 23; Edward Gordon Selwyn, *The First Epistle of Peter*, 2d ed. (1947; reprint, Grand Rapids: Baker Book House, 1981), 125; and Peter H. Davids, "The First Epistle of Peter," in *The New International Commentary on the New Testament* (Grand Rapids: William B. Eerdmans Publishing Co., 1990), 53-54.

20. Davids, "The First Epistle of Peter," 74.

21. Michaels, *1 Peter*, 68.

3:3 as it states, "Because they used to say to you, 'There will be mockers at the last time following their own ungodly desires.'" As in 2 Pet. 3:3, Jude 18 seems to have a future perspective. However, verse 19 then shifts to the present tense as it describes the mockers as people who are causing division in the Church. Though Jude might well have believed that mockers would appear at the last of time, his concern was with the presence of those mockers in his own time. This suggests that he would have understood the last time to refer to the time of his writing of the letter.

The New Testament evidence of the use of the phrases "last days," "last day," "last hour," "last times," and "last time" shows that the end times were regarded as both present and future. No consistent pattern suggests that any given phrase referred only to a present understanding of the end of time or only to a future understanding. If any pattern were to be suggested, it would be that the phrase "last days" has a present meaning in the New Testament. The study of these phrases shows that word studies or even phrase studies are not an adequate basis upon which to build an understanding of New Testament eschatology. An understanding of the way New Testament writers understood the concept of eschatology is necessary, and to that task this essay will now turn.

New Testament Eschatology

In the traditional structure of systematic theology, eschatology is the final chapter or section. The logic is simple: last things should be studied last. The truth of the future should logically follow the truth of the past and of the present. The discipline of New Testament theology approaches eschatology rather differently. Except in studies whose outline is borrowed from systematic theology, or the canonical order, eschatology is the first order of business for New Testament theologians who include the teaching of Jesus in their treatment of the New Testament.

According to the Synoptic Gospels, the main theme of Jesus' teaching was the kingdom of God.[22] This fact and the Jew-

---

22. Bruce Chilton, "Introduction," in *The Kingdom of God in the Teaching of Jesus*, ed. Bruce Chilton (Philadelphia: Fortress Press, 1984), 1.

ishness of Jesus and His ministry make eschatology a primary concern of New Testament theology.[23] It is likely that the increasing interest in eschatology near the end of the Old Testament period and throughout the intertestamental period was a product of the increasingly painful Jewish history.[24] The Babylonian captivity, the disappointing restoration period under the Persian Empire, the Seleucid attempt to destroy Judaism, and the Roman oppression were each sufficient reason for Jews to abandon hope for the present. It would be inaccurate to argue that each period was successively worse than the preceding one, but the cumulative effect of such a devastating history would have funded a growing Jewish pessimism. That Judaism increasingly turned its hope to the future intervention of God is not surprising. That Judaism continued to believe that faith in their God could make a difference in the course of human history is amazing.

Students of Judaism and early Christianity now recognize that no standard or normal form of Judaism existed by the time of Jesus, if such a Judaism had ever existed. The Jews who produced the Dead Sea Scrolls believed quite differently than did those who produced the Mishnah and Talmud. The range of theological positions reflected by the documents now considered part of the Old Testament Pseudepigrapha[25] reflect as much diversity as do contemporary Christian denominations. This diversity is true in terms of eschatology. Various forms of messianic expectation appeared portraying "a variety of figures and combinations of figures with a range of judicial and salvific functions: angels and human beings, a king, a priest, a prophet, an interpreter of the Torah."[26] It is not always clear whether the

---

23. One of the more salutary results of 20th-century studies of Jesus has been the recent recognition of the importance of Jesus' Jewishness for understanding Him and His ministry. The work of E. P. Sanders and James H. Charlesworth has led the way in this renewed emphasis.

24. See George W. E. Nicklesburg, "Eschatology (Early Jewish)" in *The Anchor Bible Dictionary*, ed. David Noel Friedman (New York: Doubleday and Co., 1992), 2:591.

25. *The Old Testament Pseudepigrapha*, ed. James H. Charlesworth (Garden City, N.Y.: Doubleday and Co., 1983, 1985), contains more than 50 separate "books" written between 200 B.C. and A.D. 200. This compares with 17 books found in the previous English translation edited by R. H. Charles and first published in 1913.

26. Nicklesburg, "Eschatology," 2:592.

various messianic figures were forgotten, reinterpreted, or preserved by the segments of Judaism who wrote about them.
Most of the Jewish apocalyptic writings between 200 B.C. and
A.D. 100 made no mention of the Messiah. Eschatology was formulated in terms of a dramatic invasion of human history by
God. In varying ways, God would destroy the present and op-
pressive foreign government and establish Jerusalem as the capital of the world and Judaism as the supreme, unhindered faith.

Given such variety in Jewish eschatology, late-20th-century
scholarship is reluctant to identify any specific beliefs as "Jewish eschatology." However, all the forms of Jewish belief are
identifiable as Jewish when compared to Greek or Roman. We
now understand Jewish and Greek to describe wide bands
along a connected spectrum of thought rather than two separate
containers of faith. The teachings of Jesus clearly reveal that He
fit within the spectrum of first-century Judaism.

One of the general distinctions that separated Greek and
Jewish thought was in the way they understood what moderns
call history. The Greek view of history was cyclical and infinite
and can be illustrated by the following figure:

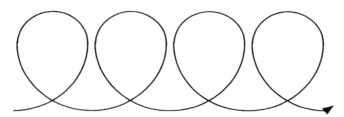

The Greek view of history: cyclical and infinite

The profound influence of this view of history on Western
thought can be seen in the traditional proverb "History repeats
itself." However, history never exactly repeats itself, and some
sense of progress and development is an essential part of the
Greek view. Thus, the spiral that never ends is an appropriate illustration.

In contrast, most of Judaism shared a view of history that
tended to be more linear, finite, and teleological. When Jewish
literature spoke of this present age, it viewed history in a way
that can be illustrated by the following diagram:

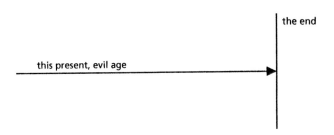

The present age was generally characterized as evil and was sometimes simply called "this age." The events of this present, evil age constitute history as the word is customarily understood. The present age would come to an end at some point that could be called only "the end of time."

Judaism, however, shared with Greek and other ancient Near Eastern cultures a persistent hope for the future. Judaism did not conceive of human existence coming to an end at the conclusion of the present evil age. Rather, existence would continue in a new age that was radically different from the present. This other age, called "the age to come," would begin shortly before the end of the present age. The following diagram illustrates the relationship between the two ages:

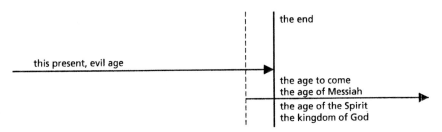

The age to come was also described as the age of the Messiah, the age of the Spirit, and the kingdom of God. When established, this coming age would be characterized by obedience to the Torah, the return of the gift of prophecy, and the sovereign rule of God on the earth. In the forms of Judaism that entertained messianic hopes, the coming age would be instituted by the Messiah.

The time of transition or overlap between the two ages was a time of conflict. The area marked by Xs in the following diagram shows the overlap of the ages:

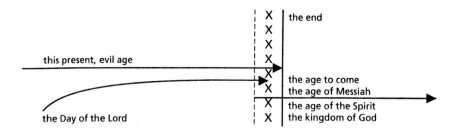

The struggle between the two ages would be accompanied by cosmic signs, such as the sun turning to darkness and the moon to blood. War between God's people and their enemies would break out, and persecution would intensify. This convulsive overlap of the ages was referred to as the Day of the Lord in Joel 2:31 and Mal. 4:5-6 and as the day of judgment in 2 Esd. 12:34.

Since the primary message of Jesus was the kingdom of God and that term was used in some forms of Judaism for the coming age, the nature of Jesus' understanding of the kingdom of God is crucial for New Testament eschatology. Twentieth-century scholarship has devoted considerable attention to this question.[27] Much of the discussion has centered around the question of whether Jesus viewed the Kingdom as a present reality or as a future hope. The view that Jesus viewed the Kingdom as present reality has been called realized eschatology and was first popularized by C. H. Dodd in the 1930s. The position that Jesus understood the kingdom of God as a future event about to take place has been called consistent eschatology or futuristic eschatology. Albert Schweitzer was the primary popularizer of this view early in the 20th century. Each view has appealed to Scripture for support.[28]

The evidence that Jesus understood the kingdom of God to have been present in His ministry is found both in comments about the Kingdom and in parables. Statements in Matt. 11:4-6, 12; Luke 11:20; 17:21; and Mark 1:15 reflect such understanding.

---

27. See Chilton, *Kingdom of God*, 1-35; and George Eldon Ladd, *The Presence of the Future: The Eschatology of Biblical Realism* (Grand Rapids: William B. Eerdmans Publishing Co., 1974), 3-42, for two helpful summaries of the research.

28. What follows is influenced by Leonhard Goppelt, *Theology of the New Testament*, trans. John Alsup (Grand Rapids: William B. Eerdmans Publishing Co., 1981), 51-67.

In Luke 11:20 Jesus states, "If by the finger of God I cast out demons, then the kingdom of God has come upon you." The context of this statement is the accusation of some that Jesus was casting out demons by the power of Beelzebub, the ruler of demons. That Jesus' ministry included demon exorcism is a clear conclusion from all the historical sources, including references in the Talmud. In Luke 11:20 Jesus interpreted that activity as an indication that the kingdom of God was a present reality.

The basic content of Matt. 11:4-6 is also found in Luke 7:18-23. The context is the question of John the Baptist in prison, delivered to Jesus by two of John's disciples: "Are you the one who is coming or do we wait for another?" Jesus replied, "When you go, tell John the things you have seen and heard. The blind see, the lame walk, lepers are being cleansed, the deaf hear, the dead are raised, and the poor have the gospel preached to them." Jesus' reference to these aspects of His ministry were not simply statements about miracles. He was alluding to the prophecies found in Isa. 29:18-19; 35:5-6; and 61:1-4. Jesus was claiming that the miracles of His ministry were signs of the presence of the great day of salvation prophesied in the Old Testament. Isa. 61:1-4 had specifically spoken of the preaching of the good news. That good news was described in Isa. 52:7 by the proclamation "Your God is King." Thus, Jesus understood His miracles as statements that the sovereign reign of God as King was present and at work in His ministry.

A few verses later, in Matt. 11:12 (Luke 16:16 provides a partial parallel), Jesus stated, "From the days of John the Baptist until now the kingdom of heaven is exercising its force, and those who use force are seizing it." The meaning of the verb *biazetai*, "exercising force," is difficult to determine. However, the tense of the verb is present. From the time of John the Baptist to the point of His comment, Jesus viewed the Kingdom as a present force.

Jesus' saying in Luke 17:20-21 is, "The kingdom of God is not coming with [signs for] observation, nor will they say, 'Behold, here,' or, 'there!' For behold the kingdom of God is in the midst of you." The words "in the midst of you" have created difficulty in interpretation. The word for this phrase allows the possibility that Jesus meant that the Kingdom was a spiritual reality "inside" each believer. However, the "you" is plural and the context of the discussion with the Pharisees makes it clear that Jesus meant the Kingdom was among them.[29] Though they did not recognize it, Jesus believed that the Kingdom was present among the Pharisees because He stood among them. He understood that the Kingdom was present because He was the bearer of the Kingdom.

The question of whether Mark 1:15 provides evidence that Jesus saw the Kingdom as present or as future has been fiercely debated in the 20th century.[30] Mark reports the opening words of Jesus' ministry as, "The time has been fulfilled and the kingdom of God has arrived. Repent and believe in the gospel." The point of debate is the meaning of the verb here translated as "arrived": *engizō*. The normal meaning of the word is "to approach, draw near, or come near," and that meaning has been used to argue that Jesus saw the Kingdom as near but still in the future. However, the tense of the Greek verb is the perfect tense, which indicates a past action that has present and ongoing results. For the Kingdom to have come near already and to be producing a present result suggests arrival.[31] If the Kingdom had arrived when Jesus began His gospel proclamation, then it was present in His ministry.

Several parables of Jesus also suggest that He understood the Kingdom to be present. The parable found in Matt. 13:31-32; Mark 4:30-32; and Luke 13:18-19 compares the Kingdom to a mustard seed, the smallest of those used in Palestine in the time of Jesus. However, though the seed is small, the mustard bush was the largest plant in a typical Palestinian garden. The parable is clearly designed to teach that the Kingdom's beginning was small but that its impact would be great. The parable is quite interesting in that it combines both a present and a future

29. Luke Timothy Johnson, *The Gospel of Luke*, in Sacra Pagina Series, ed. Daniel J. Harrington (Collegeville, Minn.: Liturgical Press, 1991), 3:262.

30. See Chilton, *Kingdom of God*, 14-15, for a summary of the discussion. Mark 1:15 was a key verse in Dodd's view of the realized eschatology of Jesus.

31. Robert H. Gundry, *Mark: A Commentary on His Apology for the Cross* (Grand Rapids: William B. Eerdmans Publishing Co., 1993), 64-66, presents a detailed argument for the case for "arrival."

aspect in Jesus' understanding of the Kingdom. As seed, the Kingdom was already present in Jesus' ministry, though it did not have the impact envisioned by Jewish eschatology. However, the promise of the Kingdom as a large bush points to a future time when it would accomplish the world-changing effects of the age to come.

In a similar fashion, the parables of the leaven in Matt. 13:33 and the seed growing by itself in Mark 4:26-29 imply the presence of the Kingdom. The leaven parable portrays the Kingdom as acting, even though it cannot be seen. The seed growing by itself, like the mustard seed, assumes the Kingdom to be present and growing without human engineering. The parables of the mustard seed, the seed growing by itself, and the leaven appear to be designed by Jesus to answer criticism that He was proclaiming the presence of the kingdom of God but that no evidence of it could be seen.

The parables of the wheat and the tares, found in Matt. 13:24-30, and the dragnet, found in Matt. 13:47-50, also assume the presence of the Kingdom. In each case, the Kingdom consists presently of a mixture of good and bad (seeds and fish). However, these parables also anticipate a future time for the Kingdom when the separation between good and bad will take place.

Based on these sayings and parables, it is difficult to avoid the conclusion that Jesus believed the kingdom of God to be present in His ministry. His personal presence was a sign of the Kingdom so that when Jesus was present the Kingdom was present as well.

The evidence that Jesus believed the kingdom of God to be future also appears in both parables and comments of Jesus. The sayings of expectation and the parables of Matt. 24—25 provide the primary evidence.

Mark 9:1 (with parallels in Matt. 16:28 and Luke 9:27) presents Jesus as saying, "Truly I say to you, there are some of those standing here who will certainly not taste death until they see the kingdom of God having come with power." The implication is that the Kingdom was not present when Jesus made the statement but that its arrival would be within the lifetime of some of His hearers. The question of how soon Jesus expected the Kingdom is debated,[32] and the question of whether the Kingdom having come with power is different from the Kingdom to come can be raised. However, Mark 9:1 and its parallels clearly point to a future expectation of the kingdom of God.

Another saying of expectation appears in Matt. 10:23—"Truly I say to you, you will not have gone through all the villages of Israel before the Son of Man comes." This verse does not mention the Kingdom but is part of a set of instructions Jesus gave His disciples before sending them on a preaching mission. Matt. 10:7 instructs them to proclaim the nearness of the Kingdom. Instructions about persecution follow, and the conclusion of verse 23 is that the whole preaching mission will not be accomplished until the Son of Man comes. The context clearly indicates that Jesus expected the Kingdom to arrive when the Son of Man arrived.

The so-called Synoptic Apocalypse found in Matt. 24, Mark 13, and Luke 21 is built around the expectation of the future coming of the Kingdom. The most specific statement of an imminent future coming of the Kingdom is in Matt. 24:34, with parallels in Mark 13:30 and Luke 21:32: "Truly I say to you, this generation will not pass away until all these things take place." This statement is part of Jesus' interpretation of the parable of the fig tree. As soon as the branch becomes tender and leaves appear, one may confidently assume that summer is near. In similar fashion, the events described in the Synoptic Apocalypse will provide a sure sign of the nearness of the Kingdom. The promise that all the events will happen in the lifetime of the listeners is a clear indication that the future Kingdom could appear shortly. All the conditions for its coming would soon be met.

Four parables dealing with preparedness for the Kingdom appear in Matt. 24 and 25 as the Matthean conclusion to the

---

32. Dale C. Allison, *The End of the Ages Has Come: An Early Interpretation of the Passion and Resurrection of Jesus* (Philadelphia: Fortress Press, 1985), 112-13, argues forcefully that Jesus expected the Kingdom in the immediate future. Allison presents an excellent list of types of future Kingdom teachings from Jesus on 112, with accompanying footnotes giving scriptural citations. On the other hand, Ben Witherington, *Jesus, Paul, and the End of the World: A Comparative Study in New Testament Eschatology* (Downers Grove, Ill.: InterVarsity Press, 1992), 36-44, argues that Jesus expected the consummation of the Kingdom in the future but had no time frame for His expectation in terms of the immediate or far distant future.

Synoptic Apocalypse. Matt. 24:45-51 presents the parable of the good and wicked servants. Matt. 25:1-13 presents the parable of the 10 virgins. The parable of the talents is found in verses 14-30, and the parable of the sheep and goats appears in verses 31-46. Parables similar to those of the good and wicked servants and of the talents appear in Luke 12:41-48 and 19:11-27 respectively, but the different context lessens the impact of the message of preparedness for the future Kingdom. Christianity very quickly interpreted these parables as teaching about watchfulness for the Second Coming. However, in the context of Jesus' own ministry, we have little indication that He taught anything explicitly about His second coming, as distinct from the coming of the Kingdom, prior to the Resurrection. From the historical context of the pre-Resurrection ministry of Jesus, the Matthean parables of preparedness call for readiness for the coming kingdom of God in the near future.

The evidence clearly points to Jesus' understanding of a future inbreaking of the Kingdom.[33] The evidence also clearly points to Jesus teaching the presence of the Kingdom in His own ministry and person. In terms of pure logic, the conclusion must be that Jesus' eschatological teaching was contradictory. However, the seed parables, among others, suggest that Jesus understood both a present and a future aspect to the kingdom of God. The Kingdom was indeed present in and through His ministry. Demon exorcism and the miracles attested to that reality. However, the cosmic effects of the Day of the Lord that Jewish eschatology expected from the inbreaking of the age to come had not accompanied Jesus' ministry. The parables of the mustard seed and the leaven are clear responses to that accusation. Jesus understood that the present reality of the Kingdom was not all the reality of the Kingdom. Its powerful, world-changing effect was yet to be seen. As a result, He taught that such a future expression of the Kingdom was on the way. His followers were to be prepared for its coming at any time.

This combination of realized and futuristic eschatology has been called eschatology in the process of realization. A less

---

33. Goppelt, *New Testament Theology*, 61, provides a helpful summary of the clarity of Jesus' teaching about the future nature of the Kingdom.

cumbersome description is inaugurated eschatology. Oscar Cullmann provided a useful illustration in his comparison of Jesus' teaching of the Kingdom to D day and V-day in World War II. The ministry of Jesus, especially including His death and resurrection, could be compared to D day. The Kingdom decisively and victoriously invaded this present age. As in the case of D day, the outcome was no longer in doubt, but the victory was not complete. Following the resurrection and ascension of Christ, the Early Church quickly understood that the final victory was yet to be consummated. The future aspect of the Kingdom, then associated with the return of Christ, would correspond to V-day.

The New Testament writers reflect this adapted understanding of Jesus' eschatology. That is why the references to "the last days" and "times" cataloged in the first section of this chapter contained both present and future points of view. The overlap of the ages in Jewish eschatology became the time of the church, the present, for the New Testament writers. The end of this present evil age would be concluded at the return of Christ, but that end had already begun with Jesus' ministry.

No scholar supposes that the New Testament writers expected the second coming of Christ to be delayed by 2,000 years or more. The uniform expectation of the New Testament was that this finalization of the end could happen at any time and would likely happen soon. The same signs that Judaism saw as evidence of the end were seen by early Christians as evidence that the Kingdom was already present and was about to be consummated. It is modern Christians—who are concerned that the 2,000-year delay must soon end—who struggle to interpret the signs of the times for an indication of the closeness of the future eschatological events.

"The Signs of the Times"

The phrase "signs of the times" is often used to describe certain events that can be understood as an indication that the second coming of Christ is about to occur. Identification of these signs with specific historical events has taken place throughout Christian history. In the past generation, however, publication, preaching, and promotion of various interpretations of the signs of the times has become a major growth industry among evangelical Christians. This is especially the case among those who describe their eschatology in dispensational terms.

The precise expression "signs of the times" (ta sēmeia tōn kairōn) appears only once in the New Testament, in Matt. 16:3: "You know how to discern the face of the heavens, but you do not know how to discern the signs of the times." In fact, verses 2-3 are not found in the two most important manuscripts witnessing to this section of Matthew, and Jerome (A.D. 345-419) stated that most of the manuscripts he knew did not include these verses. Though "most scholars regard the passage as a later insertion,"[34] a strong case can be made for including it in the original text of Matthew.[35]

The Pharisees and Sadducees had asked Jesus for a sign to demonstrate the truth of His claims. His response was a rebuke that they were able to discern the signs of the weather—a notoriously difficult undertaking—but had totally missed the signs of the times. In this context, it is clear that the signs they had missed were the signs that demonstrated the presence of the Kingdom in the ministry of Jesus. Thus, the reference to the signs of the times did not point to an understanding of the future aspects of the Kingdom. Rather, it spoke of recognition of the present reality of the Kingdom. Thus, it is ironic (and unbiblical) to call modern believers to interpret signs of the times in a way that would provide insight into the future end of time.

Hoekema points out four contemporary mistakes in attempting to understand the signs of the times in this fashion.[36] The first mistake is to see the signs of the times as referring only to the end of time understood in a future sense. The very fact that Jesus' reference to the signs of the times had a present (and past) perspective rather than future should alert the interpreter to the danger of an exclusive focus on the future. Advocates of

---

34. Bruce M. Metzger, *A Textual Commentary on the Greek New Testament* (New York: United Bible Societies, 1971), 41.

35. W. D. Davies and Dale C. Allison, *A Critical and Exegetical Commentary on the Gospel According to Saint Matthew*, in *Matthew VIII-XVIII*, vol. 2 of *The International Critical Commentary* (Edinburgh: T and T Clark, 1991), 580-81, n. 12, provides eight arguments in favor of retaining the questioned verses.

36. Hoekema, *The Bible and the Future*, 130-32.

biblical prophecy often pursue interpretations that require modern understandings of history (and science) for veracity. If such
interpretations are correct, then the prophecy must have been
utter nonsense to the original hearers. If Jesus' words from
Matt. 16:3 were meant to instruct 20th-century Christians about
interpreting the events of Iraq, Iran, and Russia, then they
meant nothing to the Pharisees and Sadducees to whom they
were spoken. Such an interpretation is extremely egotistical.

Further, if the signs mentioned in the Synoptic Apocalypse
have meaning only as keys to knowing when the end of time
will occur, their ability to call believers to preparedness
throughout Church history is gone. In fact, Christians throughout history have appealed to the signs as reminders of the need
for watchfulness in every generation. It is the nature of a biblical sign to be applicable in every period of history. König points
out that when signs are viewed as history known in advance,
they lose their message for the Church in every period prior to
that time.[37]

A second mistake in understanding biblical signs is to view
them only in terms of unusual and catastrophic events. The cosmic signs that Judaism expected in the Day of the Lord were
metaphorical references to the tremendous shift from what is
experienced in this present, evil age to the life of the age to
come. In His reply to the question of John the Baptist, Jesus
placed the preaching of the gospel alongside raising the dead as
evidence of the presence of the kingdom of God. Hoekema describes the preaching of the gospel to all nations as the "out-
standing and most characteristic sign of the times."[38] Jesus'
statement in Matt. 24:14 (paralleled in Mark 13:10), "This gospel
of the kingdom will be preached in all the inhabited world for a
witness to all the nations, and then the end will come," receives
much less attention than the more spectacular sayings. Believers
who are truly interested in the time of the Second Coming
should give themselves wholeheartedly to world evangelism as
the chief sign of the times. However, since that task requires the
daily discipline and the disappointment of being rejected, many

---

37. König, *Eclipse*, 190.
38. Hoekema, *The Bible and the Future*, 138.

believers prefer to try to ferret out future history from scattered (and unrelated) biblical passages.

The intense desire to interpret signs of the times in terms of the spectacular leaves one vulnerable to deception. The man of lawlessness described in 2 Thess. 2:1-12 will demonstrate powers, signs, and wonders. The beast of Rev. 13 will perform signs. In fact, verses 13-14 warn against being deceived by such signs. Jesus himself warned in Mark 13:21-23 against being deceived by signs and wonders. Preoccupation with unusual and abnormal signs borders on disobedience to Christ's instructions, both to evangelize the world and to give no attention to those who proclaim the spectacular.

A third error in interpreting signs is to use them to place a date on the time of Christ's return. Jesus himself taught in Matt. 24:36 and Mark 13:32 that no one, including himself, knew the time of the end of the world. Christian history is full of examples of persons who ignored that warning not to act wiser than Christ and set dates for the Second Coming. The little good accomplished has been more than offset by the skepticism toward biblical eschatology that has arisen from people who watched their mistakes.

A fourth and similar mistake is to use the signs of the time to develop timetables for end-time events. It is a persistent claim of dispensationalists that a precise pattern of events leading to the end of time is described in Scripture. Since the signs—to be authentic biblical signs—must be relevant in every period of history, they cannot follow any precise pattern.

The point of the biblical signs of the times is to enable hearers and readers of the Word to understand that God has fulfilled His promises in the coming of Christ. The end of time has already begun. It began in a stable in Bethlehem. The end of the end of time still lies in the future, but there is little we can know about it. What we must know is that the purpose and plan of God that will be fulfilled by the Second Coming has already been put in motion by the *first* coming of Christ.

Conclusion

Tremendous interest and energy is being devoted to the last days and the signs of the times in contemporary evangelical

Christianity. Too much of that interest and energy operates without a proper biblical orientation. When all eschatological attention is focused on the future, the biblical theme of the fulfillment of the times in the ministry of Jesus is diminished. Several unfortunate results occur.

Exclusive attention to the eschatological future undermines the doctrine of salvation plainly presented in the Scriptures. The New Testament writers clearly affirmed the death and resurrection of Jesus as the complete and sufficient basis for salvation. There is never the slightest hint that any schema of eschatological understanding is necessary for salvation. The amount of attention given to the last days and signs of the times in some circles is a denial of the centrality of the Cross and empty tomb for Christian faith.

Exclusive attention to the eschatological future exchanges data for relationship with Christ as the goal of Christian living. That New Testament Christians need to know the meaning of 70 weeks and 10 horns is never suggested in Scripture. That New Testament Christians are to grow up to the measure of the stature of the fullness of Christ is urged with a variety of terms by every New Testament author. Eschatological knowledge that seems more important than the pursuit of holiness is a form of idolatry. Wesleyan Christians, of all people, ought never to have the priority of holiness upstaged by eschatology.

Exclusive attention to futuristic eschatology turns attention from the daily tasks to which Christians are called. Preaching the gospel, establishing justice, showing mercy, bringing peace, and loving one's neighbor are the tasks of the Christian life. The celebration of what God has already done for us in Christ is always appropriate. Excessive concern about the future and what will happen before Christ comes is never a matter for Christian attention. Preparedness for Christ's coming is always expected of biblical Christians. Preoccupation with when He will come is never expected.

As Paul described the second coming of Christ in 1 Thess. 4, he writes in verse 18, "Encourage one another with these words." The Christian hope of Christ's return is a message of encouragement, not a mystery to be solved.

■ **JIRAIR S. TASHJIAN**

Jesus' Olivet Discourse

ACROSS A VALLEY from the Jerusalem Temple is the Mount of Olives, the site where Jesus delivered what has come to be known as the Olivet Discourse. Matt. 24—25, Mark 13, and Luke 21 provide three similar, but not identical, versions of this discourse. The Gospel of John leaves it out completely and instead substitutes a different type of farewell discourse in chapters 13—17.

For a century or so, the prevalent hypothesis among New Testament scholars has been that Mark was the first Gospel to be written, followed by Matthew and Luke, who used Mark as one of their sources.[1] Assuming the accuracy of this hypothesis, we will proceed first by examining Mark 13 as the earliest version of the Olivet Discourse. We will then take a look at Matt. 24—25 and Luke 21 and note their unique features compared to Mark 13.

---

1. According to this theory, known as the two-document hypothesis and widely accepted among New Testament scholars, Matthew and Luke depended not only on Mark but also on another source dubbed "Q," which is simply an abbreviation of "Quelle," the German word for source. "Q" was primarily a collection of the sayings of Jesus, which Matthew and Luke incorporated into their Gospels, after which "Q" disappeared as an independent document. This hypothesis is an attempt to explain the high degree of similarity and in many cases identical wording of Matthew, Mark, and Luke. For a detailed discussion of the hypothesis, see Donald Guthrie, *New Testament Introduction* (Downers Grove, Ill.: InterVarsity Press, 1970), 121-87; Werner Georg Kummel, *Introduction to the New Testament* (Nashville: Abingdon Press, 1975), 38-80.

■ *Jirair S. Tashjian is professor of New Testament at Southern Nazarene University in Bethany, Oklahoma.*

Mark 13: Analysis of Its Form and Content

The position of the Olivet Discourse in Mark is significant. It provides a link between the fast-paced public ministry of Jesus, culminating in a crescendo of controversies with Temple authorities in chapters 11—12, and the Passion narrative of chapters 14—15. Yet it is surprising that in this discourse Jesus says absolutely nothing about His impending passion. This raises some questions about the nature of the discourse, whether Jesus spoke these words exactly in their present form and at this exact point in His life.

Mark 13 is a discourse in which Jesus is giving His disciples admonition and encouragement.[2] The purpose of the address is not to predict the course of future events or to inform the disciples about exact signs of the end times.[3] The purpose is rather to provide instruction and consolation to them as they live out their lives in the world in anticipation of the final consummation. In this sense, Mark 13 is different from apocalyptic writings such as Daniel and Revelation.[4] Mark 13 is an exhortation, rather than apocalyptic speculation about the end of the world. It lacks the typical features of apocalyptic literature.[5] Instead, it is punctuated with characteristic words of exhortation that may be variously translated as "take heed," "beware," "be alert" (vv. 5, 9, 23); "do not be alarmed" (v. 7), "do not be anxious" or "do not worry" (v. 11); "pray" (v. 18); "watch," "be on guard," or "keep awake" (vv. 35, 37); and at the end of the address, a combination of two words of admonition: "beware; keep alert" or "be on guard; be alert" (v. 33).

---

2. William L. Lane, *The Gospel of Mark,* in the *New International Commentary on the New Testament* (hereafter cited as NICNT) (Grand Rapids: William B. Eerdmans Publishing Co., 1974), 444-46.

3. Werner Georg Kummel, *Promise and Fulfillment: The Eschatological Message of Jesus,* in *Studies in Biblical Theology* (London: SCM Press, 1961), 99.

4. C. E. B. Cranfield, "The Gospel According to St. Mark," in *The Cambridge Greek New Testament* (Cambridge: Cambridge University Press, 1963), 388.

5. Typical features of apocalyptic literature include an angelic being who is the agent of revelation, a recipient of revelation who is transported into heavenly realms, highly symbolic imagery that functions as a secret code understood by insiders only, and a fierce battle of cosmic proportions between good and evil. For further reading, consult Paul D. Hanson, "Apocalypse, Genre" and "Apocalypticism," in *Interpreter's Dictionary of the Bible, Supplementary Volume* (Nashville: Abingdon Press, 1962), 27-34.

It must be recognized, of course, that the address of Jesus does make references to future events and therefore is an eschatological discourse. But a number of observations must be made about these references. First, they are subordinated under the exhortations.[6] In other words, the exhortation is the main sentence; the future event is in a secondary position. Note, for example, the exhortation in verse 5 to take heed, which is the primary clause; the coming of false prophets is a subordinate statement in verse 6 to explain the reason for taking heed. In verse 7 the primary clause is "do not be alarmed"[7]; the subordinate clause is "when you hear of wars and rumors of wars." Typically, the conjunction "for" is used to subordinate a future event to an exhortation (vv. 8, 19, 22, 33, 35). The primary agenda in the Olivet Discourse is not a description of future history, but an admonition to the disciples in their present circumstances to be alert in the face of threats, dangers, and uncertainties.[8]

Second, the structure of the discourse is such that the events referred to are not really intended to be signs of the end. In fact, just the opposite is the case. This can be seen when the structure of the discourse is carefully analyzed.

The passage has two major divisions: verses 5-23 and verses 24-36, with an introduction in verses 1-4 and a conclusion in verse 37.[9] The first division consists of warnings against four types of deceptive signs of the end: (a) false prophets, wars, and natural calamities (vv. 5-8); (b) persecutions (vv. 9-13); (c) the desolating sacrilege (vv. 14-20); and (d) false Christs (vv. 21-23). The point here is that these are not the signs of the end. "Such things must happen, but the end is still to come" (v. 7). "These are the beginning of the birth pains" (v. 8). "[The one] who stands firm to the end will be saved" (v. 13). The disciples must resist the urge to speculate about the nearness of the end on the

6. Lloyd Gaston, *No Stone on Another: Studies in the Significance of the Fall of Jerusalem in the Synoptic Gospels* (Leiden: E. J. Brill, 1970), 52.

7. Unless otherwise indicated, Scripture quotations in this chapter are from the NIV.

8. James M. Robinson, *The Problem of History in Mark and Other Marcan Studies* (Philadelphia: Fortress Press, 1982), 98.

9. Lamar Williamson, Jr., "Mark," in *Interpretation* (Atlanta: John Knox Press, 1983), 237.

basis of these events. These are unfortunate developments in human history, but they are not apocalyptic signs of the nearness of the end.[10] These crises have always happened in history and will probably happen again in the future, but they are not apocalyptic signs.

It should be noted that the Temple serves as a backdrop for the discourse (vv. 1-4). In answer to the disciples' fascination with the grandeur of the Temple (v. 1), Jesus says, "Not one stone here will be left on another; every one will be thrown down" (v. 2). When the disciples ask Him about the sign as to when all these things are about to be accomplished, Jesus begins His address. Yet His reply is not neatly related to the destruction of the Temple. The connection between the disciples' question and Jesus' answer is very loose.[11] One also wonders what all is to be included in "all these things" in the disciples' question. Apparently it includes more than the destruction of the Temple. Yet in spite of such a nagging curiosity on the part of the disciples about the Temple and about "all these things," what we get is a litany of events with the constant refrain "the end is still to come"; this is just the beginning.

Why does Mark report this discourse of Jesus in the context of the disciples' question about the Temple? The implication is clear: not even such an ominous event as the destruction of the Temple should give rise to feverish speculation about end times. The disciples must resist the temptation to speculate about end times or to be unduly alarmed even when this symbol of institutional religion collapses.[12] Their hope lies elsewhere.

Third, the events of verses 5-23 are not really a reference to some mysterious, speculative, future tribulation period. These events can be perfectly understood in the historical context of the first century and the experiences of early Christians prior to and at the time of the writing of the Gospel of Mark and the

---

10. Gaston, *No Stone on Another*, 50.

11. Eduard Schweizer, *The Good News According to Mark* (Atlanta: John Knox Press, 1970), 262.

12. By the same token, even if the Temple were to be rebuilt in Jerusalem in our day, as Hal Lindsey predicted (*The Late Great Planet Earth* [Grand Rapids: Zondervan Publishing Co., 1970], 55-58), we must still resist the temptation to speculate about its significance as a sign of the end.

other Gospels. But fundamentalist interpreters who come from a Calvinist perspective have a tendency to make prophetic writings in the Bible into a prediction of a predetermined future. Accordingly, they take the statements in the Olivet Discourse out of the context and frame of reference of first-century Christians and make them into a blueprint for a future end of the world.[13]

It is necessary that we understand how the Gospels were written. As far as we know, Jesus himself did not write anything. He was a preacher rather than a writer. Furthermore, there is no evidence whatsoever that the disciples wrote anything while they were being instructed by Jesus. Jesus and His disciples lived in an oral culture. The words of Jesus were passed on by word of mouth through the avenue of preaching and teaching in the Early Church. The concern of the early disciples was not to pass on the teaching of Jesus by rote memory in a wooden and stilted fashion. Their concern was to be faithful to the spirit of His teaching and His ongoing presence with them. As the words of Jesus were passed on, they were being constantly interpreted and reinterpreted in a variety of ways, depending on the particular circumstances and needs of the Early Church. As Christians faced a new day and changing circumstances, they looked back to Jesus and His words to interpret the meaning of their bewildering experiences. The reason the words of Jesus survived in the memory of the Early Church was that they served a significant and useful function in the life of the Early Church. But the words of Jesus did not simply survive in a detached and objective manner. They shaped and in turn were shaped by the Early Church in a mutual, dynamic relationship.

It should become obvious, then, that the discourse in Mark 13 reflects not only the words and thoughts of Jesus but also the concerns, experiences, needs, historical circumstances, and the-

---

13. See, for example, Marvin Rosenthal, *The Pre-Wrath Rapture of the Church* (Nashville: Thomas Nelson, 1990), 104, who interprets Matt. 24:21, which is parallel to Mark 13:19, as a reference to "the Great Tribulation" in an effort to make the Olivet Discourse into a precise prediction of end times. Note that Matthew has no "the" before "great tribulation." It is simply "a" great affliction or suffering. Furthermore, the word "then" in this verse refers most naturally to the time of suffering described in the previous six verses (vv. 15-20), which reflect the actual experiences of Christians during the Jewish-Roman war of A.D. 66-70. More on this a little later.

ological perspectives of Christians in the 60s or 70s of the first
century when the Gospel of Mark was being formed and eventually written down. This is not to say that Mark 13 is simply
the invention and creation of the Early Church or the Gospel
writer. It is to say, however, that in Mark 13 we have the word
of Jesus as it is filtered through the heart and soul of the Early
Church. Mark 13 reflects in significant ways the experiences of
people to whom and for whom this Gospel was written.

An example will illustrate how this material developed in
the few decades between the lifetime of Jesus and the final composition of the Gospel of Mark. In verse 14, reference is made to
"the desolating sacrilege set up where it ought not to be"
(NRSV). This has puzzled many a reader of this discourse.
What makes it even more puzzling is the enigmatic statement
that follows it: "let the reader understand." It is a parenthetical
statement by the author of the Gospel. Why is he making such a
statement? What is he wanting the reader to understand?

The parenthetical statement itself makes it clear that Mark
is using an older statement of the Christian tradition and making an application of it in a new way to the circumstances of the
readers to whom he is writing. Here we find direct evidence
that as the words of Jesus were passed on, they were being used
to address new situations in the life of the Church. The words of
Jesus changed in meaning and relevance as they were told in
new and different settings. His words were not passively trans-
mitted. Likewise, the concluding statement of the discourse in
verse 37 (NRSV), "And what I say to you I say to all: Keep
awake," implies that the hearers are not limited to the first
group of disciples in the lifetime of Jesus, but includes "all"
who have heard these words in later times.

The words "desolating sacrilege" (NRSV) first occur in
Dan. 9:27; 11:31; 12:11. If the late date of the authorship of the
Book of Daniel is accepted,[14] the immediate reference of the

---

14. The traditional date for the writing of Daniel is during the Babylonian captivity.
However, critical scholars find linguistic and cultural evidence in the book that indicates that it was composed over a period of time extending from the Persian to the Hellenistic period, with the final form of the book taking shape during the Maccabean period during the first one-third of the second century B.C. (W. Sibley Towner, "Daniel," in
Interpretation [Atlanta: John Knox Press, 1984], 5-6).

phrase would be to an event in the Maccabean period that appalled Jewish people and precipitated the Maccabean war. The Seleucid ruler in Syria, Antiochus IV Epiphanes, who was in control of Palestine, had been wanting to impose Greek culture and religion on the Jewish people. It is likely that the final form of the Book of Daniel took shape during this time of crisis. In 168 B.C. Antiochus finally carried out his intentions. He forbade Jewish worship and erected an altar to the Greek god Zeus in the Jerusalem Temple and offered a pig as sacrifice (1 Macc. 1—2). The Maccabean family organized a war of resistance and succeeded in gaining power and in cleansing the Temple.

When Jesus made reference to the desolating sacrilege, He was using the phrase from Daniel but implying that the ultimate fulfillment of this prophecy would still be in the future. Critical scholars agree that Jesus must have made some sort of statement about the Temple and the city of Jerusalem, even if we may never know exactly what He said. This statement of Jesus comes to us in a variety of forms and contexts in the four Gospels. For example, according to John 2:19, Jesus says, "Destroy this temple, and I will raise it again in three days." This same saying appears in a slightly different form in Mark 14:58 (NRSV) on the lips of false witnesses at the trial of Jesus: "I will destroy this temple that is made with hands, and in three days I will build another, not made with hands" (cf. Mark 15:29). The statement in Mark 13:2 is, "Not one stone here will be left on another; every one will be thrown down." Yet in Luke 19:44 the phrase "one stone on another" is spoken not in reference to the Temple itself but to the whole city of Jerusalem.

Even if we may be uncertain about the exact words or intentions of Jesus relative to the Temple, Mark leaves no doubt as to what they meant. The Gospel of Mark was written at a time of crisis in Jewish-Roman relations in Palestine. In A.D. 66-70, war broke out between Roman troops and Jewish resistance fighters. The Roman threat to the city of Jerusalem and the Jewish nation was at an all-time high. When final negotiations failed, Roman forces under Titus took over Jerusalem and destroyed the city and the Temple in A.D. 70.

It is quite likely that the Gospel of Mark was written at this

critical point in history.[15] Mark was using words of Jesus preserved in the Christian tradition to give encouragement and exhortation to Christians who were in Jerusalem and Judea at the
time of the Jewish-Roman war and the approaching threat to
the city of Jerusalem. The instructions given in verses 14-16
make perfectly good sense in the context of that war.[16] The urgent plea to flee to the mountains, not to enter the house to take
anything, and not to return to the house from the field would be
perfectly understood by people who are fleeing the ravages of
war. They would not be thinking of some future tribulation.
Likewise, it would not be too difficult to imagine the added
complications attendant to pregnant women and inclement
weather at a time of war (vv. 17-18). What may have been a general statement on the lips of Jesus suddenly took on new and
significant meaning for Mark's audience caught in the middle
of a shattering crisis.

An important transition occurs in verse 24. This is indicated by the conjunction "but," which in Greek indicates strong
contrast with the preceding.[17] The events in this second major
division of the discourse are to be seen in contrast to the events
of the first division. The events in the first division, such as destruction of the Temple, wars, earthquakes, persecutions, or
even antichrists are not signs of the end. In contrast, this second
division does give the one true sign of the end: the coming of
the Son of Man in glory. When that happens, the end is near.

Yet when one reflects on this, it becomes clear that the coming of the Son of Man is not really a sign of the end at all. It is
the end itself.[18] It comes suddenly, without advance warnings or
signs. The events in verses 5-23 do not provide any kind of
timetable whereby to predict the coming of the end. The phrase

15. Guthrie, *Introduction*, 72-76; Kummel, *Introduction*, 98.

16. It is possible that the Olivet Discourse took shape in early Christian tradition
prior to its inclusion in Mark. There are indeed several historical occasions both in the
lifetime of Jesus as well as in the period of the Early Church, when such a saying of Jesus would have been well suited. In the lifetime of Jesus, Pilate attempted to set up Cae-
sar's standards in Jerusalem (Josephus, *Antiquities*, XVIII, iii, 1-2). In A.D. 40 the emperor
Caligula ordered the erection of his statue in the Temple (Gaston, *No Stone*, 27; Schweizer, *Mark*, 263).

17. Lane, "Mark," 473.

18. Cranfield, "Mark," 406.

"in those days" in verse 24 is an ambiguous time reference. It is a vague, stereotyped expression in the Old Testament taken over in the New Testament. Although it does have some eschatological connotations (Joel 3:1; Zech. 8:23), it has "no determined temporal value."[19]

Hence, one must be ready for the coming of the Son of Man at all times and even wait for it expectantly within one's own lifetime (v. 30), yet without a nervous attempt to find a sign of it in this or that historical event. In fact, one must guard against false messiahs and false prophets who are obsessed with an eagerness to show "signs and wonders" (v. 22, KJV).[20] False prophets "will exploit to the full the natural craving of the disciples to escape from the painful paradoxes and tensions and indirectness of faith into the comfortable security of sight."[21]

This second major division of the Olivet Discourse (vv. 24-36) begins with a bit of poetry made up of four lines (vv. 24-25). The first three lines are about the demise of the sun, moon, and stars respectively, and the last line is a summary of the first three lines. Since this is poetic and symbolic language, any interpretation that insists on a literal reading of these lines fails to reckon with the literary genre employed here. Modern scientific insights into the future of the solar system cannot be imported into the poetic symbolism of these verses.

This poetic statement is a collage of various Old Testament phrases and allusions that come primarily from Isaiah and Joel. In the Old Testament, the expectation of cosmic phenomena in the heavens, along with wars, earthquakes, and other catastrophes on earth, was associated with the judgment of God, often referred to as "the day of the Lord." Isa. 13 is an oracle about the fall of Babylon to the Persians. Her time of judgment has come. The stars, sun, and moon will cease to give their light (v. 10). Likewise in Isa. 34:4, spoken against all nations, and particularly Edom, "the host of heaven shall rot away" (NRSV). In Joel a massive locust plague is devastating Israel. Joel sees this as a

---

19. Lane, "Mark," 474.
20. Already in Deut. 13:1-3, Israel is warned not to be deceived by signs and wonders performed by false prophets, even if they do come to pass.
21. Cranfield, "Mark," 405.

judgment of God and issues a call to repentance. Again, the sun, moon, and stars are said to withhold their light (Joel 2:10; 3:15).

It would not be too difficult to imagine how such imagery may have originated. Dust, fire, and smoke during wars and earthquakes tend to darken the atmosphere. A thick swarm of locusts would likewise dim the light of the sun. Since Israel's prophets interpreted wars, earthquakes, and locusts as signs of God's judgment, the association of judgment with the cosmic phenomena of sun, moon, and stars would be close at hand.

At a more profound level, however, one must also reckon with the Old Testament perspective that sun, moon, and stars represented heavenly deities that held sway over Israel's pagan neighbors.[22] For Israel's prophets, Yahweh alone was the true, sovereign God. In His sovereignty He could even exercise His power over sun, moon, and stars.

The point of all this can now be more clearly stated in the context of Mark 13 and the Gospel as a whole. If the whole cosmos were to run its course, and if sun, moon, and stars were ultimately to fail, even this is not the ultimate end. Up to this point, Jesus has been speaking of all the horrible possibilities in history awaiting the disciples. They will be betrayed, dragged before governors and kings, beaten in synagogues, hated by all. There will be false messiahs, wars, and earthquakes. Even the Temple in Jerusalem, the symbol of God's presence, may be desecrated and destroyed. Over against these earthly sorts of events there may even be a shaking and failure of cosmic entities. Yet beyond all of these changing conditions of heaven and earth, there is the affirmation that the Son of Man will come in clouds with great power and glory (v. 26). This is another Old Testament statement coming from Dan. 7:13-14, which in turn is derived from Jer. 4:13.

The irony of Jesus' coming in divine majesty must not be lost on the reader of Mark. Mark has carefully constructed his Gospel. In chapters 8—10 he has given the reader three statements in which Jesus reveals to the disciples what sort of shameful treatment, suffering, and death awaits Him in Jerusa-

---

22. Claus Westermann, *Genesis 1—11: A Commentary* (Minneapolis: Augsburg, 1984), 127.

lem (8:31; 9:31; 10:32-34). Then in chapters 14—15, He tells the Passion story. In between these two large segments is the Olivet Discourse. To believe that this one who was despised and condemned to die on a cross will come in great power and glory all but taxes normal expectations. Yet now, the only hope held out to the disciples who would be facing an equally uncertain and calamitous future is the coming of the Son of Man. The only way they can find meaning and purpose is to hold on to that hope. In the final analysis, it is not a matter of when or how the Son of Man will come.[23] The essential point is that the disciples must live with that expectation burning in their souls.

The coming of Jesus "in clouds" reflects a rich background in Old Testament thought. Clouds are the vehicle of God's presence and glory (Exod. 16:10; Lev. 16:2; Num. 11:25; 1 Kings 8:10-11) and a symbol of His coming in judgment (Jer. 4:13).[24]

In a sense, there is no real end of the world envisioned in Mark 13. The purpose of the coming of the Son of Man is not to bring an end to the world but to "gather his elect from the four winds" (v. 27). The regathering of Israel back to their homeland after their dispersion among the nations was an Old Testament hope (Deut. 30:4; Isa. 11:12; Jer. 23:3; Ezek. 11:17). However, in Mark 13:27, the regathering of the people of God is neither to the Temple of Jerusalem nor to the land of Israel, since both are assumed to be destroyed. Nor is there any indication here that the Temple would be rebuilt or that the nation of Israel will be reestablished. Nor yet is there any hint of a "rapture" of the disciples to a heavenly realm as such. The regathering is instead around the Son of Man, Jesus himself.[25] This is the new people of God reconstituted by Jesus and brought together "from the ends of the earth to the ends of the heavens" (cf. Deut. 13:7; 30:3), which is Mark's way of expressing the universal scope of God's people, including both Jews and Gentiles.[26]

---

23. Cranfield, "Mark," 406-7.
24. R. B. Y. Scott, "Cloud," in *Interpreter's Dictionary of the Bible,* ed. George Buttrick (Nashville: Abingdon Press, 1962), 1:655; Vincent Taylor, *The Gospel According to St. Mark* (New York: St. Martin's Press, 1966), 391.
25. Lane, "Mark," 477.
26. G. R. Beasley-Murray, *Jesus and the Kingdom of God* (Grand Rapids: William B. Eerdmans Publishing Co., 1986), 332.

In verses 28-36, a number of parables and sayings of Jesus are brought together to impress on the disciples the importance of being alert. First, there is the parable of the fig tree (v. 28). When its branch becomes tender and puts forth its leaves, summer is near. This is a bit strange, because one would expect spring, not summer. Summer is the time of harvest, not the budding of trees. But perhaps the anomaly is intentional, and it does make a point. The point is that when "these things" (v. 29) begin to take place, he is "near"—near, but not quite "here." The coming of the Son of Man is always in the near future. Yet in another sense He is indeed here. Therefore, the disciples must always live at this critical point between the "already" of the Christ event that has taken place and the "not yet" that is still in the future. The present is most important. Now is the age of the fig tree.[27] The important thing is to be alert and responsible here and now with the task entrusted to us, as the parable of the servants in verse 34 makes clear. To speculate about signs of the times, apocalyptic time charts, and a golden future is a waste of energy that contradicts the very tenor of the Olivet Discourse.[28]

"These things" in verse 29 and "all these things" in verse 30 most likely refer to the events of verses 5-23. On the other hand, grammatical and syntactical considerations allow the inclusion of the heavenly phenomena and the coming of the Son of Man in verses 24-26 in "these things." However, it would be pointless for Jesus to say that when the disciples see the Son of Man coming they should know He is near.[29] Furthermore, it should

27. Bernard Brandon Scott, *Hear Then the Parable* (Minneapolis: Fortress Press, 1990), 342.

28. During the 1990-91 Persian Gulf crisis, a spate of misleading publications appeared speculating about Armageddon. Some examples: Charles H. Dyer, *The Rise of Babylon: Sign of the End Times* (Wheaton, Ill.: Tyndale House, 1991); Edgar C. James, *Arabs, Oil, and Armageddon* (Chicago: Moody Press, 1991); John F. Walvoord, *Armageddon, Oil, and the Middle East Crisis* (Grand Rapids: Zondervan Publishing House, 1990). Earlier, Hal Lindsey interpreted the budding fig tree as a specific prediction of the modern establishment of Israel as a nation, which occurred in 1948. Then he calculated that Christ would come within one generation (Mark 13:30; Matt. 24:34; Luke 21:32), or within 40 years, which made 1988 the target date (*The Late Great Planet Earth*, 53-54). Obviously he was mistaken. All such calculations are ultimately wrongheaded.

29. Cranfield, "Mark," 407; cf. Beasley-Murray, *Kingdom of God*, 334.

be noted that there is a previous mention of "these things" in the disciples' question to Jesus in verse 4. The events of verses 5-23 would be the most immediate reply of Jesus. The celestial phenomena in verses 24-26 stand apart from and in contrast to the previous events, as was argued earlier.

If this argument is correct, it would be much easier to understand the statement in verse 30 that "this generation will certainly not pass away until all these things have happened." The most natural meaning of "this generation" is the period of the first followers of Jesus. If Mark wrote his Gospel around A.D. 70, he would certainly know that the events of verses 5-23 have indeed taken place. If "these things" include the celestial phenomena and the coming of the Son of Man, it would be difficult to understand how Mark could pass on this saying of Jesus without some sort of explanation as to why Jesus has not come yet. Likewise, it would be difficult to understand how Mark could include a saying of Jesus such as Mark 9:1—that some standing there would not taste death until they have seen the kingdom of God has come in power—unless we assume that for Mark the coming of the kingdom of God in power has in some sense already occurred and therefore is not to be identified totally and exclusively with the coming of the Son of Man in clouds.[30] The kingdom of God has been inaugurated, albeit not yet consummated. Neither Jesus nor Mark thinks of the kingdom of God in terms of apocalyptic events in the future. In fact, no one knows "that day or hour" (v. 32), not even Jesus himself.[31] That ought to have put a stop to all attempts to predict the time of the Second Coming and the making of time charts, but unfortunately that has not been the case in the history of Christianity.

---

30. Taylor, *Mark*, 383-84.

31. In Matt. 24:36, which is almost identical to Mark 13:32, the words "nor the Son" are not found in any ancient manuscripts of the Gospel of Matthew. The most likely explanation is that some Christian scribes who made copies of the Gospel of Matthew had difficulty accepting the implication that Jesus was limited in His knowledge, and therefore they left those words out. These words were most likely a part of the original (Robert H. Gundry, *Matthew: A Commentary on His Literary and Theological Art* [Grand Rapids: William B. Eerdmans Publishing Co.], 492).

Unique Features of Matt. 24—25
Compared with Mark 13

Although it is impossible in this essay to discuss exhaustively all the unique features of Matthew's version of the discourse, attention will be given to some of the more significant differences between Matthew and Mark. Interestingly, the most important difference between the two versions has to do with the introduction and the conclusion.

The first thing to be noted is the question of the disciples to Jesus in Matt. 24:3. Matthew omits the names of the four disciples who are named in Mark 13:3 and instead presents the whole group of disciples as asking the question. This means that what Jesus says is significant not only for a few individuals but for the whole Church as well, both past and present.

More significantly, the question itself is different in Matthew in comparison with Mark. In Mark, the disciples ask when "these things" are to be accomplished. Matthew has changed the question into a two-pronged query: "When will this happen, and what will be the sign of your coming and of the end of the age?" Matthew has made a clear distinction between "these things" on one hand and Christ's coming and end of the age on the other hand.[32] The technical term in the Greek New Testament for the coming of Christ is *parousia*, which means public arrival or presence, and not necessarily a second coming or a return.[33] Only Matthew uses *parousia* in his Gospel, and he does this in this verse and three other times in the Olivet Discourse (vv. 27, 37, 39). Matthew is not satisfied with the ambiguous "these things" in Mark 13:3, because in the immediate context it refers to the destruction of the Temple (Mark 13:2). He wants to make it crystal clear that there is a distinction between the events surrounding the destruction of the Temple and the sign of Christ's coming.

Here in verse 3, as well as in verse 30, the "sign" of Christ's coming is singular. It is separate and distinct from the other

---

32. In Greek there is only one definite article ("the") with the coming of Christ and end of the age, thus collapsing the two into one event (Gundry, *Matthew*, 476).

33. Eduard Schweizer, *The Good News According to Matthew* (Atlanta: John Knox Press, 1975), 480.

events associated with the fall of Jerusalem and the destruction of the Temple. In verse 30 Jesus says, "Then the sign of the Son of Man will appear in heaven." In other words, the coming of the Son of Man is itself a sign of the end. There is no other sign that will usher Christ in. His own coming is the sign.[34] The implication is that Matthew even more pointedly than Mark wants to let his readers understand that the events recounted in the first part of the discourse have to do with the destruction of the Temple and are not really signs of Christ's coming or the end of the age.

The coming of Christ will be public, open, and observable by all. Matthew has two additional statements not seen in Mark that emphasize the open and public nature of Christ's coming in contrast to the false Christs and prophets who say Christ has come in the wilderness or in some inner room (vv. 23-26). His coming will be like lightning that lights up the whole sky (v. 27). The statement about the corpse and the vultures in verse 28, taken from Job 39:30, is another metaphor for the unmistakable sign of Christ's coming, just as vultures circling in the air are a sure sign that there is a corpse nearby. The metaphor should not be made into an allegory by making Christ the corpse and the people of God the vultures. In fact, in the context of verses 23-27 the imagery may be more appropriately a reference to the converging of false messiahs and false prophets as the end nears.[35]

In Matt. 24:20, Jesus tells the disciples to pray that their flight may not be in winter, which is the same as in Mark. But Matthew adds "or on the Sabbath," which would be significant for his Jewish-Christian audience who had rules against excessive travel on the Sabbath. Such a concern would make sense not at the coming of Christ or the end of the world, but for people fleeing the ravages of war such as the one in A.D. 66-70, when Jerusalem was destroyed.

We can be certain that the Gospel of Matthew was written after the fall of Jerusalem, which for Matthew was a definite, theologically significant point in the history of God's dealings with Israel. In Matt. 22:7, in the parable of the great supper, the

---

34. Gundry, *Matthew*, 488.
35. Schweizer, *Matthew*, 455.

statement is made that the angry king, whose servants had been rebuffed and killed by the prospective guests, sent his troops and destroyed those murderers and "burned their city." And in chapter 23, just before the Olivet Discourse, Matthew has a long litany of woes pronounced by Jesus on the scribes and Pharisees. At the end of that chapter, and as a transition to the Olivet Discourse, we find Jesus' lament over Jerusalem in which He says to the city, "Your house is left to you desolate" (23:38). In the opening verses of Matt. 24 Jesus is sitting on the Mount of Olives, just as in Mark, but Matthew leaves out the words "opposite the temple" in an effort to distance Jesus from the Temple (compare Matt. 24:3 and Mark 13:3).[36]

In verse 29, Matthew changes the strong conjunction "but" of Mark 13:24 to a weaker one and adds "immediately" at the beginning of the verse. Thus, according to Matthew, the heavenly portents and the coming of the Son of Man (vv. 29-31) would occur immediately after the tribulation described in verses 3-28. This means one of two things: either (a) for Matthew the coming of the Son of Man has already occurred—immediately after the fall of Jerusalem,[37] or (b) Matthew expected the coming of the Son of Man in the immediate future.[38] It would be more accurate, however, to opt for a third alternative, namely, that Christ is both present among His disciples in the world in a more hidden manner, but He will also come in a more visible and open manner in the future.

Perhaps the most significant feature of Matthew's Olivet Discourse is that he has deleted the conclusion of the discourse in Mark 13:33-37 and in its place has inserted sayings about the days of Noah (24:37-39), the two men in the field and the two women at the mill (24:40-41; v. 42 is an adaptation of Mark 13:35), the householder and the coming of the thief (24:43-44), and the good or wicked servant (24:45-51). All these sayings occur in Luke also (17:26-36; 12:39-46), but not at all in Mark. This

36. Ibid., 476.
37. Gaston, No Stone, 484. In support of this view, one can point to the last word of Jesus to the disciples in Matt. 28:18-20, where He says, "All authority in heaven and on earth has been given to me. . . . I am with you always, to the very end of the age," with no further exaltation or promise of another coming.
38. Gundry, Matthew, 487; Schweizer, Matthew, 455.

would suggest that Matthew has found these sayings in "Q"[39] and added them to what he found in Mark to compose his own version of the discourse. All of them have to do with the sudden and unexpected coming of the Son of Man.

The reason for this major departure from Mark is that Matthew was not yet ready to conclude the discourse at this point. In fact, Matthew's Olivet Discourse continues on into chapter 25, which contains the three parables of the 10 virgins, the talents, and the sheep and the goats.[40] These parables are of critical importance for our understanding of Matthew's interpretation of Christ's coming and the theological issues related to it.

The most significant point of these parables is the question as to why Christ's coming has not occurred yet. If the coming of Christ was to be soon, and even within a single generation (Matt. 16:28), why the delay? Some second- and third-generation Christians in the first century were having second thoughts and asking, "Where is this 'coming' he promised?" (2 Pet. 3:3). The Gospel of Matthew, believed to have been written around A.D. 80-90, is concerned with this pressing issue, as evidenced in the three parables in chapter 25.

In the parable of the 10 virgins (Matt. 25:1-13) we read, "As the bridegroom was delayed, all of them became drowsy and slept" (25:5, NRSV). Matthew admits that there is a delay. But his answer is not to give up the idea of Christ's coming but rather to wait for it in the right way. In this parable the right way is the decision to bring additional oil for the torches and thus have a plentiful supply for the long wait. This is what the five wise bridesmaids do. For Matthew the question is not *whether* there is a delay. Nor is the question whether the bridegroom will come. The question is *how one waits* during the delay. The parable does not specifically answer the question of how that is to be done. It simply establishes the fact that one must be prepared for a possible delay and make provision for it.

The question of how one waits during the delay is more specifically answered in the next two parables. In the parable of

---

39. See footnote 1 of this chapter.
40. Jan Lambrecht, *Once More Astonished: The Parables of Jesus* (New York: Crossroad Publishing Co., 1983), 146-50.

the talents (Matt. 25:14-30), the servants were to invest the money that was entrusted to them so that when the master returned, his money will have earned interest. The emphasis of the parable is on the third servant, who at the return of the master was condemned, because in fear he had merely hidden the master's money in the ground for safekeeping. The point of the parable is that during the master's absence the servants were to take some risks and increase the master's money. Nothing but judgment is reserved for the servant who played it safe.

The parable of the sheep and the goats (Matt. 25:31-46) depicts a scene in which all the Gentile nations (v. 32) are in the presence of the King for judgment. In Matthew, judgment awaits all people. Israel has already been judged in the destruction of Jerusalem and the Temple (23:37-38). The disciples themselves will also be judged, as indicated in the parables of the 10 virgins and the talents. Now it is time for all Gentiles to be judged.[41] The criterion of judgment is their attitude toward the disciples whom Christ has sent. The ones who are commended by the Lord are those who have received the emissaries of Christ. They have shown compassion to Christian missionaries by feeding the hungry, welcoming the stranger, clothing the naked, and visiting the sick and the imprisoned. The royal Judge will say to them, "Whatever you did for one of the least of these brothers of mine, you did for me" (v. 40).

Conversely, those who have rejected Christ's emissaries will hear the Judge say, "Whatever you did not do for one of the least of these, you did not do for me" (v. 45). The parable is a word of encouragement to Christians to persist in their witness to the world in the name of Christ.[42] Matthew has once again indicated how to prepare for the day of judgment: not by fretting about the cosmic calendar, but by doing the common acts of kindness to "the least of these."

Just as Mark, even more so Matthew has impressed upon his readers that the best way to wait for Christ's coming is not by speculating how soon or how long it will be, but by serving Christ faithfully and those who belong to him. Matthew's mes-

---

41. Ibid., 226-27.
42. Gundry, *Matthew*, 511.

sage to the Christians both of his time and of all time is that they give up their useless preoccupation with signs and calculations of time and occupy themselves with the task of living out the life of Christ in the world, in radical obedience to the commandments of Jesus given in the Sermon on the Mount (Matt. 5—7), through a deep sense of Christian identity expressed in a community of love and mutual concern (chap. 18), and continuing the mission of Jesus in the world to the end of the age (28:18-20).

Unique Features of Luke 21 Compared with Mark 13

Luke presents the eschatological teachings of Jesus in two separate sections: 17:20-37 and 21:5-36. Since most of the material in chapter 17 has parallels only with Matthew and not with Mark, we must assume that it came from "Q."[43] Most of the material in chapter 21, on the other hand, comes from Mark 13.

When we compare Luke 17 with Luke 21, we quickly discover that chapter 17 makes no reference to the fall of Jerusalem or to cosmic upheavals and other apocalyptic signs of the end, as is the case in Luke 21. Chapter 17 primarily speaks of the coming of the Son of Man and its suddenness.[44]

Since most of the material in Luke 17 and 21 is in Matthew and Mark respectively and has already been discussed, not much more need be said at this point. However, there is one segment of Luke 21 that is worth careful attention. Luke 21:20-24, which comes from Mark 13:14-20, makes explicit reference to the fall of Jerusalem. In fact, Luke does not give us the vague phrase "the desolating sacrilege" that Mark 13:14 and Matt. 24:15 use. Instead, he changes that statement to read, "When you see Jerusalem being surrounded by armies, you will know that its desolation is near" (21:20). Indeed, the whole paragraph (vv. 20-24) is a realistic description of the actual conditions that were prevalent at the destruction of Jerusalem in A.D. 70.

The words of verses 23-24 are in Luke only. In verse 23, reference is made to "great distress in the land and wrath against

---

43. See footnote 1 of this chapter; I. Howard Marshall, "Commentary on Luke," in NICNT (Grand Rapids: William B. Eerdmans Publishing Co., 1978), 656-57.

44. Fred B. Craddock, "Luke," in *Interpretation* (Louisville, Ky.: John Knox Press, 1990), 204.

this people." "Land" is a better translation here (so NASB and NIV) than "earth" (NRSV). The land of Judea is meant rather than the whole world.[45] "This people" means the Jews. In the next verse (v. 24), Luke speaks of sword and captivity. Jerusalem will be trampled on by the Gentiles "until the times of the Gentiles are fulfilled."

It appears that Luke, even more carefully than Mark and Matthew, has made a sharp distinction between the fall of Jerusalem and the coming of Christ. He did this by removing the phrase "the desolating sacrilege" (NRSV) from the discourse, making explicit statements about the fall of Jerusalem and separating all of that from the coming of Christ at the end of the world. Thus he has removed all possible misunderstanding: the fall of Jerusalem is not the end time. It is merely a historical event. Once again, historical events are not a sure sign of Christ's coming.[46]

Luke's statement about the times of the Gentiles has puzzled many readers. How does Luke understand the times of the Gentiles? And how are they fulfilled?

We must attempt to understand Luke's perspective in the context of his own time rather than read events of our own time into the biblical text. We must first recognize in Luke 21:24 several echoes of Old Testament passages such as Deut. 28:64; Ezra 9:7; Ezek. 32:9; and Zech. 12:3. The last reference is from the Septuagint, the Greek Old Testament. The Gospel of Luke is thoroughly influenced by the language of the Septuagint.[47] Although he is using Old Testament ideas in this verse, he no doubt is thinking of Jerusalem being trampled by the Romans in A.D. 70. He is describing the events of A.D. 70 in language reminiscent of the Old Testament.

This understanding of the Olivet Discourse does not necessarily deny the possibility that Jesus himself has made some sort of statement about Jerusalem and the Temple, as discussed earlier. It simply means that Luke's own experience with histor-

---

45. Joseph A. Fitzmyer, "The Gospel According to Luke" (X-XXIV) in *The Anchor Bible* (Garden City, N.Y.: Doubleday and Co., 1985), 1346; Marshall, "Luke," 773.

46. Brevard S. Childs, *The New Testament as Canon: An Introduction* (Philadelphia: Fortress Press, 1985), 111.

47. Fitzmyer, "Luke," 114-16.

ical events and his reading of the Old Testament have influenced the language of the discourse.

But what exactly did Luke have in mind in the statement "until the times of the Gentiles are fulfilled"? Many critics understand this to be a time of missionary activity among Gentiles.[48] According to Tobit, written around 225-175 B.C. and a part of the Apocrypha, Jerusalem and the Temple would be destroyed and then restored. "Then the nations in the whole world will all be converted and worship God in truth" (Tobit 14:5, NRSV). Although somewhat uncertain, the times of the Gentiles in Luke's mind may very well have been the period of the Gentile mission as Luke recounts it in the second half of Acts (note particularly Acts 28:25-28). This is also a time of judgment on Israel, as evidenced in the destruction of Jerusalem and the Temple.

However, Luke apparently does not consider Israel's judgment or the times of the Gentiles as final. In this respect he may be reflecting a Pauline understanding of salvation history, namely, that "a hardening has come upon part of Israel, until the full number of the Gentiles has come in. And so all Israel will be saved" (Rom. 11:25-26, NRSV). Luke's conception of salvation history is clearly seen in the words of Simeon, who took the infant Jesus in his arms and said in praise to God, "My eyes have seen your salvation, which you have prepared in the sight of all people, a light for revelation to the Gentiles and for glory to your people Israel" (Luke 2:30-32).[49]

A final issue to reckon with is the claim of some scholars that Luke has abandoned the expectation of Christ's imminent return by projecting it into the distant future.[50] However, in

---

48. Marshall, "Luke," 773-74; Craddock, "Luke," 246; Frederick W. Danker, *Jesus and the New Age: A Commentary on St. Luke's Gospel* (Philadelphia: Fortress Press, 1988), 335. Fitzmyer disagrees; he thinks it "can only mean the period after A.D. 70, when the city of Jerusalem and Judea are again dominated by the Romans (the pagans) after the unsuccessful revolt of the Jews" ("Luke," 1347).

49. In modern terms, Luke would advocate neither antisemitism nor Zionism. His concern is not the restoration of Jerusalem, the Temple, or Israel as a political entity. He would be neither anti-Jew nor anti-Arab. The salvation of God is for both Jew and Gentile (cf. Fitzmyer, "Luke," 187-92).

50. Hans Conzelmann, *The Theology of St. Luke* (New York: Harper and Brothers, 1960), 135.

more recent years other scholars have argued that although Luke is aware of the delay of the Parousia, he has not really relegated it to the distant future.[51] In the Olivet Discourse itself, Luke has preserved sayings of Jesus that speak of His sudden, imminent coming and the imperative to be ready at all times (21:31-32, 34, 36). Nevertheless, Luke is not crazed with an apocalyptic fever that sees signs of the end in every development in history. In fact, he discourages overzealous curiosity about such matters. Being asked by the Pharisees when the kingdom of God was coming, Jesus answers, "The kingdom of God does not come with your careful observation" (17:20).

In the introduction to the parable of the 10 pounds, Luke comments that Jesus was near to Jerusalem and people "thought that the kingdom of God was going to appear at once" (19:11). Luke wants to correct this misconception. When the disciples ask the resurrected Lord if this was the time when He would restore the kingdom to Israel, He replies, "It is not for you to know the times or dates the Father has set by his own authority" (Acts 1:7). At the time of Jesus' ascension, the two men in white robes said to the disciples, "Why do you stand here looking into the sky? This same Jesus, who has been taken from you into heaven, will come back in the same way you have seen him go into heaven" (v. 11). The implication is clear: There is no time to stand and gaze into the skies; there is work to be done. That work Luke has described in the Acts of the Apostles as a sequel to his Gospel. The task of the Church is not to stand and curiously peer into the heavens, but to carry out the mission of Jesus in the world, with the fervent hope that He will come in God's own time.

Conclusion

From this general overview of Jesus' Olivet Discourse in the three Synoptic Gospels, certain conclusions can be drawn. First, it is apparent that the three Gospels present different perspectives. Their historical setting, theological presuppositions, and literary objectives have colored the wording of the Olivet

---

51. Childs, *New Testament*, 112-13; Fitzmyer, "Luke," 234-35.

Discourse. Therefore we cannot assume that God has given us in Scripture a blueprint for the future written in concrete. What we have in Scripture is a group of people bound by time and culture who are attempting to understand what God is saying in the context of their own history and experience.

Second, it is impossible to escape the conclusion that searching for signs, making charts, and speculating about the calendar are a waste of time and energy. Time and again, people who have seen apocalyptic significance in this or that historical event have been proved wrong. In fact, such efforts are an outright rejection of the message of the Gospels and of Jesus.

Third, as the years went by between the time of Jesus and the writing of the Gospels, Christians became increasingly aware of the theological problem of the delay of Christ's coming. In response to such a problem, the Gospel writers found different ways to address the issue. None of the Gospels really gives up the hope of the Parousia. All three Gospel writers expect the coming of Christ. Yet they are also aware in different ways and varying degrees that the end of the world is not right around the corner. The Christian community must be present in the world and has work to do.

Unfortunately, in our own time so-called prophecy preachers are peddling their wares in total disregard of the theological sensitivity of the Gospel writers. Matthew and Luke in particular have found creative ways to cope with the apparent tension between Jesus' promise of an imminent coming and their own realization that such a coming has not materialized. They have much to teach us.

part II

HISTORICAL STUDIES

■ **GEORGE LYONS**

Eschatology in the Early Church

PART 1

THE WORD "ESCHATOLOGY" derives from two Greek words meaning "the doctrine of last things."[1] Within Christian theology it has traditionally treated topics associated in Scripture with the end of the world and human history. These include the second coming of Christ, the resurrection of the dead, the coming of the Antichrist, the millennium, the Last Judgment, and the intermediate and final states of the righteous and wicked. Eschatology describes the goal of soteriology, the world's and especially humanity's final attainment—individually and collectively—of God's saving purposes for His creation. Eschatology defines the Christian hope, what believers confidently expect God will do in the future.

Scripture and Speculation. Since most of the curious questions Christians—early and modern—ask concerning eschatology are not directly answered in Scripture, much of eschatology has always been speculative. Nonetheless, Christians have generally justified their speculations on last things by appeal to particular interpretations of Scripture. Often, it appears, such interpretations reveal more about the interpreters and their times than about the intentions of the biblical authors. The his-

---

1. The term was coined during the 19th century as an equivalent for the Latin title *De novissimus,* "concerning last things," traditionally used in dogmatic theology. (David Edward Aune, *The Cultic Setting of Realized Eschatology in Early Christianity* [supplements to *Novum Testamentum,* vol. 28 (Leiden: E. J. Brill, 1972)], 1, n. 1.)

■ *George Lyons is professor of biblical literature at Northwest Nazarene College in Nampa, Idaho.*

tory of Christian eschatological thought might be told as a history of the interpretation of the Bible within the Church. The earliest surviving biblical commentaries in Greek and Latin are interpretations of the Bible's two apocalyptic books: Hippolytus' *Commentary on Daniel* and Victorinus' *Commentary on Revelation*. But more influential than the Bible in shaping popular speculations concerning the end is the seventh book of Lactantius' *Divine Institutes*, whose sources range far from canonical Scripture to include various Jewish, Iranian, Egyptian, Hellenistic, gnostic, and other pagan writings and traditions.[2]

Limits and Diversity. The present essay (in two parts) attempts to summarize the eschatological convictions of the Christian Church from the 2nd through the 15th centuries. Any survey of this lengthy and formative period of the Church's history within such a brief scope runs the risk of either oversimplification or homogenization. Concern for synthesis and consensus must be balanced with an appreciation for the complexity and diversity of Christian opinion on these perennially controversial subjects.

This brief summary depends on the surviving literature, which is certainly not exhaustive of all that was written, and probably not representative of the diversity of views that existed. Some writings were accidentally lost. Others were deliberately suppressed and eliminated—sometimes, thankfully, without total success. Still others were expurgated. Eschatological views that to later readers appeared dangerous, if not heretical, were eliminated by well-intentioned church leaders even from the collected works of otherwise orthodox writers.[3]

---

2. See Bernard McGinn, *Visions of the End: Apocalyptic Traditions in the Middle Ages* (New York: Columbia University Press, 1979), 23-25.

3. For example, the millennial sections of book five of Irenaeus' *Against Heresies* were missing in the officially sanctioned collection of his works until rediscovered in long-lost manuscripts only in modern times (see Richard Landes, "Lest the Millennium Be Fulfilled: Apocalyptic Expectations and the Pattern of Western Chronology 100-800 CE," in *The Use and Abuse of Eschatology in the Middle Ages*, ed. Werner Verbeke, Daniel Verhelst, and Andries Welkenhuysen [Mediaevalia Lovaniensia, Series 1, Studia 15; Leuven, Belgium: Leuven University Press, 1988], 144).

The Eastern Church for centuries even refused to acknowledge the canonical status of the troublesome Book of Revelation (Landes, "Millennium," 163). It was not formally accepted as Christian scripture in the East until the third Council of Constantinople in 680 (Cliff Durousseau, "The Commentary of Oecumenius on the Apocalypse of John: A Lost Chapter in the History of Interpretation," in *Biblical Research* 29 [1984]: 23).

Because the Church never reached consensus on a single orthodox eschatology—as it did on the doctrines of the Trinity and Christology, considerable variety was always tolerated. The inconsistency of eschatological views within the writings of individual authors suggests that they were undecided or felt free to change their minds, as some admit they did. Some of the eschatological diversity within the Early Church arose from individual, historical, political, social, geographical, ethnic, and other differences. Marked differences existed from the beginning between the eschatology of the Eastern (largely Greek-speaking) and Western (Latin-speaking) Church. Within Eastern Christianity, the eschatologies of Asia Minor and Syria had distinctive, unique features. It is unlikely that the sophisticated views of those whose views were preserved in writing adequately reflect the breadth of popular opinion, whether of the average clergy or the laity.

This chapter depends on a firsthand reading of a great deal of the relevant primary literature.[4] No selective survey of the eschatology of the Early Church, however accurate and objective, can claim to be totally unbiased. This essay focuses on the major features of the emerging consensus of orthodox Christian eschatological thought during the patristic period.[5]

It also notes the many variations of interpretation and emphasis that existed, as well as the names of the more important writers on last things. Some attention is given to views that re-

---

For other examples of Western expurgations, see Landes, "Millennium," 161, n. 97. For a thorough treatment of Eastern eschatology from the 4th through 11th centuries, see Paul J. Alexander, *The Byzantine Apocalyptic Tradition,* Dorothy deF. Abrahamse, ed. (Berkeley, Calif.: University of California Press, 1985).

4. Because of the sheer volume of this literature and space constraints, I generally cite the summaries found in full-length, scholarly treatments rather than the primary documents themselves. I am particularly indebted to Brian E. Daley's recent survey, *The Hope of the Early Church: A Handbook of Patristic Eschatology* (Cambridge: Cambridge University Press, 1991). All quotations from this source are reprinted with permission of Cambridge University Press. Readers interested in studying the primary documents for themselves may consult translations of selected works in *The Library of Christian Classics* (Philadelphia: Westminster Press, 1953 ff.); *The Ante-Nicene Fathers* (Buffalo, N.Y.: Christian Literature Publishing, 1885-86); *The Fathers of the Church* (Washington, D.C.: Catholic University Press, 1972).

5. Traditionally the patristic period of early Christian literature includes all the theological writers, orthodox and heretical, Western and Eastern, through the seventh century (Johannes Quasten, *The Beginnings of Patristic Literature,* vol. 1 of *Patrology* [Westminster, Md.: Newman Press; Utrecht-Antwerp, Belgium: Spectrum Publishers, 1962], 1).

mained controversial and undecided during this period. Only the most significant new developments in medieval eschatology are noted.[6]

Organization. This survey is organized thematically, rather than historically, and in seven sections. Generally, the various positions reported within each of the thematic discussions are arranged in roughly chronological order. In order to provide for those unfamiliar with the various writers and writings cited, it seems advisable to involve minimal historical orientation. Both those readers well versed in the history of Christian thought and those not curious about the historical circumstances that contributed to the development of eschatology within the Early Church may wish to skip **The Historical Context of Early Christian Eschatology.** Those who are interested in knowing who said what and why and when he said it will probably want to read this section and refer back to it as the names appear in the subsequent discussions.

The various topics of early Christian eschatology are so closely interrelated that it is impossible to avoid a certain amount of overlapping. They are organized as responses to a series of questions concerning the end with the answers early Christian writers offered to them. These questions are as follows: "When will the end come?" found in **The Date of the End;** "What will become of the dead before the end arrives?" found in **The Intermediate State;** Where is the millennium? found in **The Millennium;** How will the end come? found in **The Parousia and the Resurrection of the Dead;** Who will face the Last Judgment and what will be their final destiny? found in section **Eternal Destiny;** and, Why must there be an end? in **Practical Implications of the Christian Hope.**

The Historical Context of Early Christian Eschatology[7]

Patristic Eschatology. Some anonymous early Christians were responsible for preserving, rewriting, and expanding a

---

6. See McGinn, *Visions;* and Alexander, *Byzantine Apocalyptic Tradition.*

7. All dates cited within this section are A.D. unless otherwise noted. I depend for these dates on a variety of standard sources within Church history. Many dates are only approximate; a few are controversial. Dates cited alone refer to that of a particular writing cited or to the death of the named individual.

number of eschatological writings that were Jewish in origin, and ascribing them to some ancient worthy who lived during the "period of inspiration."[8] This was an attempt to increase their own authority by affecting the appearance of antiquity. Among these pseudepigraphal writings treating apocalyptic-eschatological subjects were 4 Ezra (= 2 Esdras), the Martyrdom and Ascension of Isaiah, the Sibylline Oracles, 2 Baruch, and the Odes of Solomon.[9] The complicated literary history of these writings makes it difficult to distinguish clearly between pre-Christian and Christian features. Whether created by them or borrowed, these writings apparently document the views of certain marginal, syncretistic, Jewish-Christian groups during the late first through the third centuries.[10] The most important Christian apocryphal writings treating the subject of eschatology were the Apocalypse of Peter, probably written in Syria about 135, and the Epistula Apostolorum, written in Asia Minor about 160.[11]

The Apostolic Fathers date from the late first and early second centuries. They traditionally include 1 Clement (96), the Didache (= Teaching of the Twelve Apostles, 70-150), seven Epistles of Ignatius of Antioch (110), the Letter of Polycarp (110), the Epistle of Barnabas (120-35), so-called 2 Clement (150), the Martyrdom of Polycarp (156), and the Epistle to Diognetus (120-200). Despite its traditional classification, the last named work would be more appropriately grouped with the apologists (see below). The Shepherd of Hermas and the so-called Epistle of Barnabas (both

---

8. It was a common Jewish belief that the Spirit of Prophecy (inspiration) withdrew from the world at the time of Ezra, who established the Jewish religion on the basis of the Law.

9. Despite official efforts to suppress such writings, many accidentally survive. Quotations follow James H. Charlesworth, ed., The Old Testament Pseudepigrapha, 2 vols.; vol. 1: Apocalyptic Literature and Testaments; vol. 2: Expansions of the "Old Testament" and Legends, Wisdom and Philosophical Literature, Prayers, Psalms and Odes, Fragments of Lost Judaeo-Hellenistic Works (Garden City, N.Y.: Doubleday and Co., 1983-85).

10. Norman Cohn, The Pursuit of the Millennium (Fairlawn, N.J.: Essential Books, 1957), 7, notes that these Jewish apocalypses had "a wider circulation amongst Christians than amongst Jews."

11. Quotations are found in Edgar Hennecke and Wilhelm Schneemelcher, eds., New Testament Apocrypha, 2 vols.; vol. 1: Gospels and Related Writings; vol. 2: Writings Related to the Apostles: Apocalypses and Related Subjects, R. McL. Wilson, trans. and ed. (Philadelphia: Westminster Press, 1963-65). For a fuller discussion, see Adela Yarbro Collins, "The Early Christian Apocalypses," Semeia 14 (1979): 61-121.

140) were apparently considered a part of the New Testament in Alexandria, where they were included in Sinaiticus, an important late-fourth-century biblical codex. Similarly, *1* and *2 Clement* are included within the fifth-century biblical codex Alexandrinus.[12]

The apologists were second-century Christian theologians who attempted to defend Christian practices and beliefs—including eschatology—in terms intelligible to contemporary pagans. In roughly chronological order, they include Aristides of Athens, Justin Martyr of Shechem in Palestine, Tatian the Syrian, Athenagoras of Athens, and Theophilus of Antioch.

The Church's formulation of its eschatological hopes was fundamentally shaped during the second and subsequent centuries by two extremist theological movements: Montanism[13] and gnosticism. Because both were eventually condemned as heretical, few of their writings have survived.[14] The most important orthodox Church theologian of the second half of the second century was Irenaeus of Lyons (135-70). The first significant Latin Christian writer was the north African Tertullian (160-220), who left the Catholic community to join the Montanists early in the third century. Hippolytus was a Greek-speaking bishop of a schismatic church in Rome (he died a martyr in 235). Cyprian was the bishop of Carthage in north Africa during the middle of the third century (248-58).

The earliest representatives of the influential Alexandrian tradition of Greek Christian thought were Clement of Alexan-

---

12. See Kurt Aland and Barbara Aland, *The Text of the New Testament: An Introduction to the Critical Editions and to the Theory and Practice of Modern Textual Criticism*, 2nd ed., rev. and enl., trans. Erroll F. Rhodes (Grand Rapids: William B. Eerdmans Publishing Co., 1989), 107-8.

13. It is interesting that John Wesley expressed sympathy with the Montanists as creating opposition because they were a "faithful testimony against the general corruption of Christians." He concludes, "I believe his [Montanus'] grand heresy was, the maintaining that 'without inward and outward holiness no man shall see the Lord'" (*The Works of John Wesley*, 3rd ed. [1872; reprint, Kansas City: Beacon Hill Press of Kansas City, 1978], 6:261).

14. Only brief quotations in the works of orthodox writers survive of Montanism. This was also true of gnosticism until the discovery in 1945 of a small gnostic library in upper Egypt. Quotations are those in James M. Robinson, gen. ed., *The Nag Hammadi Library in English*, trans. members of the Coptic Gnostic Library Project of the Institute for Antiquity and Christianity (San Francisco: Harper and Row, 1977).

dria (215) and Origen (253). Both reinterpreted traditional Christian eschatological hopes allegorically, drawing upon the speculative intellectual resources of Platonism and Stoicism. Greek theologians in the late third and early fourth centuries, until the Council of Nicaea (325), were either admirers or critics of Origen's "radically spiritual, internalized reinterpretation of the eschatological tradition."[15] The divisive issue almost always revolved around the interpretation of the millennium.

Dionysius, a pupil of Origen and bishop of Alexandria (265), responded to an attack on Origen's allegorical interpretation of Rev. 20 written by Nepos, a millenarian Egyptian bishop whose followers had formed a schismatic church largely on the basis of eschatological differences.[16] Origen's friend Julius Africanus (240) appropriated the cosmic week tradition, often associated with millennialism, in his *Chronology*. Methodius of Olympus (late third/early fourth centuries) opposed Origen's conception of the resurrection body but shared his allegorical interpretation of the millennium, despite his theological roots in Asia Minor.[17]

The savage and widespread persecution of Christians under Decius was followed by a "long peace" during the latter half of the third century. Preoccupied with unprecedented church growth and building programs, the Latin West showed little enthusiasm for eschatology during this period. But without warning, everything changed—violent Diocletian persecution was accompanied by famine, plagues, depopulation, and wars. Such events during the first decade of the fourth century (303-13) revived Western interest in eschatological speculation. Both of the leading contributors had close connections with the millenarian tradition of Asia Minor. The earliest surviving biblical commentary in Latin was on Revelation and was written by Victorinus of Pettau (304). Lactantius (317) was a well-read but theologically untrained lay adult convert to Christianity.[18]

---

15. Daley, *Hope*, 60.
16. Eusebius, *Ecclesiastical History* 7:24-25.
17. Charles E. Hill, *Regnum Caelorum: Patterns of Future Hope in Early Christianity.* Oxford Early Christian Studies (Oxford: Oxford University Press, 1992), 32-34. This and all subsequent quotes from this source are reprinted with the permission of Oxford University Press. Daley, *Hope*, 60-64), assumes that Methodius expects a literal millennium.
18. Daley, *Hope*, 65-68.

"In the midst of black hopelessness there came relief which could only be ascribed to heaven."[19] The Church's situation changed dramatically after 313, when Constantine unexpectedly granted it freedom of worship. By the last quarter of the fourth century, thanks to Theodosius I (378-95), Christianity was virtually the empire's official religion. The end of persecutions, which made it easy and respectable to be Christian, prompted two different responses in the Eastern Church. First, in Egypt and Syria it contributed to the popularity of the "voluntary," "bloodless" martyrdom of monastic asceticism. One prominent theme in early monastic writings was "the importance of frequently meditating on death and judgment, heaven and hell, in the most vivid images one could muster, as a way of confirming one's motivation to follow the ascetic life."[20] Syria, where the ascetic tradition was much older, was the home of two significant eschatological writers—Aphrahat (345) and Ephrem (306-73).

Second, the new security after Constantine's accession and its preoccupation with the Arian controversy contributed to a de-emphasis of eschatology in Greek theology. Bitter debates over the Nicene definition of the relationship between the Father and the Son preoccupied most theological writings. Among those who contributed to the Early Church's understanding of "last things" during this period were Athanasius (295-373), Eusebius of Caesaraea (339), Cyril of Jerusalem (386), Apollinarius of Laodicaea (310-90), and the Cappadocian Fathers: Basil of Caesaraea (330-79), Gregory of Nazianzus (330-90), and Gregory of Nyssa (335-94). During his lifetime, Eusebius, the Church's first historian, witnessed the "long peace," the Diocletian persecution, the "conversion" of Constantine, and the changing fate of eschatology during these circumstances. Critically sympathetic with Origen and impatient with millenarians, Eusebius represents the Church's eschatological mainstream.

By the second half of the fourth century the legacy of Origen had become as controversial in the eschatology of the Latin

---

19. Ian Gillman, "Eschatology in the Reign of Constantine," *Reformed Theological Review* 24 (1965): 45.

20. Daley, *Hope*, 70, provides the documentation.

West as in the East. Among the fourth-century Latin writers who contributed to the Church's eschatological tradition were Firmicus Maternus, Hilary of Poitiers (315-67), Ambrose (334-97), and Jerome (331-420).

The Christological controversies dominated Greek theological writings from the fifth through the seventh centuries. The pre-Chalcedon Eastern writers who addressed eschatological questions included John Chrysostom (345-407), Cyril of Alexandria (444), Theodore of Mopsuestia (352-428), and Theodoret of Cyrus (393-466). In 431 the Council of Ephesus condemned millenarianism as a superstitious aberration.[21] After the Council of Chalcedon (451), eschatological views in the East appeared largely in anonymous or pseudonymous literature, including the *Teaching of St. Gregory* by "Agathangelos" (430-60), the *Theosophia* (491), and the *Oracle of Baalbek* by the "Tiburtine Sibyl" (505). Two popular pseudonymous writings, apparently written in the Greek East sometime before the fifth century—the *Apocalypse of Paul* and the *Apocalypse of Thomas*—have survived. The earliest extant Greek commentary on Revelation, written by Oecumenius sometime during the sixth century, collected the traditional views of earlier eschatological writers.[22] Origenist eschatology became the focus of renewed theological debate during the second quarter of the sixth century.[23]

Massive barbarian invasions during the final decade of the fourth century and the sack of Rome by Alaric in 410 cast a dark shadow over the Roman Empire. Average Christians took every natural disaster and military defeat as signs of Christ's soon return.[24] Wars and violence brought Roman civilization—now officially Christian—to the brink of extinction. Sophisticated pagans raised difficult questions about the plausibility of Christianity.[25] In the face of all this, most fifth-century Western Christian writers seemed convinced that the end was near.[26]

---

21. Cohn, *Pursuit*, 14.

22. Daley, *Hope*, 179-80. For a fuller discussion, see Durousseau, "Commentary of Oecumenius," 21-34.

23. See Daley, *Hope*, 188-204, for a discussion of the issues.

24. See ibid., 247, n. 1, for references in the primary documents from the period.

25. Ibid., 150.

26. See Daley's survey of Latin eschatology during the fifth century: ibid., 124-31, 150-67.

Nevertheless, the fifth-century theologian who most influenced subsequent Latin eschatology, Augustine of Hippo in North Africa (354-450), refused to speculate as to the nearness of the end. Among his contemporaries who addressed eschatological issues were the African Donatist Tyconius (330-85), Maximus of Turin (415), Sulpicius Severus (420), Hilarianus, Commodian (450), Salvian of Marseilles (470), and Peter Chrysologus (380-450).

Continuing violence, social turmoil, political unrest, together with a general decline in the availability and quality of education in the West during the sixth century, brought an end to the originality and intellectual sophistication of eschatology. During the medieval period—the so-called Dark Ages—from the beginning of the seventh century, eschatology became a central Christian concern.[27]

Three major innovations appeared in the eschatology of the Middle Ages, but with no biblical foundation. They were the traditions of (1) the "Last Roman Emperor," (2) Muslims as the armies of Antichrist, and (3) the "Angel Pope." Each of these attempted to validate "the most significant developments of the period—the conversion of the Roman Empire, the onslaught of Islam, and the emergence of the high medieval papacy."[28] The single most influential contributor to medieval eschatology was Joachim of Fiore (1135-1202).[29]

Medieval Eschatology. Inconceivable before the "conversion" of Constantine and the emergence of the "imperial theology" that linked the fates of Church and empire, the "Last Roman Emperor" became a standard fixture in both Eastern and Western eschatology. The expectation was that at the end of time a Roman emperor would decisively defeat a hostile army to become unchallenged ruler of the world. Then he would surrender his imperial power to God, usually in Jerusalem, more specifically at Golgotha, and die. With the end of the empire, the Antichrist would appear to persecute the faithful, his schemes thwarted only by the return of Christ.

---

27. Ibid., 205.
28. McGinn, *Visions,* 33; see 41.
29. Ibid., 126-48. McGinn, 158, suggests that "by about 1250, it was almost as difficult to ignore Joachim as it was to neglect Daniel or the Book of Revelation."

The emperor's enemies were at first interpreted to be pagans, occasionally Jews. But beginning with the Syriac *Pseudo-Methodius*, the enemies were described as "Ishmaelites," Arabs and later Turks—Islam.[30] No foe before Islam was as enduring, successful, and violently anti-Christian. "The sudden appearance of this new foe in the seventh century, at a time when Christianity seemed to have achieved almost universal domination, obviously invited an apocalyptic explanation."[31] In time, this explanation became a powerful stimulus for the Crusades to recapture Jerusalem,[32] either to delay or to hasten the end, depending on one's eschatology.

The 11th and 12th centuries witnessed a prolonged struggle between the popes and emperors for domination of Western Christian society. During the 13th century the "Angel Pope" emerged as an eschatological figure to validate the new universal role given the papacy in the Great Reform movement. Appearing as his counterpart and far too like many of the pontiffs of the time was the "Papal Antichrist."[33] The key theorist in this development in Western eschatology was Joachim of Fiore.

This latest innovation proved to be more enduring than the earlier for at least two reasons. First, the Last Emperor came to be interpreted in increasingly nationalistic ways throughout the 14th and 15th centuries. French and German rivals for the role of Christendom's ultimate savior vilified one another as Antichrists. The emperors' efforts to diminish the power of their papal opponents by confiscating church property proved to be their undoing. Second, scriptural warrant existed for a more ancient view of the emperor as a persecuting Antichrist (Rev. 13).[34] By the eve of the Protestant Reformation, a series of incompetent emperors and a corrupt Church left most Christians divided on the question "Who is on the side of the angels and who is on the side of the Antichrist?"

---

30. Alexander, *Byzantine Apocalyptic Tradition*, 151-84.
31. McGinn, *Visions*, 34. See also the chapter titled "Moslems, Mongols, and the Last Days," 149-57.
32. Ibid., 88, 90-93.
33. McGinn, *Visions*, 34 and 94-102. See also McGinn's "Angel Pope and Papal Antichrist," *Church History* 47 (1978): 155-73.
34. McGinn, *Visions*, 148.

The Date of the End

Imminent. Christians of virtually every century, though troubled by the delay of the Parousia, have continued to expect Christ to come again within their lifetimes. Only a few of the numerous early examples may be cited. The *Shepherd of Hermas* was an urgent call for fallen church members to repent before the imminent end, briefly delayed for this purpose.[35] Justin insisted that the end was very near, but that "God has delayed" the coming judgment until "the number of those who are foreknown by Him . . . is complete."[36] Tertullian reported as credible a number of eyewitness accounts of the New Jerusalem seen suspended in the dawn sky over Judea, confirming the nearness of the millennium.[37] Cyprian "believed, especially as the dreaded but never-materialized persecution of Gallus approached, that the return of Christ and the coming of the kingdom were imminent."[38] He was the first of many early Christians to adopt the Stoic conviction that the world is dying of old age.[39] The time allotted the created order is nearly over; the prophesied signs of the end are already appearing.[40]

Signs of the End. Early Christians identified prophesied signs of the end by appeal to Jesus' "Apocalyptic Discourse," preserved in the Synoptic Gospels (Matt. 24—25; Mark 13; Luke 21). During times of external oppression, these signs were most often identified as persecution, famine, cosmic disasters, wars, and rumors of war—recalling Matt. 24:3-13.[41] During times of internal strife within the Christian community, the signs were found in the appearance of false prophets, seducers, apostasy,

---

35. *Similitudes* 9:14.2; 10:4.4.

36. *Apology* 28; 45; see 32; 40. *4 Ezra* 4:36 and 6:6 likewise assume that the end will occur when the predetermined number of the elect is complete. According to *2 Baruch* 23:4-5 even "the number of those to be born" as children of Adam was "fixed" after his fall.

37. Daley, *Hope,* 35.

38. Hill, *Regnum,* 144-45, cites the primary documents.

39. Daley, *Hope,* notes references to this *senectus mundi* theme in the writings of Cyprian (41), Origen (48), Lactantius (67), Ambrose (98), Jerome (101-2), Augustine (133), and others (152, 161, 166, 211).

40. Daley, *Hope,* 41. Firmicus Maternus, writing in 346, makes an almost identical claim (Daley, *Hope,* 93).

41. See ibid., 8, 33-34, 41, 65-68, 97, 123, 126, 163, 172, 179, 211.

and heresy—recalling Matt. 24:23-24.[42] Satan was presumed to stand behind both kinds of signs, frequently through the work of his agent, the Antichrist.[43]

After the Church's relationship to the state was fundamentally altered in 313, another sign became more prominent as advocated by Eusebius of Caesarea. Throughout his writings, Eusebius strongly emphasized the Second Coming and his belief in the nearness of the end,[44] but he considered the earlier, negative signs mistaken. The evidence that buoyed his hopes was the positive victory of Christ over the powers of darkness. He saw in Constantine God's agent to enable the Church to spread the gospel throughout the world and prepare the way for the return of Christ—recalling Matt. 24:14. His *Ecclesiastical History* is an account of the progress that had come into the world since Christ. When his hopes for Constantine were disappointed, he turned to the emperor's sons. Although the label is anachronistic, Eusebius may be termed a postmillennialist,[45] his optimism continuing even during the dark days of later emperors Constantius and Julian.[46] Chrysostom, another eschatological optimist, referred to the advance of the gospel throughout the world as evidence that the end was near.[47]

---

42. For some of the earliest writings, see *Didache* 16:1-7; *Ascension of Isaiah* 3:21-31; *Epistula Apostolorum* 37; *Sibylline Oracles* 2:168ff. See also ibid., 49, 101, 129, and 211.

43. See the classic study by Wilhelm Bousset, *The Antichrist Legend* (1896; reprint, New York: AMS Press, 1982). See Daley's *Index* for Early Church references, 288; and elsewhere in the present chapter.

44. Gillman, "Eschatology," 46-47; and Frank S. Thielman, "Another Look at the Eschatology of Eusebius of Caesarea," *Vigiliae Christianae* 41 (1987): 226-37.

45. Paulus Orosius, in his *Historia adversus Paganos*, attempted to document the argument of his friend Augustine's *City of God* (Book III) that the lot of humanity has improved since the coming of the Christian faith (Daley, *Hope*, 151-52), which is the essential point of postmillennialism. The modern view by this name, however, apparently appeared first during the 17th century (Robert Clouse, ed., *The Meaning of the Millennium: Four Views* [Downers Grove, Ill.: InterVarsity Press, 1977], 11).

46. Gillman, "Eschatology," 48-50, cites the primary documents. Efforts to salvage the dashed hopes of the *Tiburtine Sibyl*'s enthusiastic identification of Constantine as the messianic king probably launched the tradition that came to expect a righteous "Emperor of the Last Days." He plays a prominent role in the end-time drama prophesied in *Pseudo-Methodius*, late seventh century (Cohn, *Pursuit*, 15-18). See Paul J. Alexander, "The Last Roman Emperor," in *The Byzantine Apocalyptic Tradition*, ed. Dorothy deF. Abrahamse (Berkeley, Calif.: University of California Press, 1985), 151-84.

47. Daley, *Hope*, 106.

Jerome cited as signs that he was living in the last days the appearance of Gog and Magog—Arian and Origenist heretics assaulting the Church and worldwide barbarian invasions threatening the empire's survival. He assumed the traditional interpretation of the enigmatic "Restrainer" in 2 Thess. 2:6-7 as a reference to the Roman Empire, destined to last until the end. Thus, he concluded that Antichrist would soon overthrow Rome and rule the world. But he did not despair, for the end of the world could only mean the return of Christ and the transformation of the world into something better.[48]

Augustine insisted that Christians have been living in the last days since the first Christian Pentecost. He rejected both catastrophes and progress as signs of the end. He asserted that there is "no essential relation between God's plan of salvation and the destinies of secular kingdoms and empires."[49] His reluctance to associate biblical prophecies with current, much less, future historical events arose from his conviction that fulfillment can only be recognized retrospectively.[50] He remained agnostic about when the world would end and skeptical about all attempts to calculate its date from Scripture and contemporary events.

Augustine frequently appealed to Acts 1:7 and Matt. 24:36 to argue that God wills human ignorance about the end: "Apocalyptic signs of the end seem always to be appearing, and those who try to compute from them the exact time of the cataclysm are always disappointed." Truly eschatological events are beyond human powers of prediction because they lie on the boundary between time and eternity, he noted. "To insist that the Lord is coming soon and to be wrong" can damage one's own and one's neighbor's faith. It is better "to long for the Lord's coming but to believe it will be long delayed." This "gives one grounds for both patience, if one is right, and for a happy surprise, if he *does* come soon." It is best to admit that one does not know whether Christ's coming will be soon or delayed; to hope for the first, be resigned to the second, and be wrong in neither.[51]

48. Ibid., 101; McGinn, *Visions*, 33.
49. McGinn, *Visions*, 26.
50. *City of God* 20:19; 20; and 30.
51. Daley, *Hope*, 134-36.

Eschatological Calculus. Despite the prohibitions of Scripture against speculating concerning the timing of the Second Coming, obviously mistaken predictions strew the Church's history. Some writers set dates within their own lifetimes; others set dates well beyond. The former betrayed an overconfident sense of the imminence of the end; the latter may have been motivated by other needs and interests.

During the difficult days of persecution faced by Jewish Christians following the Second Jewish Revolt (132-35), two early Christian writings predicted the coming of the end as around 150.[52] A period relatively free of threat followed the death of Marcus Aurelius (180) only to be succeeded by the Severan persecution. This first empirewide oppression of Christians early in the third century (201-2) was accompanied by renewed eschatological anticipation. Most parts of the empire during the third century were comparatively peaceful until 235, when barbarian attacks, economic disasters, and political conflict began a period of violence that continued until 284. During the persecutions, numerous would-be prophets urged the faithful to expect the Parousia immediately—setting dates in 202 and 236.[53]

It is in this environment early in the third century that Hippolytus of Rome and Julius Africanus propose a chronology based on the presumed age of the world, *Annus Mundi* (AM I). They assumed that the Incarnation occurred 5,500 years after the Creation, placing themselves in the early 5700s AM I.[54] They appealed to the "cosmic week" tradition, first documented in Christian circles in the *Epistle of Barnabas* (15:4-5). This originally pagan conception of history as a "week" of ages[55] is found in earlier Jewish apocalyptic literature. *Jubilees* (4:30) and *2 Enoch* (33)

---

52. The *Epistula Apostolorum* (65-72) foretells the end as 120 (Coptic) or 150 (Ethiopic) years after Christ's resurrection. The *Sibylline Oracles* (8:147-61) predicts its arrival during the closing years of the reign of Antoninus Pius (147-61) (Daley, *Hope*, 8). The predicted date could be 195 (J. J. Collins, "Sibylline Oracles [Second Century B.C.—Second Century A.D.]: A New Translation and Introduction," in *Old Testament Pseudepigrapha*, ed. Charlesworth, 1:421, n. *u*).

53. Daley, *Hope*, 33, notes other dates as well. For the primary documentation, see Daley, *Hope*, 232, n. 1; and David G. Dunbar, "The Delay of the Parousia in Hippolytus," *Vigiliae Christianae* 37 (1983): 314-15 and 324, nn. 9-15.

54. Landes, "Millennium," 137-38 and 145.

55. Daley, *Hope*, 11.

combine Genesis (1:1—2:4), where a six-day creation is followed by a seventh day of rest, with Ps. 90:4 (cited in 2 Pet. 3:8), where the Lord's day is 1,000 years. From this they conclude that by dating the world's creation one can know the time of its end.

Although clearly antimillennial in his eschatology,[56] "Barnabas" began within the Church the tradition of the cosmic week. According to Irenaeus' Christianized Jewish millenarianism, "In as many days as this world was made, in so many thousand years shall it be concluded." The world "will come to an end at the sixth thousand year."[57] The seventh day is the seventh millennium, the kingdom of the just, during which the renewed creation will become incorruptible.[58]

Hippolytus exploited the cosmic week tradition, not as a millenarian, but in an effort to undo the damage done by the failed prophecies of the millenarian preachers who had set a date for the Parousia during the coming year.[59] One had claimed, "If it does not happen as I have said, then no longer believe even the scriptures, but each one of you do whatever you please."[60] Hippolytus insisted that the problem is not with

---

56. The eschatology of "Barnabas" leaves no room for an earthly interim. He interprets Gen. 2:2, "God rested on the seventh day," to indicate that "when His Son returns, He will put an end to the years of the Lawless One, pass sentence on the godless, transform the sun and moon and stars, and then, on the seventh Day, enter into His true rest," and "usher in . . . a new world" (15). Quotations are from the translation by Maxwell Staniforth, revised by Andrew Louth in *Early Christian Fathers* (New York: Penguin Books, 1987).

57. *Against Heresies* 5.28.3.

58. Ibid., 5.36.3. Among the other early Christians who presumed (or, at least employed the popular presumption of) the "cosmic week" tradition, Daley mentions Hippolytus (39), Cyprian (41), Julius Africanus (61), Methodius (62), Victorinus (65), Lactantius (67), Apollinarius of Laodicaea (80), Firmicus Maternus (93), Hilary of Poitiers (94), Theodoret of Cyrus (117), the apocryphal *Gospel of Nicodemus* (123), Gaudentius of Brescia (124-25), Sulpicius Severus (126), Hilarianus (127), the early Augustine (133), Commodian (163), "Agathangelos" (169), and the writers of the *Theosophia* (178-79). Hill, *Regnum*, 113, cites the evidence that Origen knew and allegorically reinterpreted the tradition. Few, other than the Alexandrians and Ambrose, are courageous enough to reject the widespread view (Daley, *Hope*, 97-98).

59. Landes, "Millennium," 147. It should be noted that millenarians have not had a monopoly on the hazardous game of proximate date-setting. Tyconius interprets the "three and one-half days" of Rev. 11:9 as "the three hundred and fifty years of oppression and subtle blasphemy that must elapse between Christ's passion and the revelation of the Antichrist." Thus, he predicted the end within just a few years, during his own lifetime (Daley, *Hope*, 130).

60. *Commentary on Daniel* 4:19, as cited in Dunbar, "Delay," 325, n. 21.

Scripture but with those who trust visions instead.[61] Scripture implies, he argued, that the Second Advent would not occur until the dawning of the seventh millennium, that is, around 500.[62] Under similar circumstances two centuries later, Apollinarius of Laodicaea likewise pointed to 500 as the crucial year.[63]

Hippolytus was the first early Christian writer "to reject explicitly the hope of an imminent Parousia."[64] But his motivation was sincere pastoral concern—to protect his flock from the disillusionment aroused by misguided date-setting, not theological skepticism. But while Hippolytus' postponement of the end for 300 more years relieved the apocalyptic fever of his contemporaries, it elevated that of a later generation as the predicted date eventually drew near.

Sulpicius Severus, writing around 395, cites both negative and positive end-signs traditions. He claimed, "Nine of the ten prophesied persecutions [are] already past." Various false prophets have appeared in Spain and the East. "Antichrist" has already been born and is in his boyhood, ready to assume power when he comes of age. And yet, remarkably, "the Christian religion is flourishing."[65] At about the same time Hilarianus (397) predicted the second coming of Christ for the year 500, on March 25—the same date on which contemporary Christians believed He was conceived and crucified.[66]

As the fateful year 500 drew near, the *Theosophia*—"a curious compilation of pagan oracles and Christian pseudo-oracles"—written shortly before 491, repeated the century-old prediction.[67] But as Landes asks, does eschatological calculus give the Church "a new lease on life, or rather, a new mortgage on

---

61. Dunbar, "Delay," 316.

62. *Commentary on Daniel* 4:23, cited in Landes, "Millennium," 145.

63. Daley, *Hope*, 80. Among other writers cited by Landes, "Millennium," 151-52, who use the "cosmic week" tradition as only a delaying tactic to refute those predicting an immediate end are Julius Africanus, Lactantius, and Hilarianus.

64. Dunbar, "Delay," 313. Landes, "Millennium," 148, however, is quite certain that Hippolytus "never expected the world to last *another* three centuries."

65. Quoted in Daley, *Hope*, 126.

66. Ibid., 127.

67. Ibid., 178-79. It is difficult to know how to classify the pseudonymous writings from the period because of their complicated literary histories. E.g., the longer version of the *Apocalypse of Thomas*, which probably dates from the early 400s, also predicts the end for 500.

time"?[68] Whatever the motivation for date-setting, however distant or near the dates, all the notes eventually come due.

Adjusting the Calendar. The Church had accepted Hippolytus' AM I system for nearly two centuries in both East and West. In the AM I 5900s, the West replaced the AM I calendar with one that Eusebius and Jerome had championed a century earlier. This AM II calendar turned back the world's age once again to the 5700s. But in the AM II 5900s, the West once again adjusted its chronology by adopting the calendar of Dionysius Exiguus and the Venerable Bede. This was the *Annus Domini* (B.C./A.D.) calendar, still in use, which employs the Incarnation rather than the Creation as its starting point. Thus, the West twice conveniently adjusted its calendar just in time to avoid the dawning of the seventh millennium.[69] The necessity of recalculations suggests just how tenacious millenarianism is in the West.[70]

As the various target dates for the dawning of the fateful seventh millennium according to the AM I chronology approached and passed, reports of natural catastrophes (an earthquake in Constantinople in 398), political chaos (the barbarian sack of Rome in 410), and alleged heavenly portents provoked panic among a populace preoccupied with a proximate Parousia.[71] In response to such confusion, Augustine vainly tried to rid the Church of this belief.[72] Nevertheless, the accumulation over several centuries of predictions of the end for around 500 not surprisingly made the reign of Emperor Anastasius (491-518) "a time of fervent, if short-lived apocalyptic anxiety."[73]

Those inclined to set dates are seldom put off by failed predictions, preferring instead to fine-tune their calculations. The *Tiburtine Sibyl* (505) predicted the coming of the predecessors of the Antichrist in 522.[74] Eschatological hysteria again ran ram-

---

68. Landes, "Millennium," 160.
69. Ibid., 140-41.
70. Ibid., 182. Landes (184-85) notes that the repeated "documentary repression" of failed predictions suggests that the sense of apocalyptic imminence was deep-seated even among leading theologians.
71. Ibid., 155-59, 201.
72. Ibid., 156.
73. Ibid., 179.
74. Ibid.

pant as the world approached 6000 AM II. Signs of the approaching end were seen in numerous unusual prodigies,[75] and some remarkable religio-political "headlines": Muslims Invade; Irene Usurps Throne in Constantinople (797); Pope Flees Rome (798); and Charlemagne Coronated (800 = 5999 AM II).[76] All these called for various measures to defuse the time bomb.[77] In the final decade of the sixth millennium AM II (A.D. 703) the Venerable Bede proposed new calendrical calculations based on numbers derived from the Hebrew Bible rather than the Greek Old Testament. He attempted to place the Incarnation in 3952 AM III, but this was immediately and violently rejected. He then warned his critics not to be misled by the "vulgar" and nonscriptural opinion that the world would endure only 6,000 years or that the seventh millennium would bring an earthly sabbatical millennium. But Bede's major contribution to medieval chronology was not AM III; it was the reintroduction of the *Annus Domini* dating system proposed first by Dionysius Exiguus in 526.[78]

Ironically, Augustine's limited success in disarming the misguided millennial prophets during the 5th century contributed to renewed apocalyptic anxiety during the 10th. By then, much of the Christian world had accepted his symbolic interpretation of the millennium (Rev. 20:4-6) as the era between the Incarnation and the Parousia. But as the first millennium drew to a close, the prospect of Satan's release, the onslaught of the hordes of Gog and Magog, and Judgment Day at the end of the thousand years (Rev. 20:7-15), made A.D. 1000 a year of foreboding. Signs and omens, corrupt clergy, violence, wars, famines, and epidemics throughout the 10th century persuaded many that Judgment Day was near.[79]

Death. From the earliest days of the Church, Christians have offered another answer to the question, When will the end come? Irenaeus claims, "The business of the Christian is noth-

---

75. See ibid., 191-92.
76. Ibid., 196-203.
77. Ibid., 165-96.
78. Ibid., 175-78; see also 196-203.
79. See McGinn, *Visions*, 88-90.

ing else than to be ever preparing for death."[80] Hippolytus at times interpreted cosmic language in a personal sense, suggesting that since each of us reaches our end at death, we should recognize that when we leave this world, "the consummation has come."[81] Chrysostom reasoned that if the nearness of the end is an appropriate cause for Christian concern, then we should repent now, for our deaths may be nearer still, and this "has the same meaning."[82] Jerome repeatedly "takes apocalyptic predictions of the end of history as referring primarily to the individual's confrontation with death."[83]

The Intermediate State

Introduction. The Christian hope is intimately associated with the end. Only at the end will Christ come again in glory and the dead be raised. This inevitably raises the question of the status of the dead between their deaths and the resurrection. Virtually all the early Christian eschatological writings presumed the Greek distinction between body and soul, and sometimes instead, or also, spirit.[84] Thus, the question became "What is the fate of disembodied souls in the interval between death and the eschaton?" This postmortem state is clearly an intermediate one because it anticipates a future resurrection as the necessary preparation for the ultimate state of blessedness or damnation.

Early Christians apparently inherited their views of the intermediate state from those espoused in different contemporary sects of Judaism. According to Josephus, first-century Jewish historian, Pharisees believed the souls of the dead await the res-

---

80. *Fragment*, 11, *Ante-Nicene Fathers.*

81. *Commentary on Daniel* 4:18, as cited in Daley, *Hope*, 39.

82. Cited in ibid., 106.

83. Ibid., 101.

84. Jaroslav Pelikan, *The Shape of Death: Life, Death, and Immortality in the Early Fathers* (Nashville: Abingdon Press, 1961), 51, correctly notes that "the Bible has no original and consistent doctrine of the soul. Yet the Bible does speak about the soul, and thus obligates its interpreters to speak about the soul too." This chapter makes no attempt to resolve the problem of the "body-soul" relationship. Readers may consult any standard Bible dictionary for a discussion of the diverse uses of the Hebrew (*nephesh* and *ruach*) and Greek terms (*psyche* and *pneuma*) often translated "soul" and "spirit" in English Bibles.

urrection "under the earth" in Sheol or Hades.[85] Apocalyptic writings, generally considered Pharisaic in their orientation, also looked forward to an intermediate messianic kingdom to precede the dawning of the eternal order.[86] The Essenes, however, assumed that only the souls of the wicked are detained in Hades; the souls of the righteous look forward to the resurrection in a heavenly paradise.[87] The late first-century *Similitudes of Enoch* (= *1 Enoch* 37—71) also locates the righteous dead in heaven.[88] It does not express an expectation of an earthly intermediate kingdom but that, after the resurrection and Last Judgment, the elect will inherit a transformed earth.[89] The later rabbinic tradition generally presumed that the souls of the dead reside in heaven, under the altar, awaiting the resurrection.[90]

Justin distinguishes three different Christian views of the future hope coexisting during the second century. First, those "who are right-minded Christians on all points"—of course, including himself—are "assured that there will be a resurrection of the dead and a thousand years in Jerusalem." Second, "many" others, "who are Christians of pure and pious mind," accept the resurrection but deny the millennium.[91] Third, gnostics, who claim to be Christian but are actually godless heretics, deny both the resurrection and the millennium.[92]

Later in the same century Irenaeus also acknowledged the existence of "orthodox" Christians who, unlike himself, deny the millennium.[93] Their "error," in his view, is the claim that the

---

85. *Antiquities of the Jews* 18:1.14. "Sheol" is the Hebrew word used to identify the shadowy "nonworld" of the dead, usually conceived as a pit somewhere under the earth's surface. "Hades" is the Greek term representing a similar subterranean "holding area." See *2 Baruch* 11:6.

86. See the discussion of *4 Ezra* and *2 Baruch* in the section The Millennium in Part 2.

87. Josephus, *Jewish War* 2:120.

88. 39:4-5; 45:2; 47:2; 61:12; 70:3-4.

89. *1 Enoch* 45.4-6; 51.1-5. See Hill, *Regnum*, 50.

90. Hill, *Regnum*, 53-57.

91. See Sec. 4. The Millennium, below.

92. *Dialogue with Trypho* 80:2. Justin believed that very soon "Christ will appear in Jerusalem" (*Dialogue with Trypho* 85) to destroy his enemies, including "the man of sin" (ibid., 32; see 121). But he is not entirely consistent on the millennial issue. "In *1 Apol.* 52 and in *Dial.* 45.4; 113.3-5; 139.5 Justin awaits a general resurrection, a final judgement and the establishment of an eternal (not a temporary) kingdom on the renewed earth to ensue upon the parousia." Hill, *Regnum*, 20. So also in *1 Apology* 11.

93. *Against Heresies* 5.30.4; see 5.31—32.1.

souls of the pious dead immediately enter heaven. The omission of the millennium leaves out an essential step in "the order of the promotion of the righteous." The Valentinian gnostics, whom he identified as "heretics," both deny the resurrection and affirm that, immediately upon death, believers enter heaven. "The common ground with the heretics, the reason why certain orthodox cannot acquiesce to millennialism, is evidently the belief that the righteous go immediately after death into the presence of God in heaven."[94] According to Irenaeus, the heavenly intermediate state of his orthodox opponents' eschatology takes the place of the earthly millennium in his.[95]

This suggests that "the doctrines of the millennium and the intermediate state" have "a close internal relationship to one another." The central issue is whether "the interim reign of Christ" has as its capital "the terrestrial or the celestial Jerusalem."[96] We turn now to these two distinctive hopes, that of the heavenly intermediate state and of the earthly interim.

Heavenly Interim State. Most ante-Nicene Christian writers expected righteous souls to enter heaven immediately after death, and none of them were millenarians.[97] They include Clement of Rome, Ignatius of Antioch, Polycarp of Smyrna, the *Shepherd of Hermas, 2 Clement, Epistle to Diognetus*, Melito of Sardis, the *Ascension of Isaiah* (6—11), *4 Ezra, Apocalypse of Peter, Epistula Apostolorum, Odes of Solomon, Acts of Thaddeus, Acts of Thomas, Apocalypse of Thomas*, the *Martyrdom of Polycarp*, the *Epistle of Vienna and Lyons*, Hippolytus, Clement of Alexandria, Origen, Dionysius of Alexandria, and Cyprian.[98] In brief, they believed that all the dead of former times descended into Hades. But when Christ died and entered Hades, He delivered those who awaited His coming. Now only the wicked enter Hades. At death the righteous immediately join Christ in heaven and reign with Him there.[99]

---

94. Hill, *Regnum*, 14.
95. Ibid., 18.
96. Ibid., 10.
97. Ibid., 64.
98. For a discussion of the primary documentation of those writers not discussed more fully below, see ibid., 70-112, 141-43, 180-81.
99. Ibid., 142. For the primary documentation on the amillennial interpretation of the reign of Christ in Rev. 20:4-6, see 190-91.

Ignatius of Antioch described his eschatological hope in terms of personal union with the divine—"to get to God"[100] or "coming to Jesus Christ."[101] He expected this hope to be fulfilled immediately upon his approaching martyrdom, although he still looked forward to the resurrection of the dead.[102] Ignatius also claimed that "the prize" he sought—"immortality and eternal life" (Polycarp 2:3)—are already partially realized in the celebration of the Eucharist, "the medicine of immortality, and the sovereign remedy by which we escape death and live in Jesus Christ" (Ephesians 20:2).

The Martyrdom of Polycarp (117:1) similarly assumes that martyrs immediately enter into the presence of the Lord and receive the "prize" of "a crown of immortality." It is not clear whether this immediate reward is a special compensation for martyrs only, as Tertullian explicitly asserted, or represents a particular variety of eschatological hope for all believers.

Cyprian explicitly took issue with Tertullian, insisting that all believers enter their heavenly reward at death, although martyrs (and virgins) enjoy a greater heavenly reward than ordinary believers.[103] Such descriptions of the heavenly interim as "reigning with Christ" clearly interpret Rev. 20:4-6 in a nonmillenarian fashion. For Cyprian, the thousand-year reign is the heavenly kingdom, where the dead in Christ are with their King.[104] Hippolytus adopted the traditional language of the millennium to portray neither a transitional era, nor the intermediate state, but the ultimate order of blessedness.[105]

The Alexandrian eschatological tradition, preserved in Clement and Origen, far from an allegorizing innovation, seems to preserve "a solidly entrenched and conservative" amillennial tradition present in the Church from its beginning.[106] Clement frequently alluded to Christ's heavenly kingdom and reign, en-

100. Ephesians 10:1; 12:2; Magnesians 1:2; 14:1; Trallians 12:2; Romans 1:2; 2:2; 4:1; 9:2; Smyrnaeans 9:2; 11:1; Polycarp 2:3; 7:1.
101. Romans 5:3; 6:1; 8:3; Philadelphians 5:1.
102. Smyrnaeans 5; Trallians, Introduction.
103. Daley, Hope, 42.
104. Hill, Regnum, 153.
105. Commentary on Daniel 4:18. See Daley, Hope, 38-41.
106. Hill, Regnum, 184.

tered by believers at death. "Heaven is the 'chosen land' that saints will inherit and rule over."[107] He explained why the intermediate state is necessary. If the soul were reunited with a body prior to the coming of the new age, it would find a new opportunity to sin. Only at the resurrection will pious souls be made incorruptible and receive their bodies again, finally incapable of sinning.[108]

Origen interpreted the millennium of Rev. 20 as referring to the intermediate state, claiming that millenarians "take those promises meant to instruct us of the intermediate state of the blessed in heaven and transmute them into a crass hope of an earthly paradise." Origen's quotations from Hippolytus' lost *Commentary on Revelation* and other earlier writings make plausible his claim that he preserves a primitive Christian belief that the souls of the righteous go immediately to heaven at death.[109] This is confirmed by a broad spectrum of later Christian writers otherwise unsympathetic with Origenists.

Methodius used traditional millenarian language in a nonmillenarian sense.[110] In his comments on 2 Cor. 5:1 he concluded that when we die "we shall have the habitation which is before the resurrection—that is, our souls shall be with God."[111] He interpreted the millennium allegorically as the intermediate state in the heavenly world. Ambrose also interpreted the millennium of Rev. 20 as referring to the interim state. He, however, limits the participants in the "first resurrection" to the saints who enter heaven immediately after their deaths. Sinful believers must spend the interim in the purging fires of hell until the "second resurrection" or longer if need be.[112]

The Greek monastic classics (late fourth/early fifth centuries), the Pseudo-Macarian homilies, assume that the "first resurrection" affects the soul immediately after death; the "second," the body when it is rejoined by the soul at the final resurrection.[113] Jerome had no doubt that the dead enter their reward

---

107. *Stromata* 5:14.139.1, as cited in ibid., 124.
108. Daley, *Hope*, 46.
109. Hill, *Regnum*, 143. See Daley, *Hope*, 49.
110. Hill, *Regnum*, 32-34.
111. *Resurrection* 2:15.7, as cited in ibid., 32.
112. Daley, *Hope*, 99, 101.
113. Ibid., 118.

or punishment immediately after death. Christ brought an end to the detention of the saints in the underworld.[114] Peter Chrysologus conceded that the dead were confined in separate compartments of the underworld before the death of Christ. But Christ descended into Hades to release the just and admit them to paradise. Ever since, all the saints enter this temporary reward immediately upon death.[115] Although Chrysostom held a similar view, he emphasized that "the joy of the blessed will not be complete until they are joined by the whole company of the saved, at the end of human history."[116]

Augustine was also convinced that "the rewards of the good and the punishments of the wicked after death are only a partial anticipation of what they will be when body and soul are eternally reunited at the end of history."[117] Origen could not imagine that the souls of the righteous, "unclothed by bodies," are merely at rest in a heavenly paradise. They intercede in prayer for the living and are involved with Christ in His struggle to purify those who serve Him. Jerome, despite his opposition to Origenism, shares the same view.[118]

Earthly Interim State. Several variations existed among Christian writers who assigned the dead to an earthly intermediate state. Virtually all indisputably millenarian ante-Nicene writers assumed this intermediate state of the dead in Hades. And conversely, those who conceived of Hades as the intermediate state were all millenarians.[119] In addition to those dis-

---

114. Ibid.; 103.
115. Ibid., 166.
116. Ibid., 109.
117. Ibid., 142.
118. Ibid., 56, 103.
119. Methodius, discussed above, and the *Apocalypse of Paul* are the only possible exceptions to the correlation of millennialism and the subterranean intermediate state. The confused eschatology in the latter, a "carelessly compiled work" developed between the third and fifth centuries, is not surprising (Hugo Duensing, "Apocalypse of Paul" in *New Testament Apocrypha*, 2 vols., ed. Edgar Hennecke and Wilhelm Schneemelcher, 2:757). Here angels, leading the souls of the righteous dead to the seventh heaven to worship God, stop "for a while" on the way in the second heaven to see the "land of promise." This is the already existing new earth that will replace the old at the Second Coming, where they will live during Christ's millennial reign. The various heavens provide separate dwelling places for translated saints, patriarchs, monks and

cussed more fully below, these include Papias, Commodian, Novatian, Victorinus, and Lactantius.[120]

Fourth Ezra conjectures that, after people die, their spirits leave their bodies and briefly visit what will be their eternal home after the resurrection. Then they return to "sleep" in the subterrestrial "chambers" of Sheol until the end (2:31-35; 7:75-101, 112-15).[121] Only at the Parousia will the gates of Hades open to release the dead kept there, so souls and bodies may reunite to rise in the flesh (4 *Ezra* 4; so also *Sibylline Oracles* 8:226-27; 2:221-51; *Epistula Apostolorum* 19; 21—25).

The apologists Tatian and Justin, both Syro-Palestinians, considered the human body and soul to be mortal. God alone is immortal and His Spirit the only source of immortal life.[122] According to Tatian, after the fiery "consummation of all things," the souls and bodies of all humans will be reconstituted and granted immortality for the purpose of receiving eternal reward or punishment.[123] "God the Sovereign, when He pleases, will restore to its pristine condition the substance that is visible to Him alone."[124]

Eusebius mentions heretical Arabian Christians who believed that both soul and body are mortal and must be re-created at the resurrection.[125] This view is a radically anti-Hellenic position, which brings the resurrection into even greater prominence than the view that assigns souls to a conscious existence in Hades.[126] It survived in the later Syrian writers, Aphrahat, Ephrem, and Theodore of Mopsuestia, all of whom conceived of

---

nuns, martyrs, and others. But the majority of the righteous souls apparently await "the day of resurrection" in "the city of Christ" or "the paradise of jubilation," in "the third heaven." Wicked souls are punished in "outer darkness . . . until the great day of judgment." On the day of resurrection, all return to their fleshly bodies to receive their reward or punishment (14—16; 19; 21).

120. Hill, *Regnum*, 39. Hill cites the primary documentation for Papias (18-19), Commodian (29-31), Novatian (31-32), Victorinus (34-37), and Lactantius (37-39).

121. All quotations from 4 *Ezra* are from the NRSV.

122. Tatian, *Address to the Greeks* 12; 13; 15; Justin, *Dialogue with Trypho* 5. Apologist Theophilus of Antioch argues that humans are "by nature neither mortal nor immortal . . . but . . . capable of both" (*To Autolycus* 2:27).

123. *Address to the Greeks* 13. Athenagoras (*On the Resurrection of the Dead* 25) makes the same point.

124. *Address to the Greeks* 6.

125. *Ecclesiastical History* 6:37.

126. Hill, *Regnum*, 139-41.

souls in Hades as inactive, in a refreshing, dreamlike state of "sleep."[127] Its only noteworthy Latin representative was Hilary of Poitiers.[128]

According to Irenaeus, the "law of the dead" dictates that at death all human souls—including Christ's—separate from their bodies and "go away into the invisible places allotted to them by God" beneath the earth to await resurrection. He knows and specifically rejects the Christian eschatological hope of immediate entrance to heaven upon death, a hope he had earlier espoused himself.[129] "Only one momentous cause, towering above all others, is capable of accounting for this departure: the increasing urgency of the confrontation with Gnosticism."

The orthodox eschatology he rejected allowed the gnostics to deny the redeemability of the material world.[130] "Marcionite and Valentinian eschatologies depended on the outlines of existing Church eschatology." Marcion claimed that when Christ rose from Hades, He took with Him to heaven only the enemies of the Old Testament God (*Against Heresies* 1.27.3). He agreed that Christians were now in heaven but held that they were Marcionites, not Catholics. When he wrote Book 1, Irenaeus did not object to the idea of souls in heaven—only Marcion's notion of who was there. Valentinians, however, admitted Catholics to heaven but claimed that they occupied an inferior level compared to the gnostics (*Against Heresies* 1.7.1). The millennialism Irenaeus adopted was "tailor-made for refuting gnostics, providing at once a tremendous apologetic for the goodness of the material creation and, with its attendant conception of the intermediate state, an antidote to the aggravating gnostic pretensions to a super-celestial existence after death."[131]

---

127. Daley, *Hope*, 72-76, 114.

128. Ibid., 95.

129. *Against Heresies* 5.31.1-2. This obviously had not always been his view, for in 3.16.4 and 4.33.9 he refers to the pious dead entering heaven directly. In 5.5.1 he restricts the human residents of heaven to those still in their flesh, who like Enoch and Elijah were translated to heaven without dying. In 5.32.1 he specifically denies any special dispensation to martyrs permitting them an early entrance to heaven, in an unmistakable allusion to Ignatius' hope of "getting to God" by his death.

130. Hill, *Regnum*, 187.

131. Ibid., 188.

Tertullian also conceived of the intermediate state, in which the souls of the dead anticipate their final punishment or reward, as in Hades.[132] His *Treatise on the Soul* describes it as "a vast deep space in the interior of the earth" (55), divided into "two regions," one of refreshment for the righteous and another of suffering for sinners (56; see 58). He insisted that heaven is opened to no one until the end, with one exception (55).[133] He interpreted Paul's statements in Phil. 1:23 and 2 Cor. 5:6-8, which contradict this view, as referring to martyrs only.[134] Like Irenaeus, Tertullian had once believed that all the righteous would go to heaven at death but changed his eschatology in his battle with Valentinianism and Marcionism.[135]

---

132. Daley, *Hope*, 37 and 36.
133. Tertullian, like Irenaeus, also allowed that the translated saints are already in heaven. *On the Resurrection* 58; *Against Marcion* 4:22; 5:12.
134. Hill, *Regnum*, 26 and 27, n. 47.
135. Ibid., 16 and 62. He refers to the primary documentation on 26, nn. 45 and 46.

■ GEORGE LYONS

Eschatology in the Early Church

PART 2

The Millennium

*T*HE TERM "MILLENNIUM" derives from two Latin words meaning "1,000 years."[1] It is preferable to define millennialism so as to highlight the shared features of both its Christian and earlier Jewish expressions. To encompass both of these forms, millennialism may be defined as the "belief in a temporary, earthly, messianic kingdom to be realized sometime in the future: temporary, for, whereas it covers an extended period of time, it is not viewed as the ultimate state of things; earthly, as it takes place on this earth, typically with Jerusalem as its capital; and messianic, as an individual deliverer(s) plays a central role in it." In Christian writings, influenced by the Book of Revelation, the duration of the millennium is almost always 1,000 years; but in Jewish writings it ranges from 40 to 7,000 years.[2] In both schemes, the capital of the messianic kingdom is generally a renewed Jerusalem.

Jewish Precedents. Early Christians preserved and interpolated two originally Jewish apocalyptic writings dating from the last third of the first century, *4 Ezra* and *2 Baruch*. Between the present, evil, dying age and the new, eternal age *4 Ezra* anticipated a period of great tribulation (6:7-24; 8:63—9:13) to be followed by 400 years of earthly messianic salvation, to be experi-

---

Footnote abbreviations used in Part 1 are continued here.
1. The words *milia anni* translate the Greek terms *chilia ete* in Rev. 20:3 and 7. Thus, the beliefs associated with millennialism are sometimes identified as chiliasm.
2. Hill, *Regnum*, 5.

enced only by those alive at the time (6:25-28; 7:26-48; 13:1-24). After this all humans, including the Messiah, will die and the world will return "to primeval silence for seven days" (7:30). Then "the city that now is not seen shall appear, and the land that is now hidden shall be disclosed" (7:26). Only then will the dead be raised (7:32) and after seven days of judgment, the evil ones are assigned to "the furnace of hell" and the just to the heavenly "paradise of delight" (7:33-48). Similarly, *2 Baruch* presumes that only believers who survive the final tribulation will experience the messianic era, which will precede the final consummation (29:1-3; 32:1-9; 39:7; 40:3; 42:2). At the end of the interim period the Messiah will return to heaven and the dead will rise again; first, the righteous to eternal joy; last, the wicked to fiery torments (30:1-5; 44:15).[3]

Christian Origins in Asia Minor. Central and western Asia Minor was the hotbed of Christian millennial speculation. Some Christian communities in this region expected a "millennium" following the second coming of Christ during which all believers—living and risen—would enjoy an Eden-like earthly paradise of luxury and sensual delights. In most millennial schemes, the final consummation and renewal of creation followed a decisive defeat of Satan at the end of this period.[4]

The alleged scriptural basis for such a millennium was the Book of Revelation, traditionally associated with Asia Minor. But as we have already seen, early Christians interpreted Rev. 20:1—21:5 in a variety of ways.[5] Based on the surviving evidence, the earliest millenarian was Cerinthus, a Jewish-Christian gnostic leader who was active in Asia Minor at the end of the first century.[6] Third-century opponents of millennialism

---

3. Was it in response to such views that Paul assured the Thessalonians that those who died in advance of the Parousia would be at no disadvantage compared to those who were alive at the time (1 Thess. 4:13-18)?

4. This view has been called "historic premillennialism" to distinguish it from "premillennial dispensationalism," which first appeared only in the 19th century. See Clouse, *Meaning of the Millennium*, 9-13, 17-40.

5. Rev. 20:4 does not locate the millennial reign of Christ on earth. Rev. 5:10, which does refer to all the saints reigning on earth, does not mention the millennium. Rev. 20 does not refer to those who reign with Christ as all the saints, but only to the beheaded. No millennial view is without its difficulties.

6. Eusebius, *Ecclesiastical History*, 3:28. See Daley, *Hope*, 18 and 229, nn. 43-44.

voiced their opposition by attributing the Revelation to the heretic Cerinthus. Eusebius, who quotes the opinion of Dionysius of Alexandria to this effect, accepted the Western consensus that the Apocalypse was canonical scripture but questioned its traditional authorship and literal interpretation.[7]

Eusebius also identified Papias, an early second-century bishop in Asia Minor, as a millenarian: "He says that there will be a millennium after the resurrection of the dead, when the kingdom of Christ will be set up in material form on this earth." Despite Papias' primitive status and alleged contacts with the apostle John, Eusebius dismissed his ideas as "a perverse reading" of the symbolism and Papias himself as "a man of very little intelligence." But he conceded that Papias influenced "many Christian writers after him," including most notably Irenaeus of Lyons, to adopt "the same opinion."[8] He also noted that Montanism, a millenarian Christian sect originating in Asia Minor during the last third of the second century, considered heretical on other grounds, expected the new Jerusalem to descend from heaven to Asia Minor, on the Phrygian village of Pepuza.[9] Eusebius, like the millenarians Justin and Irenaeus, attempted to discredit the opposing eschatology by associating its origins with ignorance and heresy.[10]

Descriptions of the Millennium. According to Irenaeus, when Christ returns, the righteous dead will be raised in the "first resurrection" to participate with living believers in an earthly kingdom of 1,000 years. This will give them time to progress in incorruption, in the familiar setting of a renewed earth, until they become "accustomed gradually to partake of the divine nature." At the end of this millennium of progress, in the "second resurrection," the rest of the dead will be raised and the final judgment will occur.[11] Justin described the millennium as "a

---

7. *Ecclesiastical History* 7:24-25.
8. Ibid., 3:39.12-13. Quotations from Eusebius are based on the translation of Kirsopp Lake in the Loeb Classical Library.
9. Daley, *Hope,* 18-19.
10. See the introduction to the section on The Intermediate State.
11. *Against Heresies* 5.32.1.

thousand years in Jerusalem" before "the general," that is, "the eternal resurrection and judgment of all men."[12]

The *Apocalypse of Paul* describes the setting of the millennium as "the land of promise," a now invisible land "flowing with milk and honey," where risen saints will enjoy a vegetarian diet (22).[13] Paul's angel guide informs him, "When Christ . . . comes to reign, then by the fiat of God the first earth will be dissolved and this land of promise will be shown." Christ "will come with all his saints to dwell in it and he will reign over them for a thousand years" (21).

Irenaeus quotes Papias' account of the millennium, allegedly derived from the Lord on the authority of the apostle John.

> The days will come in which vines shall grow each having ten thousand branches, and in each branch ten thousand twigs, and in each true twig ten thousand shoots, and in each one of the shoots ten thousand clusters, and on every one of the clusters ten thousand grapes, and every grape when pressed will give five and twenty metres of wine. . . . And . . . all other fruit-bearing trees, and seeds and grass, [will] produce in similar proportions.[14]

This description of the incredible fruitfulness of the millennial earth is remarkably similar to those in the earlier Jewish apocalypse, *2 Baruch*, and in the *Apocalypse of Paul:*

> The earth also shall yield its fruit ten thousandfold; and each vine there shall be a thousand branches, and each branch shall produce a thousand clusters, and each cluster produce a thousand grapes and each grape produce a cor of wine *(2 Baruch 29:5).*

> Each vine had ten thousand branches, and each branch had on it ten thousand bunches of grapes, and each bunch had ten thousand grapes. And there were other trees there . . . and their fruit was in the same proportion (*Apocalypse of Paul* 22).

According to the *Apocalypse of Paul* this promised land "is for the married who have kept the purity of their marriages in acting chastely. But to virgins and to those who hunger and thirst after righteousness and afflict themselves for the name of the Lord, God will give things seven times greater" (22). Different degrees of reward also figured in Tertullian's version of the

---

12. *Dialogue with Trypho* 81.
13. This is interpreted allegorically in the *Epistle of Barnabas* 6.
14. *Against Heresies* 5.33.3-4.

millennium. But he expected believers to rise at various times throughout the thousand years, depending on their deserts.[15] The commentary of Victorinus on the Revelation takes chapters 20 and 21 fairly literally, in the tradition of Papias and Irenaeus, while opposing overly sensual interpretations of the millennial hope, like those preserved in Lactantius and Commodian.[16]

The final book of Lactantius' *Divine Institutes* (7) vividly presents his apocalyptic expectations. They are "a systematic synthesis of earlier Latin eschatological speculation, the Asian millenarian tradition, and a wide range of ancient philosophical and literary speculations on the afterlife."[17] His descriptions of the millennial Kingdom depend more on Virgil's *Fourth Eclogue*, the *Sibylline Oracles*, the Hermetic tractate *Asclepius*, and the Zoroastrian *Oracles of Hystaspes*, than on the Christian scriptures.[18]

According to Lactantius, the world must come to an end after 6,000 years, which he calculated to be 200 years in the future (7:14; 25). As the end draws near, the restraining rule of Rome will collapse before "Antichrist," a son of Satan, who will appear to persecute the faithful for three and one-half years (7:17; 19). Then Christ will return, destroy Antichrist and his forces, and usher in an age of peace (7:17—19). The Christian dead will be raised in the "first resurrection." Those whose sins outweigh their good deeds will be consigned to hell. The truly righteous will reign with Christ. Dead non-Christians, who are "already judged and condemned," will be raised to eternal punishment only after the millennium (7:20; see 21 and 26). During this 1,000 years of peace and prosperity, living saints will propagate "an infinite multitude" of holy offspring. Risen saints will rule over all the living, including enslaved unbelievers (7:24). At the end of the millennium, Satan will be released to rally his forces in one last, futile attack against the saints. After God defeats Satan and his forces, He will grant the saints seven more years of peace before renovating the world and transforming believers so that they become like angels (7:26).[19]

---

15. Daley, *Hope*, 35.
16. Ibid., 65-66.
17. Ibid., 67.
18. Ibid., 68.
19. See ibid., 67-68.

According to Commodian, even risen saints will marry and beget children during the millennium. He expected fire to fall from heaven at the end of the millennium and cleanse the earth of all the wicked who survive. After seven months, the Second Coming and the "second resurrection" will occur—the righteous will meet Christ in the air and the wicked be thrown into hell.[20] Hilarianus believed that in the final conflict at the end of the millennium, heavenly fire will kill all living humans, just and unjust, before the "second resurrection."[21]

Opponents of Millennialism. Despite the primitive origins of millennialism, from the fourth century onward official Church spokesmen openly rejected it as incredible, potentially destructive, and even heretical—but without much success, since millennial speculations continue to thrive even to our day. It must be emphasized that the rejection of millenarian interpretation did not begin with Alexandrian allegorists nor with fourth-century triumphalists who imagined that the kingdom of God had dawned with the conversion of the Roman Emperor Constantine. Nonmillenarian interpretations of Revelation were at least as early and geographically more diverse than were the millenarian.

During the early centuries of the Church, millennialism was one, but only one, of several viable eschatological views. Some writers, like Augustine, who acknowledged that they once held millenarian views report their change of mind on the matter. Others—even avowed millenarians—use millenarian terms in a nonmillenarian or, at least, inconsistent manner.[22]

Justin sometimes interpreted the millennium of Rev. 20 literally as a reference to a transitional kingdom;[23] at other times he applied it figuratively to the Christian's eternal reward.[24] Although Book Five of Irenaeus' *Refutation and Subversion of Knowledge Falsely So Called*, better known as *Against Heresies*, is thoroughly millenarian, his earlier writings were not. Both

---

20. Ibid., 163-64.
21. Ibid., 127.
22. For documentation, see the introduction to the section on The Intermediate State above.
23. *Dialogue with Trypho* 81.
24. Ibid., 113; 139.

Justin and Irenaeus during the second century acknowledged the existence of orthodox Christians who, unlike the gnostics, accepted the resurrection of the dead but denied the millennium.[25] Tertullian was not consistently millenarian in his eschatology. He often interpreted biblical passages figuratively that Justin and Irenaeus applied literally to the millennium.[26] Both Irenaeus and Tertullian adopted millenarian eschatology as a weapon in their debates with the antimaterialistic gnostics.

In addition to the ante-Nicene nonmillennial Christian writers mentioned earlier, some of the more significant later opponents of millennialism may be noted. Jerome rejected millenarian literalism as a Judaizing heresy and even interpreted the new Jerusalem of Rev. 21 as referring allegorically to the historical Church.[27] Origen, Jerome, Tyconius, and Augustine interpreted the "first resurrection" of Rev. 20:5-6 symbolically as the "resurrection" of the soul to new life in baptism. Earlier Ignatius, Hippolytus, Origen, Methodius, and Ambrose understood it as "the rising of the soul to heaven at death," a view that "does not surface again, after Augustine's epoch-making exposition of the passage, until Berengaudus, a commentator of the eighth or perhaps the twelfth century."[28]

Tyconius proposed a "spiritual" interpretation that referred all the threats and promises of the Book of Revelation to the Church, ideal and real. The millennium is the Christian era, a period of indefinite length between Christ's first and second coming. In this era, all of humanity is divided invisibly into two opposing cities—of God and of the devil. All the blessings of the future are already spiritually available to believers in the Church. The world's last days will involve "struggle and persecution for God's people all over the earth," "growth and ambiguity." They will be concluded when the "full number of the saints" is complete. At the close of this spiritual millennium,

---

25. *Against Heresies* 5.31.1. See the introduction to the section The Intermediate State above.

26. See *On the Resurrection of the Flesh* 26.

27. Daley, *Hope*, 102.

28. Hill, *Regnum*, 191. See Daley, *Hope*, 51 and 55.

"Satan will be released from the spiritual 'abyss' where he is now confined—'the secret depths of the human heart.'"[29]

Forty years later, Augustine similarly interpreted Rev. 20 in terms of the Church, virtually equating the institutional Catholic Church and the kingdom of God. The "first resurrection" is the raising of "dead souls" from sin through baptism, conversion, and the acceptance of God's grace. This marks the beginning of Christ's temporal kingdom. The "second resurrection" is the "final raising of reanimated bodies from death, when Christ will come again."[30] "The 'thousand years' stand for all the years of the Christian era."[31]

Other symbolic interpretations of the millennium were less widely circulated. According to "Agathangelos," the seventh day in the cosmic week is not a transitional period of 1,000 years, but represents "eternal beatitude."[32] According to Oecumenius' novel interpretation of the millennium, the "thousand years" of Rev. 20:1-7 represent the period of Christ's earthly sojourn. Satan's release in verses 7-10 refers to "the relatively short time between the life of Jesus and the end of the world."[33]

The Parousia and the Resurrection of the Dead

The Second Coming of Jesus Christ. On the eschatological event par excellence, the Early Church has almost nothing to say that is not simply a repetition of New Testament descriptions.

The Consummation of Salvation. In one development, several early writings conceived of the Parousia as the appearance of Christ in the heavens on a glorified cross. This conception probably depended upon an interpretation of Rev. 1:7, with allusions to John 19:37 and Zech. 12:10. The association of the Cross and the Parousia seems to be presumed in the *Didache* (16:6); *Epistle*

---

29. Daley, *Hope*, 128-31. On Augustine's appropriation of these views, see also 133-34.

30. Ibid., 134 and 136.

31. *City of God* 20:7.

32. Daley, *Hope*, 169.

33. Ibid., 180. See Durousseau, "Commentary," 28-29. For the primary documentation on other early amillennial interpretations of the binding and release of Satan in Rev. 20:1-3, 7-8, see Hill, *Regnum*, 189-90.

of Barnabas (12:2-4); *Apocalypse of Peter* (1); *Epistula Apostolorum* (16); *Sibylline Oracles* (8:68-72); and *Teaching of St. Gregory* in "Agathangelos" (471; 502; 676). This is a theologically important reminder of the intimate connection between the first and second advents, Christ's comings in humility and in glory. Like the wounds visible in the body of the risen Jesus (John 20:20, 25, 27), the association of the Cross and the Parousia emphasizes the continuity between Jesus of Nazareth—the Crucified One who came and died—and the Exalted Lord—the Coming One whom the Church worships and expects to consummate the salvation He began.

The Realization of the Kingdom of God. Eusebius has preserved the story, credited to Hegesippus, of the trial of Jude's grandsons before the emperor Domitian at the end of the first century. "They were asked concerning the Christ and his kingdom, its nature, origin, and time of appearance, and explained that it was neither of the world nor earthly, but heavenly and angelic, and it would be at the end of the world, when he would come in glory to judge the living and the dead and to reward every man according to his deeds. At this Domitian did not condemn them at all, but despised them as simple folk."[34]

Most early Christians *were* "simple folk." Living before the Enlightenment, they seemed completely untroubled by the prescientific imagery used in New Testament descriptions of the Parousia, such as heavenly portents, clouds, and splitting skies. For his more sophisticated audience, Origen attempted to explain the "real meaning" of the Parousia by means of a spiritual reinterpretation. It means that Christ and His divinity will one day become obvious to all humanity. He will not appear in a given place, like Jerusalem, but to everyone everywhere. Every nation will appear before His throne in the sense that all will acknowledge His Lordship.[35] Whatever else may be said of Origen's attempt at demythologization, he correctly emphasized

---

34. Eusebius, *Ecclesiastical History* 3:20.4-5. English translation by Kirsopp Lake in the Loeb Classical Library.

35. J. N. D. Kelley, *Early Christian Doctrines*, 2nd ed. (New York: Harper and Row, 1960), 473.

the close connection between Parousia and kingdom of God in the Early Church.

The *Didache* includes as part of its eucharistic prayer the petitions: "Let your Church be brought together from the ends of the earth into your Kingdom. For yours is the glory and power through Jesus Christ forever" (9:4); and "Remember, Lord, your Church, to save it from all evil and to make it perfect by your love. Make it holy, 'and gather' it 'together from the four winds' [Matt. 24:31] into your Kingdom which you have made ready for it. For yours is the power and glory forever. Let Grace come and let this world pass away" (10:5-6).[36] Such affirmations affirm, but do not explain, the relationship between the present and future Kingdom and between the Lordship of Jesus Christ and the sovereign rule of God the Father.

According to Hilary of Poitiers, "The resurrection will mean the realization of the Kingdom of God in each of us, a Kingdom that . . . will only be realized more fully, not ended, when Christ 'hands over his Kingdom to the Father.'" Christ's "subjection" to God in 1 Cor. 15:24-28 will not require Him to resign His power. Rather, it will require the God-man to become "once again wholly God." As a result, His Body, the Church, will be transformed into "the perfect image of God."[37]

The Resurrection of the Dead. Hilary presumed what virtually all early Christians took for granted, that the Parousia of Christ will effect the resurrection of the dead. These two final events of history will occur simultaneously. What divided Christians was generally not when the resurrection would occur or whether resurrection was possible, but what resurrection *means.*

By the Power of God Alone. Paul's defense of the future resurrection of the dead in 1 Cor. 15 was decisive for virtually all subsequent early Christian discussions. Clement of Rome was only the first of many writers to affirm his faith in the resurrection by repeating and supplementing Paul's analogies from na-

---

36. Cyril C. Richardson, trans. and ed., *Early Christian Fathers*, vol. 1 (Philadelphia: Westminster Press, 1953).

37. Daley, *Hope*, 96, notes that Hilary is the first Latin Christian to appropriate the Greek goal of "divinization" into his eschatology. See Eternal Destiny, Heaven, below.

ture.[38] He cites the phoenix as decisive proof, a legendary bird believed to live 500 years, die, and from its decaying flesh produce a worm that would become a phoenix to begin the cycle again (1 Clement 24—25). "Shall we, then, imagine that it is something great and surprising if the Creator of the universe raises up those who have served him in holiness and in the assurance born of a good faith, when he uses a mere bird to illustrate the greatness of his promise?" (26).[39]

Justin rejected the widely held pagan belief that "souls are still conscious after death," insisting, "We believe in God not less than they do, but rather more, since we look forward to receiving again our own bodies, though they be buried in the earth, declaring that nothing is impossible to God" (1 Apology 18).[40] Origen and the Alexandrians accepted this pagan belief, agreeing that the possibility of the resurrection depends on the postmortem survival of the soul.[41] Nevertheless, Justin's simple affirmation of the resurrection, possible by the power of God alone, is far more common, repeated by Athenagoras, Irenaeus, Tertullian, Hippolytus, Ephrem, Cyril of Jerusalem, Ambrose, Augustine, and others.[42]

Realized Eschatology. In the radically personal and realized eschatology of the *Odes of Solomon*, "resurrection" is conceived in gnostic fashion as consummated in the believer's present experience of salvation. The odist exults, "The Lord renewed me with his garment, and possessed me by his light. And from above he gave me immortal rest" (11:11-12a).[43] "I have put on incorruption through his name, and stripped off corruption by his grace" (15:8). "I stripped off darkness, and put on light" (21:3). "I was covered with the covering of your spirit, and I removed from me my garments of skin" (25:8). He can even express his

---

38. See ibid. for other Christian writers who appeal to analogies from nature to validate the resurrection faith: Theophilus of Antioch (24), Cyril of Jerusalem (80), Ambrose (99), Chrysostom (106), Augustine (144), and others (160, 165, and 175).

39. Trans. Cyril C. Richardson in vol. 1, *Library of Christian Classics*.

40. Trans. Edward Rochie Hardy in vol. 1, *Library of Christian Classics*, ed. Cyril C. Richardson.

41. Daley, *Hope*, 53-54, 191, 194.

42. See ibid., 23, 30, 34, 40, 75, 80, 99, 144, 160-61, 165, and 194.

43. Quotations of the *Odes of Solomon* depend on the translation of J. H. Charlesworth in *The Old Testament Pseudepigrapha*, vol. 2.

experience of immortality in millenarian terms (11:16-24; 20:7). "Eternal life has arisen in the Lord's land, and it has become known to his faithful ones" (15:10). "And I became like the land which blossoms and rejoices in its fruits" (11:12b).

Clement of Alexandria insisted that in this life Christians may be perfected in the love of God so as to anticipate the fullness that awaits the resurrection. "Through love, the future is . . . already present."[44] Realized eschatology was a distinguishing feature of both gnostic and Alexandrian Christianity. But this view also appeared occasionally in earlier and later orthodox Christian writers—Ignatius, Cyprian, Augustine, and the desert Fathers.[45]

By the mid-second century, most Christians considered the growing numbers of gnostic Christian groups a serious threat to the survival of traditional Christian faith and practice. Gnosticism's elitist religious thought, rejection of the Old Testament Creator-God, and world-denying philosophy were incompatible with the Christian gospel. Gnostic eschatology[46] in general looked forward to the restoration of heavenly reality to its precreation, ideal state. Thus, it expressed hope for the elimination, not the renewal, of the material cosmos and denied any realistic doctrine of the resurrection of the dead.[47]

The gnostic *Treatise on the Resurrection*, for example, reinterpreted the Christian hope of resurrection as the present saving enlightenment that allows believers to disregard material existence.[48] Not surprisingly, death, far from the "last enemy" (1 Cor. 15:26), was conceived as a blessed release from matter.[49] "In so far as we may speak of a single eschatological hope in Gnosticism at all, its heart is . . . in the promised continuity between

---

44. *Stromata* 6:9.77.1, as cited in Daley, *Hope*, 45.

45. Daley, *Hope*, 12, 15-16, 43, 46, 54-55, 71-72, 118, 120, 130, and 218. John Wesley's doctrine of Christian perfection is clearly indebted to this ancient Alexandrian tradition.

46. The diversity and esoteric character of the numerous gnostic systems make it impossible to survey adequately the full breadth of their eschatologies. See Daley, *Hope*, 25-28; and Francis T. Fallon, "The Gnostic Apocalypses," *Semeia* 14 (1979): 123-58.

47. Gnosticism represents an outright rejection of traditional biblical eschatology (Dunbar, "Delay," 314).

48. 146:30 ff.; 47:2-12. See Robinson's *Nag Hammadi Library*.

49. Daley, *Hope*, 27.

the present enlightenment claimed by the sect and an eternal sharing in a saving, but largely hidden, truth."[50]

Material. The presentation of the Christian hope in Irenaeus' *Against Heresies* "must be seen above all as a polemical response to the typical Gnostic understanding of God, the world and human salvation."[51] He affirmed that God will resurrect human beings in their unified wholeness—body, soul, and spirit—to final salvation (5.6.1). He carefully refuted the gnostic interpretation of 1 Cor. 15:50, which understood Paul's statement "Flesh and blood cannot inherit the kingdom of God" to mean that the resurrection is of incorporeal spirits only. Irenaeus insisted that "flesh and blood" refers to unbelievers, who do not possess the Spirit of God, not to the physical bodies of Spirit-filled believers (5.9.1): "The flesh, therefore, when destitute of the Spirit of God, is dead, not having life, and cannot possess the kingdom of God. . . . Inasmuch, therefore, as without the Spirit of God we cannot be saved, the apostle exhorts us through faith and chaste conversation to preserve the Spirit of God, lest, having become non-participators of the Divine Spirit, we lose the kingdom of heaven" (5.9.3).

Irenaeus cites several apropos Pauline passages[52] in support of this exegesis. His conclusive appeal was to the full and sinless humanity of Jesus Christ, whom God raised from the dead (5.14—21). Paul's point, he argued, is that immorality may disqualify one-time believers from the final Kingdom, not that bodily existence is excluded in this Kingdom. "For as the flesh is capable of corruption, so is it also of incorruption; and as it is of death, so it is also of life" (5.12.1).

Tertullian also discussed the proper interpretation of 1 Cor. 15. Although he was willing to acknowledge "the similarity of the Christian eschatological hope to the speculations of pagan literature and philosophy about the future,"[53] his polemic

---

50. Ibid., 28.
51. Ibid.
52. They include Rom. 8:9-13 (in *Against Heresies* [AH] 5.10.2); Gal. 5:19 (AH 5.11.1); Col. 3:5-9 (AH 5.12.3); 1 Cor. 15:53 (AH 5.13.3); Phil. 3:21 (AH 5.13.4); and 2 Cor. 4:11 (AH 5.13.5).
53. Daley, *Hope*, 38. Tertullian vigorously attacks the pagan theory of metempsychosis, the transmigration and reincarnation of souls (*Apology* 48), as does Hippolytus (ibid., 40). Origen, however, considers it "a theoretical possibility" (ibid., 58).

against the gnostics made the reality of the flesh of the resurrected body his major concern.[54] He insisted on both the identity
of the risen body with the present one and that it will be "like
the angels" (Matt. 22:30, NIV).[55]

The amillennial *Apocalypse of Thomas,* despite its different
conception of the interim state, preserved a similar conception
of the resurrection, but with allusions to 1 Thess. 4:13-18. When
Christ returns,

> The spirits and souls of the saints will come forth from par-
> adise and come into all the earth, and each go to its own body
> where it is laid up . . . and the bodies of the saints who sleep will
> rise. Then their bodies will be changed into the image and like-
> ness and honour of the holy angels and into the power of the im-
> age of [the] holy Father. Then they will put on the garment of
> eternal life. . . . Then they will be carried off in a cloud of light in-
> to the air," where they will "remain" forever with the Lord.[56]

The tradition of heavenly garments figured prominently in
a variety of Jewish and Christian descriptions of the resurrection (see 1 Cor. 15:53-54; 2 Cor. 5:1-10; Rev. 7:9 and 13). The *Martyrdom and Ascension of Isaiah* insisted that resurrected saints
wear only angelic "garments which are stored on high in the
seventh heaven" (4:16-17; cf. 8:14-15, 26; 9:2, 9-11, 26; 11:40).[57] In
4 Ezra, the fleshly resurrection of the just is conceived as a putting on of "glorious," "white," "immortal" garments suited for
life in "the celestial kingdoms" (2:30-48). The *Similitudes of
Enoch* refers to resurrection as putting on "garments of glory" or
"garments of life" (62:15-16).[58] The *Apocalypse of Peter* describes
angels clothing the righteous "with garments of eternal life"
(13).[59] Tatian said of such "clothing": "It is possible for every one
who is naked to obtain this apparel" (*Address to the Greeks,* 20).

---

54. *Against Marcion* 5:9-10.

55. *On the Resurrection of the Flesh* 51-56; 62.

56. Trans. A. de Santos Otero and Ernest Best, in *New Testament Apocrypha,* vol. 2,
ed. Edgar Hennecke and Wilhelm Schneemelcher.

57. Trans. M. A. Knibb, in *The Old Testament Pseudepigrapha,* vol. 2, ed. James H.
Charlesworth. Its date is between the second and fourth centuries.

58. Trans. E. Isaac, in *The Old Testament Pseudepigrapha,* vol. 1, ed. James H.
Charlesworth.

59. Trans. Hugo Duensing in *New Testament Apocrypha,* vol. 2, ed. Edgar Hennecke
and Wilhelm Schneemelcher, trans. and ed. R. McL. Wilson.

The meaning of this imagery is made apparent in *2 Baruch.* In the coming new age, "everything corruptible will pass away, And everything mortal will disappear" (44:9-12). "Time shall no longer age" risen saints (51:9). God will so transform them "that they look like angels" (51:5).[60]

Spiritual. Origen conceived of his interpretation of the resurrection body as an appropriate middle course between gnostic and materialistic extremes. The risen body will be "like the angels" in that it will be "spiritual" and "heavenly" (1 Cor. 15:35-50). It will be perfectly suited for life in heaven—utterly different in form, new and better in every way as compared to the present body, yet recognizable as the same individual. Resurrection means that the unique form of our present bodies will be created in a new materiality, not that the same matter that constitutes our present bodies will be reassembled. Although Origen interpreted the "first resurrection" (Rev. 20:6) as both the heavenly ascent of the soul at death and the anticipation of the future promise experienced by believers in their baptism,[61] neither intermediate nor realized eschatology makes unnecessary future bodily resurrection.[62] Resurrection must await the eschaton, because it effects the salvation of the whole church, not simply of individual believers. In some of his writings, Origen implied that the risen body is not an integral part of ultimate human salvation but merely a transitional stage before bodily existence is finally abandoned.[63]

Gregory of Nyssa conceived of the human person, created in the image of God, as "a true composite of spiritual and material dimensions which . . . depend on each other for their full existence." Thus, the resurrection of the body is the first stage of the "restoration of humanity to its original and ideal form."[64] Gregory expected the risen body to be "identical with the present body, and recognizable as such . . . yet it will be 'subtle and

---

60. Trans. R. H. Charles, rev. L. H. Brockington, in *The Apocryphal Old Testament*, ed. H. F. D. Sparks (Oxford: Clarendon, 1984).
61. Jerome, Tyconius, and Augustine also accept the latter interpretation.
62. Daley, *Hope*, 51-55.
63. Ibid., 54.
64. Ibid., 87.

ethereal' in texture, 'with a brighter and more entrancing beauty.'" It will lack the characteristics that result from sin and the sexual differences necessary for procreation. It will be freed from the processes of change that make for aging and decay. Risen people will be consumed by an insatiable desire for God.[65]

Eternal. As over against Origenism, Jerome insisted that the resurrection body will be identical to the present one in every way. Humans will not become angels but will be enabled to act in angelic ways. He rejected the Origenist conception of the risen body as spiritual in character, emphasizing that it will be a material body of flesh made glorious.[66] Augustine understood resurrection as quite literally the process of reassembling the particles of matter that made up each individual, the restoration of all the organs of the present body—including the sexual.[67] He excluded from this restoration discarded body parts, such as hair and nails, and present disfigurements. He maintained that the risen body will be both "identical" to the present "material" body and yet "spiritual." The flesh will at last be perfectly subject to and integrated with the spirit.[68]

Absolutely crucial for Augustine was the insight that resurrection means the end of human existence in time as restless, changeable, fallen souls. Resurrection will confirm "the present, historically conditioned order of loves in the changelessness of eternal beatitude or eternal self-destruction." God will effect this "without destroying human identity as flesh and spirit" and "without annihilating the world in which that identity has been realized."[69] Resurrection will utterly transform the dead so that they may enter a new phase for created existence, crossing the threshold from time to eternity.[70]

Augustine deferred the truly eschatological fate of individuals until the end of time so that it will be "simultaneous with the collective judgment and transformation of the whole community of rational creatures. Consequently, he distinguishes

65. Ibid., 88.
66. Ibid., 102-3.
67. Ibid., 144.
68. Ibid., 143-44.
69. Ibid., 132.
70. Ibid., 144.

clearly between the fate of those now dead, who still belong to the realm of time and are subject to its limitations, and the finality of eternal reward or punishment." The dead in their interim state will receive only a small portion of the reward or punishment that awaits them at the end of time.[71]

Eternal Destiny

The Last Judgment. Millennialism places the time of the Second Coming and "first resurrection" 1,000 years before the "second resurrection" and final judgment. But according to most amillennial interpreters, the Second Coming and the resurrection of the dead will occur simultaneously with the final judgment. The Creed of the Council of Nicaea represents the early fourth-century Church's consensus that the purpose of the Parousia is "to judge living and dead."[72] According to Cyril of Jerusalem, resurrection effects the judgment, for although believers rise from the dead transformed, sinners rise unchanged.[73] Augustine held that the Last Judgment merely seals the consequences of the decisions people make while alive.[74] The distinctions between the intermediate states of the just and unjust—reward and punishment—begin upon the separation of soul and body immediately at death. Thus, in effect, people are judged during their lifetimes by their acts. Hilary of Poitiers, Zeno of Verona, Ambrose, and Paulinus of Nola expected formal judicial proceedings only in cases of ambiguity. Hilary insisted that, despite the universality of the final judgment, there will need only be a genuine trial for "those who are midway between the faithful and the unfaithful," who will have already saved or condemned themselves.[75] Ambrose similarly theorized that only the "sinful believer" will need to be judged at the Second Coming.[76]

---

71. Ibid., 137.
72. Trans. Joseph Cullen Ayer, ed., *Source Book for Ancient Church History* (New York: Charles Scribner's Sons, 1913).
73. Daley, *Hope*, 110.
74. Ibid., 137-41.
75. Ibid., 94.
76. Ibid., 98; see 97 and 159.

Augustine believed that "the souls of some of the dead, who are condemned to punishment immediately after death because of their sins, will be released" before the end. Because final judgment is delayed to the end, because the dead still belong to time, their fate is not hopeless. Their sufferings may purge them of self-love, or God may yet forgive them in response to the prayers, alms, and Eucharist of the living Church. "Hell is not a permanent state . . . until the common passage of all creatures from time into eternity." Thus "the resurrection of the dead is, for Augustine, the one genuinely eschatological event."[77]

Daley (131-32) argues that the key feature of Augustine's eschatological hope was his Neoplatonist metaphysical distinction between time and eternity. Eternity is not endless duration, as in Origen, but freedom from duration, an unchanging present. Thus, Augustine conceived of "the end of the world" as more correctly "the end of history" and the dawning of the "eternal Sabbath."

The intimate connection between the various eschatological events in Jewish Christian thought[78] may account for the unexpected delay of the resurrection and judgment to the end of the millennium in *4 Ezra* and *2 Baruch*. In some of Justin's works, the general resurrection and final judgment usher in the eternal Kingdom on the renewed earth.[79] He also believed that the souls of the righteous and unrighteous reside in better and worse places in Hades awaiting the resurrection and the day of final judgment.[80] The concurrence of judgment and resurrection is presumed in the variety of Syrian millennialism that adopted "soul sleep" as the intermediate state.[81]

Hell. Early Christians for the most part were reluctant to describe the nature of the suffering in hell beyond the descriptions included in the New Testament. Tertullian conjectured that the torments of hell would be suited to each person's

---

77. Ibid., 138-41.
78. Ibid., 6, 8-9.
79. *1 Apology* 52; *Dialogue with Trypho* 5; 45:4; 113:3-5; 139:5.
80. *Dialogue with Trypho* 5.
81. Daley, *Hope*, 73.

crimes.[82] Both the *Apocalypse of Peter* (3—13) and the *Apocalypse of Paul* (31—44) offer graphic descriptions of the various punishments of sinners in hell, torments inflicted by pitiless angels to fit the crimes of those confined there.

Ephrem suggested that the damned in hell suffer most from the realization that they have lost all hope of sharing in the beauty and happiness of heaven.[83] Chrysostom insisted that the principal suffering will not be the inexpressible physical agonies, but "exclusion from the presence of the Lord and the company of the saints in heaven."[84] Oecumenius similarly stressed deprivation rather than physical pain as the chief punishment of the damned.[85] Augustine refused to hazard a guess as to the nature of hell's fire or as to its location. He conceived of the misery and pain of hell as not only corporeal but also psychological torture of "fruitless repentance."[86]

Although part of the joy Tertullian expected in heaven was "the sight of this 'spectacle' of divine retribution,"[87] most Christians from the earliest days of the Church have been troubled by the prospect of eternal punishment for sinners. They often appealed to an interpretation of Matt. 12:32 that reasons—although sins "against the Holy Spirit will not be forgiven, either in this age or in the age to come," other sins may be. Some proposed various ways in which they hoped God would forgive and soften His judgment of sinners.

According to the *Apocalypse of Paul*, Christ will graciously grant the tormented "a day and a night of ease" every Lord's Day (44).[88] The Christian *Sibylline Oracles* express an expectation that God would allow the just to intercede for their loved ones in hell and eventually permit them to share in heaven's comfort (2:330-38). Perhaps in this same tradition of compassion for the damned is *Didache* 16:7, which claims that only the righteous

---

82. *The Shows* 30; see also Daley, *Hope*, 36.
83. Daley, *Hope*, 76.
84. Ibid., 107.
85. Ibid., 181.
86. Ibid., 148.
87. *The Shows*, 30, as cited in ibid., 36.
88. A similar hope is found in Christian poet Aurelius Prudentius Clemens, c. 348-405 (ibid., 158).

dead will be raised in the resurrection.[89] It is unclear whether it, like the *Apocalypse of Thomas*, presumes that the final destiny of the wicked will be annihilation, or like Ignatius, conceives of a continuing phantomlike, bodiless existence as a part of the punishment of the wicked (*Smyrnaens* 2:1).

Although the Alexandrian Fathers spoke at times using the traditional language of "the punishment of eternal fire," they introduced a new dimension into the Christian reflection on hell. Origen sometimes referred to hell in a purely moral or psychological sense, as the torments sinners brought upon themselves by their rebellion against God. Clement and Origen generally viewed punishment after death as medicinal, educative, corrective, beneficial, and thus temporary. The progress of every soul toward the knowledge of God involves a long and painful purification process. The "wise fire" of hell is intended to purify souls of their sinful inclinations so that they may ultimately reach heaven.[90] Both held out the optimistic hope of universal salvation. On occasion, Origen went so far as to imply that even the devil himself may finally be saved.[91]

Gregory of Nyssa affirmed and refined Origen's hope of ultimate universal salvation, which he described as "the restoration of intellectual creation to an 'original' unity with God in contemplative beatitude."[92] He rejected Origen's notion that the original state was "a prehistorical existence of unembodied souls, and that our present corporeal existence is the result of a 'fall.'" What is to be restored in the resurrection is the fulfillment of the perfection possible of every one of God's human creatures.[93] Gregory's rationale for conceiving of hell as temporary was not emotional—sympathy for the lost—but philosophical. "Evil, being the corruption or disfigurement of what is good rather than a substance in its own right, must eventually come to an end. Only the good, as genuine being, has the positive charac-

---

89. This reflects older Jewish rabbinic and apocalyptic notions. Daley, *Hope*, 227, n. 29.

90. It should be emphasized that during the patristic period there is no notion of purgatory as a separate place between heaven and hell. Ibid., 223.

91. Ibid., 46-47, 56-58.

92. Ibid., 85.

93. Ibid., 86.

teristic of permanence." The likeness of the human soul to God and its capacity to share in his life make it "axiomatic that this capacity cannot be permanently frustrated."[94] He believed that the restoration of the disfigured image of God in humans requires "a difficult and painful process of 'cleansing.'" If it is not experienced before death, it must occur after the resurrection "in the purifying fire," so that reconstituted human beings may be prepared to participate fully in the life of God.[95]

Ambrose held no consistent "position on the nature, purpose, and duration of punishment after death." In some of his writings he merely repeated the Church's traditional teaching about eternal punishment. But in other writings he adopted the Alexandrian views concerning medicinal and temporary postmortem punishment and universal salvation.[96] Jerome's position on universal salvation was also inconsistent. At least in his mature writings, he leaves it to God to decide whether unbelievers may finally be saved. But he consistently affirmed that all baptized believers will ultimately be admitted into heaven, although sinful believers must first be purged in fire.[97] This belief, called misericordism, was defended also in Maximus of Turin.[98] Chrysostom, who self-consciously opposed Origen's notion of hell as temporary, nonetheless "urges his hearers to continue the traditional practice of praying for the dead, . . . [for] 'it is possible . . . that his punishments will be lightened.'"[99]

Augustine asserted that "the ability of the dead to profit from the prayers" offered for them by the living depends on how they lived during their lifetime.[100] Such prayers are unnecessary for proven saints and ineffectual for hardened sinners. He rejected the notion of the "tender-hearted" that all punishment is healing and only temporary. Suffering—before and after death—is "purgative" only if it leads sinners to repent.[101]

---

94. Ibid., 87.
95. Ibid., 88-89.
96. Ibid., 98-99.
97. Ibid., 104.
98. Ibid., 126.
99. Ibid., 108.
100. Ibid., 137; see 149.
101. Ibid., 138-41.

Although Augustine appealed to 2 Macc. 12:43 as scriptural evidence for the Latin church's long practice of intercessory prayers for the dead, he was reluctant to interpret 1 Cor. 3:10-15 as referring to purgative judgment. To those who imagine that God's mercy extends even to hardened sinners, Augustine conceded that God "will let them suffer less horrible punishments than what they deserve."[102] "To those who ask how one can reconcile the proclamation of a God of 'manifold mercy' with the prospect of eternal punishment, Oecumenius suggested that no sinner is punished, even eternally, to the degree he deserves, and probably not as strictly as Scripture threatens."[103]

Heaven. A few early Christian writers conceived of the final destiny of believers in spatial terms, often blending the language of Revelation with pagan hopes. In the *Apocalypse of Peter*, Christ promises, "Then will I give to my elect and righteous the baptism and salvation for which they have besought me, in the field of Akrosja (= Acherusia) which is called Aneslasleja (= Elysium). They shall adorn with flowers the portion of the righteous and I will . . . rejoice with them. I will cause the nations to enter my eternal kingdom and show to them that eternal thing to which I have directed their hope" (14).

The *Apocalypse of Paul* includes a detailed description of heaven as a massive, golden "city of Christ," bounded on its four sides with rivers of honey, milk, wine, and oil (22—30). Ephrem described heaven as an enclosed garden with trees offering shelter, food, fragrance, delicate flowers, refreshing breezes, and the continual presence of Christ. Outside the walls of paradise a grassy border will serve as the home for "those who have sinned without full knowledge."[104]

But according to Irenaeus, the real reward of the just will be unending communion with God.[105] He expected different degrees of blessing in the eternal world—from life "in heaven" to "in paradise" to in "the city"—and eternal progress until all such distinctions end.[106] Jerome also stressed the "personal and

---

102. Quoted in ibid., 149.
103. Ibid., 182.
104. Ibid., 75.
105. *Against Heresies* 5.27.1; 5.36.1.
106. Ibid., 5.36.1; see 2.28.3.

social, rather than the material, aspects of heavenly joy, . . . the company of Jesus and the angels and saints."[107] For Justin, the experience of heaven will be to "exist in freedom from suffering, from corruption, and from grief, and in immortality"[108] and to enjoy "fellowship" with God.[109] Theophilus of Antioch argued that God made people free to disobey and bring death upon themselves, or to obey and "become God."[110] Thus, he was the first theologian "to speak of Christian fulfillment expressly in terms of divinization," language that came to dominate Eastern eschatological discussion.[111]

The Alexandrians, Clement and Origen, conceived of the Christian life in terms of growth, development, and process rather than of eschatological crisis. Clement's eschatological goal was seeing God, loving fellowship with Him, and ultimately "assimilation" to Him.[112] According to Origen the one activity of heaven will be "to apprehend God."[113] Gradually, across the endless ages of eternity, evil will cease to exist, all division will end, the Church will be one, all things will be reunited with God, and the original harmony of creation will be reestablished. "God will ultimately be the totally satisfying object of every mind's activity."[114] "Nothing will disrupt the final unity and harmony of God's creation."[115]

The Cappadocian Fathers continued the Alexandrian tradition. Gregory of Nyssa described heaven as "eternal self-transcendence,"[116] "the eternal movement of endlessly knowing and loving God" more fully.[117] Gregory of Nazianzus sympathized with Origen's spiritual interpretation of traditional images of eschatological language, yet he tends to "revel still in those images' pictorial power, rather than to explain them away by alle-

---

107. Daley, Hope, 103.
108. Dialogue with Trypho 45; see 1 Apology 21.
109. 1 Apology 10.
110. To Autolycus 2:27.
111. Daley, Hope, 24. See 40, 84, 96, 183, 201-2, 204, 218, and 251, n. 32.
112. Stromata 2:23.236.6; 7:3.13.1
113. Commentary on John 1:16.92.
114. Daley, Hope, 51. See Kelly, Early Christian Doctrines, 485-86.
115. Daley, Hope, 59.
116. Ibid., 50.
117. Ibid., 88.

gory." Gregory emphasized that "the goal of the divine econo-
my is our participation, as human creatures, in the Godhead."[118]
The perfection toward which Christians presently strive is their
ultimate eschatological goal, to "be wholly like God, receptive
of God as a whole and of God alone."[119]

For Chrysostom, heaven will be "the nearness of the just to
God, and their ability to see God."[120] For Cyril of Jerusalem, in
the tradition of the Greek Fathers, it is "direct knowledge of
God," which will be rest, glory, and delight.[121] Theodore of Mopsuestia conceived of salvation as a strictly future, eschatological
reality, awaiting the resurrection. For the present, all believers
possess is the "certain hope of immortality." As a result of the
transformation the Spirit will effect at the resurrection, in heav-
en believers will experience "the destruction of sin, even as a
possibility" and the gift of holiness in its fullness.[122] For Theodoret of Cyrus, heaven will grant believers "a real union" with
God that will endow them with "the stability and changelessness" that are His naturally. God's personal presence will ban-
ish all corruption and sin.[123]

For Augustine, heaven will be "the direct contemplative vision of God."[124] This will not mean eternal passivity. "Heaven
will have a kind of activity all its own, perfectly compatible
with eternal rest: the activity of praise." In heaven, humans will
share in God's nature. Freed from the effects of the Fall, fully integrated with and fully subject to God, peace will reign within
and between every individual so that sin will be no longer possible. Humans will find their "ultimate happiness" and "highest
good" there. The saved will become "the equals" and eternal
companions of angels. Although there will be different orders of
heavenly happiness and blessing, there will be no envy or dis-
content, but only perfect harmony and everlasting love. God
alone will be "our common sight, . . . our common possession,

---

118. Ibid., 84.
119. Ibid., 85.
120. Ibid., 108.
121. Ibid., 110.
122. Ibid., 112-13.
123. Ibid., 115-16.
124. Ibid., 145.

. . . our common peace."[125] Oecumenius' description is similar: In heaven, the saints will enjoy the contemplation of God, His indwelling presence, friendship with Him, and the company of the saints and angels.[126]

Practical Implications of the Christian Hope

Motivation. Numerous early Christian writings recognized the importance of the Christian hope in motivating moral behavior. The *Didache* urges Christians to live in a state of ethical readiness for the Parousia (16:1-2). The essential message of the *Shepherd of Hermas* is an urgent call to his church to repent in the present in view of the future God is about to bring. In a view characteristic of but not exclusive to the apologists, Aristides claims it is the eschatological hope of Christians that motivates them to live righteous and holy lives.[127]

Even Origen recognized "the enormous importance of the 'deterrent' of eternal fire in shaping the ordinary Christian's moral behavior." Thus, he considered it "incautious" to discuss openly his reservations about a literal, eternal hell. But he does this at times in order to refute the gnostic distortions of God's judgment as cruel.[128]

Basil of Caesarea sometimes followed Origen's "tendency to interpret the traditional images of the Christian hope in psychological or spiritual terms." But he was also "keenly aware of the importance of the prospects of judgment and retribution in the moral life of Christians." After a vivid description of the punishments of hell, he appealed to his community, "Fear these things: and trained by this fear, rein in your soul from its desire for evil."[129] Maximus of Turin regarded the perils of life in northern Italy during the barbarian invasions a warning of the approaching day of judgment. Thus, he urged, "There is still more to fear. For while we are cautious with regard to what we see,

---

125. Ibid., 146-47.
126. Ibid., 182-83.
127. *Apology* 15-16. Repeated by Cyril of Jerusalem during the fourth century and by Commodian during the fifth. Daley, *Hope,* 161.
128. Daley, *Hope,* 57.
129. *Homily on Psalm 33:8,* cited in ibid., 81-82. See also Kelly, *Early Christian Doctrines,* 483.

we are made still more cautious with respect to what we hope for." "Think of the imminent day of judgment and the inextinguishable fires of Gehenna, the terrible gnashing of teeth and the final torture of darkness, and then, if you can, leave the Church and involve yourself in worldly cares!"[130]

Salvian of Marseilles contended that a strong eschatological faith motivates Christians to deep social concern, austerity, and moral uprightness. "The fact that so many Christians are more concerned to preserve their wealth for their heirs than to care for the poor is, in Salvian's view, simply a proof of the weakness of their eschatological faith."[131] During the 10th through the 12th centuries, Cluniac monasticism placed heavy emphasis on eschatology. Reflecting upon the Last Judgment should motivate people to change their lives and the world. "Cluny made it almost impossible for society to ignore its need to change and, consequently, the desirability of change."[132]

Consolation in the Face of Death. Justin noted that since Christians do not place their hopes in the present, they are not troubled by undeserved suffering or death for doing right—all must die in any case. The fulfillment of Christ's prediction that His followers would be persecuted only persuades them that all He has promised will surely come to pass.[133] Augustine considered the promise of the Second Coming "the main legitimate source of consolation for Christians who rightly mourn the death of their loved ones."[134]

Divine Justice and Human Responsibility. The apologists stressed that the relevance of the Christian hope is not simply to motivate believers to do right and avoid evil or to comfort them in the face of persecution and death. If there were no judgment administered by a just and all-knowing God, history would be finally unintelligible[135] and human moral choices incoherent.[136]

---

130. Quoted in Daley, *Hope*, 125.
131. Ibid., 154-55.
132. Patricia Ranft, "The Maintenance and Transformation of Society Through Eschatology: Cluniac Monasticism," *Journal of Religious History* 14 (1987): 249-50.
133. *Apology* 11-12, 17.
134. Daley, *Hope*, 135.
135. Justin, *1 Apology* 43-44.
136. Athenagoras, *On the Resurrection of the Dead* 19.

But as it is, the resurrection and judgment affirm the incomparable value of human life.[137]

Chrysostom insisted that "if goodness is not rewarded and evil punished after this life . . . then our most basic sense of justice will be rendered absurd, and our faith in God's provident care of the world contradicted." He considered it "proof of God's providential care for us that he has appointed punishments terrible enough to deter any reasonable person from sin." "The very fact that God holds us responsible for our deeds with the prospect of just sanctions is a sign of human dignity; otherwise, we would be no different from the other animals. . . . Punishment . . . is God's way of upholding the noblest human instincts, and so is a proof of his goodness."[138] According to Peter Chrysologus, the resurrection and judgment are necessary "to allow God to fulfill his justice by rewarding the just and punishing sinners in the flesh that they now possess."[139]

Augustine affirmed this ancient Christian tradition that "emphasizes the need for a judgment to reveal the justice and goodness of God's providence, which are often concealed in the present life." Judgment will be the "unmasking of human history," the inauguration of "the irreversible distinction between the saved and the damned, between lovers of God and lovers of self."[140] "Human salvation is the achievement, by God's gracious gift, of the union with God for which alone humanity was made." "The only genuine meaning of human history is to be found in God's eternity."[141]

Future Destination and Present Occupation. In the difficult days of the Decian persecution, Cyprian called Christians to look beyond the suffering of this world to the security of their future hope. Convinced that hope may be a present force in the lives of believers, he urged his readers to persevere: "That which you shall be, you have already begun to be. You possess already in this world the glory of the resurrection."[142]

---

137. Athenagoras, *Plea for the Christians* 31.
138. Daley, *Hope*, 106, 107-8.
139. Ibid., 165.
140. Ibid., 135.
141. Ibid., 150.
142. *The Dress of Virgins* 22, as cited in ibid., 43.

Origen intended his controversial attempts to reinterpret Christian eschatology to be constructive, reverent, and relevant. His search for "deeper" meanings in biblical texts and traditional doctrines was motivated by genuine pastoral concern. He assumed that "eschatological statements must have a present as well as a future relevance." Christians' future destination should fundamentally shape their present occupation. Origen emphasized "the continuity between the present Christian life and its eschatological . . . goal"—"providentially guided growth towards union with God."[143] For Origen, eschatology is "simply a part of a larger picture: the grace-filled finality of the mystery of growth towards God that is already the heart of Christian faith and practice."[144]

Conclusion

Given the lengthy time period and the variety of writers surveyed, the wide range of opinion on the subject of eschatology within the Early Church should come as no surprise. To this day, the Church has not approached the unanimity on the formulation of its future hope achieved in the patristic era on the Trinity and Christology. If Augustine is correct, it probably never will—until history passes into eternity. But for all the lingering diversity, there also seems to be a considerable measure of continuity and consensus.

The future hopes of early Christians were inextricably bound to their faith in Jesus Christ. Eschatology is finally the conviction that He will bring to a proper conclusion the salvation He began. The resurrection of Jesus Christ is God's decisive vindication of all Jesus said and did—including His death on the Cross—not its undoing. Just so, Christian eschatology is the confidence that human life, in the body, in the Church, in the world, within history, on this planet is ultimately relevant and that the final judgment on the worth of human life will be determined by God.

---

143. Ibid., 48.
144. Ibid., 60.

Early Christians agreed that history has meaning because it has a destination determined by God. They agreed that material existence created by God is an integral part of human identity and, thus, must have a role in the consummation of salvation. They agreed that, to the extent that humans are free to choose the kind of persons they are and become, they are accountable for their choices before their Creator, who is also the Judge of the universe. They agreed that "the final state of human existence, after God's judgment, will be permanent and perfect happiness for the good, and permanent, all-consuming misery for the wicked."[145]

But early Christians also disagreed on eschatology. They disagreed about whether the end was near or far away and about how one may know when it is finally approaching. They disagreed about the current status of the dead and about the precise character of resurrection existence. And they disagreed about the extent and finality of eschatological salvation.

We may not reasonably hope that all Christians will ever agree on the precise formulation of their future hopes. But perhaps this chapter may serve as a reminder that, with rare exceptions, the Church has been remarkably tolerant of harmless, private speculations about the future. We would do well, however, to remember that there are exceptions—speculations that are contrary to love or contrary to Scripture. Visions of the future, however attractive, that may not be validated by appeal to Scripture are not tolerated—nor are predictions that, if proven wrong, may damage one's own faith or that of a neighbor.

---

145. Ibid., 221.

■ WILLIAM M. GREATHOUSE

John Wesley's View of the Last Things

THE REV. THOMAS HARTLEY, a friend of Countess Selina Huntington, in 1764 published a 476-page volume titled *Paradise Restored: A Testimony to the Doctrine of the Blessed Millennium*, in which he advocated that Christ will return, set up the Kingdom, and visibly reign on earth for a thousand years.[1]

In the *Methodist Magazine*, John Wesley published a letter he wrote Hartley: "Your book on the millennium was lately put into my hands. I cannot but thank you for your strong and seasonable confirmation of that comfortable doctrine: of which I cannot entertain the least doubt, as long as I believe the Bible."[2]

This would seem to prove, as Tyerman believed, that Wesley was a premillennialist.[3] Further evidences of his presumed premillennialism are Wesley's *Notes* on the Book of Revelation, in which he incorporated Johann Bengel's highly speculative interpretation of chapters 4—20. The German scholar understood this portion of the Apocalypse to prophesy in amazing detail the history of the Christian Church from the time of the apostle John to the return of Christ, which Bengel predicted would occur in 1836.

Wesley adopted Bengel's detailed interpretation of the apocalyptic language of woes, calamities, and destruction, be-

---

1. Luke Tyerman, *Life and Times of the Rev. John Wesley* (London: Hodder and Stoughton, 1876), 2:519.
2. *Methodist Magazine*, 1783, 498; cited by Tyerman, *Life and Times*, 523.
3. Ibid.

■ *William M. Greathouse is general superintendent emeritus in the Church of the Nazarene.*

ginning at chapter 4, as descriptive of the Germanic invasions, the destruction of Rome, and the spread of "Mohammetanism [sic]." Chapters 9—17 then depict the severe persecutions of true Christian believers before and after the Reformation. The Roman papacy of the late Middle Ages qualified as the Antichrist. The only portion of the Apocalypse remaining to be fulfilled was its final chapters. The Beast and the False Prophet could appear in Rome at any time, and surely before the end of the century, but were destined to be destroyed by Christ in His return in glory.

The allegation that Wesley was a premillennialist, however, has not gone unchallenged. His *Notes* on the Gospels, Acts, and the Epistles, along with several of his sermons as well as his journal and letters, reveal an understanding of the last things that has led reputable scholars to argue that Wesley was a postmillennialist.[4] His published works contain no sermon on the Second Coming, and a study of his other writings indicates he had anything but "a premillennial mind."

In his *Notes* on the Apocalypse, following Bengel, Wesley indulges in fanciful speculation and proposes a dual millennium—a thousand-year period when Satan is bound and the Church flourishes on earth [20:2, 3, 7] and a thousand-year period when the saints rule with Christ in heaven [20:4-6].[5]

It is instructive to read Wesley's preface to Revelation, in which he confesses his dependence on Bengel and acknowledges his own ignorance concerning the greater part of "this mysterious book." Listen to Wesley:

> It is scarce possible for any that either love or fear God not to feel their hearts extremely affected in seriously reading either the

---

4. The list includes Harris Franklin Rall (*Modern Premillenialism and Christian Hope* [New York: Abingdon, 1920]); Jerry Mercer ("The Destiny of Man in John Wesley's Eschatology," *Wesleyan Theological Journal*, Spring 1967); W. Ralph Thompson ("The Millennium," *Contemporary Wesleyan Theology*, 1987). See Kenneth O. Brown, "John Wesley—Post or Premillenialism?" *Methodist History* 28 (October 1989): 1.

5. John Wesley, *Explanatory Notes upon the New Testament* (London: Epworth Press, 1950), 1038-39. A 1976 reprint of this book is available from SCM Press Ltd. of London. Hereafter, references to the *Notes* will normally be indicated by citing in brackets the book, chapter, and verse of scripture to which they refer after the quotation or allusion. Since there are several editions of the *Notes*, this will enable the reader to check the reference in whatever edition is available.

beginning or the latter part of the Revelation. But the intermediate parts I did not study at all for many years; as utterly despairing of understanding them, . . . and perhaps I should have lived and died in this sentiment had I not seen the works of the great Bengelius. The following notes are mostly those of that excellent man. . . . All I can do is, partly to translate, partly abridge, the most necessary of his observations. . . . Yet I by no means understand or explain all that is contained in this mysterious book.[6]

In his *Journal* for December 1762, Wesley acknowledges further unresolved questions in his mind: "Monday the sixth and the following day, I corrected the Notes upon Revelation. Oh, how little do we know of this deep book. At least how little do I know. I can barely conjecture, not confirm, any one point concerning the part of it which is yet unfulfilled."[7]

And although Wesley incorporated Bengel's observations as if in total agreement with him, he later appears to draw back from some of his interpretations. After being accused of setting a date for the end of the world in a sermon, Wesley wrote the following letter:

My dear brother, I said nothing—less or more—in Bradford Church concerning the end of the world, neither concerning *my own* opinion. What I said was that Bengel had given it as *his* opinion, not that the world would end, but that the millennial reign of Christ would *begin* in the year 1836. I have no opinion at all upon that topic. I can determine nothing about it. These calculations are far above, out of my sight. I have only one thing to do, to save my own soul and those that hear me.[8]

This last sentence provides a key to understanding Wesley. As Clarence Bence observes, "For Wesley, theology is soteriology." Noting Colin Williams' statement that the saving work of Christ and the human appropriation of that work is the central focus of Wesley's theology, he states, "Wesleyan eschatology must be developed out of the Wesleyan understanding of salvation, both in its individual and its broader socio-historical orien-

6. Ibid., 932.

7. *The Journal of the Rev. John Wesley,* ed. Nehemiah Curnock (London: Epworth Press, 1938), 4:540.

8. John Wesley, *The Works of John Wesley,* 3rd ed., 14 vols. (1872; reprint, Kansas City: Beacon Hill Press of Kansas City, 1978), 12:319.

tation."[9] For Wesley, eschatology and soteriology are two parts of one system of understanding.

Christ the King

The publication of Gustaf Aulén's *Christus Victor* earlier in this century signaled a fresh appraisal in the Church's thinking about the Atonement.[10] Previously, Anselm of Canterbury's satisfaction theory had been considered the first thought-out doctrine of Atonement in the history of dogma. Anselm repressed, even if he could not overcome, the patristic account of Christ's work as a *victory* over the devil, which had developed into the ransom theory. Aulén argues that "the view of the Atonement which is summed up in such phrases as 'Christus Victor,' and 'God was in Christ reconciling the world to Himself'—the view that sets the Incarnation in direct connection with the Atonement, and proclaims that it is God Himself who in Christ has delivered mankind from the power of evil"—is the view that dominates the New Testament and finds strong, clear, and consistent expression in the early Fathers. This, Aulén insists, is a doctrine that has every right to be called the "classic" idea of the Atonement.[11]

While the death of Christ is at the center of the Atonement, it is not His death in isolation. Rather,

> It is death seen in connection, on the one hand with the life-work of Christ as a whole, and on the other hand with the Resurrection and Ascension; the death irradiated with the light of Easter and Pentecost. . . . The Resurrection is . . . first of all the manifestation of the decisive victory over the powers of evil, which was won on the cross; it is also the starting point for the new dispensation, for the gift of the Spirit, for the continuation of the work of God in the souls of men "for unity and communion of God and man."[12]

9. Clarence Bence, "Processive Eschatology: A Wesleyan Alternative," *Wesleyan Theological Journal,* Spring 1979, 47.

10. Gustav Aulén, *Christus Victor,* trans. A. G. Hebert (New York: Macmillan, 1951). This is a translation of lectures given by Aulén, professor of theology in the University of Lund, before the University of Uppsala in March and April 1930.

11. Ibid., v.

12. Ibid., 31-32.

The foregoing summary of the teaching of Irenaeus, whom McGiffert calls "the most influential of all the early Fathers,"[13] represents at its best the "classic" idea, which also finds strong expression in Wesley's writings.

Wesley generally viewed Christ's atoning work in terms of propitiation. But "alongside this judicial scheme of thought," John Deschner writes,

> There is also in Wesley a pervasive tendency to view Christ's work on Good Friday and Easter, but also today and in the future, in terms of the military metaphor: Christ is a king who has won and wins a victory for us over sin and evil. Much attention has been given to the power of the Holy Spirit in Wesley's doctrine of sanctification. *It needs to be more clearly recognized that the sanctifying Spirit is the Spirit of the victorious as well as the suffering Christ.*[14]

Deschner gives a clear and comprehensive summary of the Christus Victor idea as it appears in Wesley. While Christ's victorious power is repeatedly demonstrated in His earthly ministry (Matt. 12:28-29),

> The grand revelation of Christ's kingship is not in the miracles but in the cross, resurrection, and ascension. It is before Pilate, as Wesley emphasizes, that Christ is revealed to be king (Mt. 27:11, Jn. 11:50), and the cross is the decisive encounter between Christ, Satan, and sin, before which the kingdom could not be set up (1 Cor. 15:26, Lk. 12:50). The resurrection, which is a victory over death (1 Cor. 15:26), is the beginning of the kingdom (Lk. 22:16, Acts 2:31), and its power will raise men to new life in regeneration, and to eternal life in the general resurrection (Rom. 6:5, Eph. 1:19, 1 Cor. 15:20). The ascension signifies Christ's elevation to rule from the right hand of the Father (Acts 2:33, Eph. 1:21-22), until He comes to judge the world, in a form appropriate to His majesty (Rev. 1:7, Heb. 9:28). After the judgment, Christ will return the mediatorial kingdom to the Father, without ceasing to rule eternally with Him (1 Cor. 15:24).[15]

---

13. A. C. McGiffert, *A History of Christian Thought* (New York: Charles Scribner's Sons, 1949), 1:132.

14. John Deschner, *John Wesley's Christology* (Dallas: Southern Methodist University Press, 1960), 116 (emphasis added). Used with permission. All rights reserved. All Scripture references included in quotations of this source (in this and successive notes) are placed in parentheses and refer to John Wesley's comments in his *Explanatory Notes upon the New Testament.*

15. Ibid., 117.

For Wesley, this view of Christ's victory over the powers of evil that have dominated humanity since the Fall is at the same time a doctrine of sanctification. Although he did not formulate this motif into a Christus Victor theology of sanctification, all the elements of this theology are to be found in his *Explanatory Notes upon the New Testament*, sermons, and various other writings.

1. *Christ's Defeat of Satan.* Wesley spoke of the world Christ entered as "Satan's house" [Matt. 12:29]. Although Christ is sovereign Lord of the universe, Satan is now "the god of this world" [2 Cor. 4:4]. By his seduction of our first parents and their fall into sin, he gained a right, a claim, and a power over man.[16]

"*Unde malum?* 'How came sin into the world?'" Wesley asks in his sermon titled "The End of Christ's Coming." "It came from 'Lucifer, son of the morning.' It was the work of the devil. 'For the devil,' saith the apostle, 'sinneth from the beginning'; that is, was the first sinner of the universe, the author of sin, the first being who, by the abuse of his liberty, introduced evil into the creation."[17]

In the Garden the devil "transfused" his own self-will and pride into our parents.[18] The devil was "self-tempted,"[19] but man fell from temptation *outside* himself. Induced by the devil to revolt against God, man came under the *guilt* and therefore the *power* of sin.[20] It is thus that Satan gained control of man.

The end of Christ's coming, first of all, was to redeem the race from Satan's dominion and control. Commenting on Matt. 12:29, Wesley says, "So Christ coming into the world, which was then eminently the strong one's, Satan's house, first bound him, and then took his spoils" (see *Notes*). Casting out demons by the Spirit of God was the beginning of Christ's work of binding Satan. It was His cross and resurrection, however, which constituted His *decisive* victory.

"Now is the judgment of this world," Jesus said of His coming death on the Cross; "now shall the prince of this world be

---

16. Deschner, *Christology*, 120.
17. Sermon 62, "The End of Christ's Coming," *Sermons*, Albert Outler, ed. (*The Works of John Wesley*, Frank Baker, gen. ed. [Nashville: Abingdon Press, 1985]), 2:476.
18. Sermon 28, "The Deceitfulness of the Human Heart," *Sermons* 1:152.
19. Sermon 62, *Sermons* 2:476.
20. See Note 21.

cast out" (John 12:31, KJV). Commenting on this announcement, Wesley says, "Satan, who had gained possession of [the world] by sin and death, is judged, condemned, *cast out* of his possession, and out of the bounds of Christ's kingdom" (see *Notes*).

Christ's holiness was the one thing damnatory of Satan. "The prince of this world is coming—To make his grand assault. But he hath nothing in me—No right, no claim, or power," Wesley comments. He then explains the words of Christ: "There is no guilt in Me to give him power over Me; no corruption to take part with his temptation" [John 14:30].[21]

The moment of Satan's apparent victory, when he made his "grand assault" at Calvary, was actually that of his own defeat, for in his pride he overreached himself. The Father raised Christ from the dead by His own right hand, making Him Lord and through Him sending the Holy Spirit [Acts 2:33]. Referring to the promised Spirit, Jesus said, "He will convince the world of judgment, . . . because the prince of this world is judged." For those who believe, Satan is "dethroned, deprived of the power he had long usurped over men" [John 16:11].

2. *Christ's Destruction of Sin.* The end of Christ's coming, in the second place, was the abolition of sin. "For this purpose the Son of God was manifested, that he might destroy the works of the devil" (1 John 3:8, KJV)—that is, "sin and its fruits."[22]

Through His Incarnate Son, God has done what the Law of Moses could never do. "Incapable of conquering our evil nature" [Rom. 8:3] as those fallen in Adam, the law is powerless against the sin that indwells and "tyrannizes over" us [Rom. 7:17]. Under the law, "we with our sinful flesh were devoted to death. But God, sending His own Son in the likeness of that flesh, *condemned* that sin which was *in our flesh:* gave sentence, that sin should be destroyed, and the believer wholly delivered from it" [Rom. 8:3].

The foregoing *Notes* leave no doubt that, for Wesley, Christ's atonement makes possible our deliverance from the

---

21. "The guilt and power of sin" is a frequently occurring formula in Wesley. The two terms must not be taken as two parallel aspects of sin but rather as "the guilt, and therefore, in principle, the power of sin" (see Deschner, *Christology,* 141, n. 3).

22. *Sermons* 2:477.

frustrating struggle of Rom. 7. The implied reference to the Incarnation and Pentecost in 8:1-4 presupposes that the Atonement embraces the *entire* Christ event. The freedom from sin
that Christ made possible *for* us as the incarnate Son offered up
on the Cross He now works *in* us as the glorified Lord of the
Church, provided "we walk not after the flesh, but after the
Spirit" He gives us.

The Son of God was manifested "that he might destroy the
works of the devil." For Wesley, this is a promise of complete
deliverance from sin—from both its power and its inbeing—in
order to bring about our full restoration of the forfeited image
of God. In John's text he finds "in the clearest, strongest light,
what is real religion." It is

> a restoration of man by Him that bruises the serpent's head, to all
> the old serpent deprived him of; a restoration, not only to the
> favour but likewise to the image of God, implying not barely de-
> liverance from sin, but the being filled with the fullness of God. It
> is plain . . . that nothing short of this is Christian religion. . . . Take
> no less for [Christ's] religion, than the "faith that worketh by
> love" all inward and outward holiness.[23]

We must not, therefore, be content with any religion that
does not imply the destruction of all sin. Sin "need not remain:
this is the work of the devil, eminently so called, which the Son
of God was manifested to destroy in this present life."[24]

3. *Christ's Victory over Death.* Christ has not only defeated
Satan and condemned sin, but He has also destroyed our "last
enemy, death" [1 Cor. 15:26]. "Death, 'the devil's sergeant,' is
conquered, abolished, destroyed, forever; without sin, which is
its sting, death can have no more power. Moreover, Christ
turned death into a blessing (Heb. 2:14, 1 Cor. 15:26, 54, 56, 2
Tim. 1:10)."[25] Now even the enemies of Christ must confess that
He is Lord [Phil. 2:10-11]. And the positive scope of this victory
Wesley describes as a recapitulation of "all angels and men,
whether living or dead, in the Lord" under Christ, their common Head [Eph. 1:10].

---

23. Ibid., 482-83.
24. Ibid., 483.
25. Deschner, *Christology,* 122.

4. *Eschatological Consequences.* Although Satan, sin, and death have been decisively defeated, Wesley does not underestimate the provisional, remaining power of evil. "The deliverer has come, but not the full fruit of His coming" [Rom. 11:26]. Satan has been dethroned and robbed of his power, "yet those who reject the deliverance offered them will remain slaves of Satan still" [John 16:11]. Although the evil angels have been bound with chains, "still those chains do not hinder their often walking up and down seeking whom they may devour" [2 Pet. 2:4].

A state of war remains between "the Church warring under Christ, and the world warring under Satan" [Rev. 6:9]. But since Christ has won the decisive battle, the outcome of this war is already determined: in both heaven and earth, God's kingdom stands and Satan's is being destroyed [Mark 9:40; Luke 10:18-19]. Nor is Satan able to keep from Christ those who follow His "drawings" [John 12:32] or hinder anyone from attaining the heights of God's love [Eph. 3:18].

"Because a victory has been won in principle, while the eschatological consequences are not yet fully evident, sanctification has the character of spiritual warfare."[26] Although the Spirit and the flesh are at war in the justified believer, true believers in Christ have *"crucified the flesh*—nailed it, as it were, to a cross, whence it has no power to break loose, but is continually weaker and weaker" [Gal. 5:24]. Christ has been manifested in our hearts to destroy the works of the devil in us—"all sin" [1 John 3:8]—and this He will perform in all who trust Him.[27]

But He does *not* destroy the whole work of the devil *in this life:* "We know weakness of understanding, and a thousand infirmities, will remain while this corruptible body remains."[28] Infirmities and death are destroyed only at the resurrection. "The Son of God, manifested in the clouds of heaven, shall destroy this last work of the devil."[29] "Universal holiness," understood as the mind of Christ, stands, however, as "the general preservative against the devil."[30]

---

26. Ibid., 123.
27. See Sermon 43, "The Scripture Way of Salvation," *Sermons* 2:162-9.
28. *Sermons* 2:483.
29. Ibid., 482.
30. Sermon 72, "Evil Angels," *Sermons* 3:27.

Christ's final victory over Satan will come at the last day [1 Cor. 15:24]. Satan has already been judged in Christ's death and resurrection; it is only "the great mystery of God" that has permitted him this interval [Rev. 20:3]. But on that last day our accuser will be "taken away" and "the whole world and all its kingdoms" returned to its rightful Master [Rev. 11:15].

Toward a Wesleyan Eschatology

Let us return to the question of John Wesley's eschatological position. Was he a premillennialist or postmillennialist? Scholars seem equally divided on this issue, and a final resolution of the question seems unlikely.

Tyerman was certain Wesley was a premillennialist who believed that Christ would reign *visibly* on earth a thousand years before the final consummation. Commenting on Wesley's letter to Hartley in which Wesley apparently endorsed the latter's millennialism, Tyerman says: "With such a statement, in reference to such a book, there can be no doubt, that Wesley, like his father before him, was a millenarian, a believer in the second advent of Christ, to *reign* on earth, visibly and gloriously, for a thousand years."[31]

Wesley's curious view of a dual millennium, however, seems to refute Tyerman. The first millennium promised in Rev. 20:2, 3, 7, Wesley holds (following Bengel), will be a time when the Church on earth will flourish as "never yet seen." *After this,* the martyred saints will be raised from the dead to "live and reign with Christ a thousand years," *not on earth, but in heaven* [Rev. 20:4-6].

The vision of a thousand-year period when the Church will enjoy an unprecedented success before "the first resurrection" lends itself to a kind of postmillennialism consonant with Wesley's frequently proclaimed optimism concerning "the general spread of the Gospel." The second millennium then becomes a kind of transition between the mediatorial kingdom of grace Christ established by His first coming and the kingdom of glory to be ushered in by His second advent. An interesting point to keep in mind is Wesley's observation that the beginnings of

---

31. Tyerman, *Life and Times*, 523.

these two millennia will not be known by the peoples of the earth, since the divine transactions initiating these periods take place "in the invisible world" [Rev. 20:5].

Wesley's *Notes* on Rev. 20 are his only attempt to unravel the mystery of the last things. And what he says there is difficult to integrate with what he says elsewhere. Donald W. Dayton seems to be true to Wesley when he claims that the latter's thinking is "probably better captured by the less apocalyptic and more postmillennial schemes of thought." He then suggests, "Wesley was so oriented to soteriology that his followers could combine a basically Wesleyan scheme of salvation with a variety of eschatologies without an obvious sense of betrayal."[32]

Several recent studies tend to see Wesley from different theological perspectives. Colin Williams argues that Wesley "stressed realized eschatology more than any other western theologian."[33] Since for Wesley, "Justification, sanctification, perfection all lead in a sequenced order toward the eschatological realities of death, glorification, paradise and eternal glory," Clarence L. Bence thinks his position is best understood as "processive eschatology."[34] Cyril Downes argues that a better term for Wesley's view would be "anticipated eschatology."[35] More recently Roger L. Hahn has argued, "It would be more accurate to characterize Wesley's soteriological eschatology in terms of 'inaugurated eschatology' rather than 'realized eschatology.' This means that the promises and blessings of the last days have already been secured by means of Christ and in that sense the future hope has been 'realized.' It also means a steadfast grip on the future consummation of that hope."[36]

From our examination of the Christus Victor motif, the accuracy of Hahn's characterization of Wesley's doctrine seems abundantly sustained. The tension between the "already" and the "not yet" is basic to Wesley, in both Christ's kingly reign

---

32. Donald Dayton, *Theological Roots of Pentecostalism* (Grand Rapids: Francis Asbury Press, 1987), 153.

33. Colin Williams, *John Wesley's Theology Today* (London: Epworth Press, 1960), 194.

34. Bence, "Processive Eschatology," 48.

35. Brown, "John Wesley," 60.

36. Roger Hahn, "A Wesleyan Approach to Eschatology," paper presented at the Eighth Theology Conference, Kansas City (February 28, 1992), 4.

and sanctifying work, as it is in Jesus and Paul. In Christ's victory over the powers of evil, the Kingdom has actually been *inaugurated* in history, even though its final consummation awaits His return in glory. As we look more closely at Wesley's doctrine of the kingdom of God, the rightness of this view should become even more apparent [Rom. 8:17-24].

The One Kingdom of God

At first glance, Wesley's use of the term "kingdom" seems to have a remarkable looseness of meaning. Sometimes it means the heavenly kingdom, sometimes inward religion, sometimes the gospel dispensation, as well as "a person, or thing relating to any of these" [Matt. 13:24]. Deschner avers, "Upon closer analysis, a doctrinal pattern begins to emerge, and this pattern, once seen, is found with remarkable consistency throughout Wesley's writings."[37]

The crucial note is on Matt. 3:2, John the Baptist's announcement, "The kingdom of heaven is at hand" (KJV). Wesley comments:

> The kingdom of heaven and the kingdom of God are but two phrases for the same thing. They mean, not barely a future happy state in heaven, but a state to be enjoyed on earth; the proper disposition for the glory of heaven, rather than the possession of it. . . . It properly signifies here, the gospel dispensation, in which subjects were to be gathered to God by His Son, and a society to be formed, which was to subsist first on earth, and afterwards with God in glory. In some places of Scripture the phrase more particularly denotes the state of it on earth; in others, it signifies only the state of glory; but it generally includes both [Matt. 3:2].

The Kingdom is a both a state on earth and a state in heaven. This is a distinction Wesley makes throughout the *Notes*, where the terms are frequently "the kingdom of grace" and "the kingdom of glory." In his sixth homily on the Sermon on the Mount, Wesley urges on the petition "Thy kingdom come" in the Lord's Prayer:

> It is meet for all those who "love his appearing" to pray that he would hasten the time; that this his kingdom, the kingdom of

---

37. Deschner, *Christology*, 127.

grace, may come quickly, and swallow up all the kingdoms of the earth; that all mankind receiving him for their king, truly believing in his name, may be filled with righteousness, peace and joy, with holiness and happiness, till they are removed hence into his heavenly kingdom, there to reign with him for ever and ever.

For this also we pray in those words, "Thy kingdom come." We pray for the coming of the everlasting kingdom, the kingdom of glory in heaven, which is the continuation and perfection of the kingdom of grace on earth.[38]

Wesley's interpretation of Daniel's 70th week in his *Explanatory Notes upon the Old Testament* reveals how far he was from modern dispensationalism. The 70th week is no literal seven-year period expected only at the end of the Church age, but the whole of the Christian dispensation. For Wesley, the divine covenant-maker of Dan. 9:27 is not Antichrist—but Christ! He explains:

Christ confirmed the new covenant, 1. By the testimony of angels, of John the Baptist, of the wise men, of the saints then living, of Moses and Elias. 2. By his preaching. 3. By signs and wonders. 4. By his holy life. 5. By his resurrection and ascension. 6. By his death and blood shedding shall cause the sacrifice to cease— all the Jewish rites and levitical worship. By his death he abrogated and put an end to his laborious service forever.[39]

The first half of Daniel's 70th week, which some dispensationalists believe will be the first half of a seven-year "Great Tribulation" period, Wesley understands has already been fulfilled in Jesus' three-and-a-half-year public ministry. The "covenant" of Dan. 9:27 is not a future peace treaty to be signed by Jews and the Roman antichrist; it is the Christian gospel, which promises "to bring in justification by the free grace of God, and sanctification by his Spirit, . . . To abrogate the former dispensation of the law, and to ratify the gospel covenant (Dan. 9:24-27)."[40] Moreover, this covenant is not limited to the Jews but is for the "many," all those for whom Jesus shed His blood.

---

38. *Sermons* 1:582.
39. John Wesley, *Explanatory Notes upon the Old Testament* (Salem, Ohio: Schmul Publishers, 1975), 3:2456-57.
40. Ibid., 2456.

The second half of Daniel's 70th week embraces the entire Christian dispensation stretching between Christ's resurrection and His second advent. The 70th week, therefore, is a dispensational continuum for the entire Christian age, which in his *Notes upon the New Testament* Wesley calls Christ's mediatorial "kingdom of grace" and "the gospel dispensation."

The Kingdom of Grace

John's announcement of the kingdom's being "at hand" was for Wesley "as if he had said, God is about to erect the kingdom spoken of by Daniel (2:44 and 7:13-14), the kingdom of the God of heaven" [Matt. 3:2]. "It properly signifies here," he continues, "the gospel dispensation," its spiritual nature shown by John's demand for repentance" [Matt. 3:2].

The Kingdom was present in Christ himself, "the King of heaven" [Matt. 25:14] and the Son of Man promised in Dan. 7:13 [Matt. 8:20]. By His casting out demons [Matt. 12:28-29], preaching the gospel [Matt. 13:24], and teaching in parables [Matt. 25:14], the Kingdom was beginning to break into history. Thus, Jesus could announce to His hearers, "Behold, the kingdom of God . . . is now in the midst of you: it is come" [Luke 17:21]. In theological terms, this means that the future eschatological kingdom had already begun in Jesus' ministry.

The full erection of the Kingdom, however, awaited His passion, resurrection, and ascension. "Before I can set up My kingdom," Wesley hears Jesus saying in Luke 12:50, "I must suffer first." Observing the Passover with His disciples shortly before His death, Jesus said He would not partake with them again "till it be fulfilled in the kingdom of God." Here Wesley observes, "The kingdom of God did not properly commence till His resurrection" [Luke 22:16]. And Wesley understood Jesus' prediction that some of His hearers would not taste death until they should see "the kingdom of God coming in power" to refer to the Day of Pentecost [Mark 9:1]. The parallel passage in Matthew means that these persons would see "the Messiah coming to set up His mediatorial kingdom with great power and glory," setting aside the Temple and Judaism [Matt. 16:28].

The Day of Pentecost, which marked the coming of the kingdom of God "in power," ushered in "the last days" that

would continue until the day of judgment. The Spirit's outpour-
ing was "not on the day of Pentecost only" but was the beginning of "the last dispensation of divine grace," when the Spirit
would be poured out "on persons of every age, sex, and rank"
[Acts 2:16-20].

Wesley's favorite text on the Kingdom was Paul's declaration in Romans: "For the kingdom of God is not meat and
drink; but righteousness, and peace, and joy in the Holy Ghost"
(14:17, KJV). The Kingdom is nothing less than "the image of
God stamped on the heart; the love of God and man, accompanied with the *peace* that passeth all understanding, *and joy in the
Holy Ghost*" [Rom. 14:17]. This was not only Wesley's definition
of the present kingdom but also what he meant by holiness.
Here his eschatology and his soteriology are one.

In his sermon "The Way to the Kingdom," Wesley gives a
full exposition of Rom. 14:17.[41] In explaining "joy in the Holy
Ghost," he clearly indicates the relation of salvation to eschatology. The Holy Spirit "inspires the Christian soul with that even,
solid joy, which arises from the testimony of the Spirit that he is
a child of God; and that gives him to 'rejoice with joy unspeakable, in hope of the glory of God'; hope both of the glorious image of God, which is in part and shall be fully 'revealed in him';
and of that crown of glory which fadeth not away, reserved in
heaven for him."

> This holiness and happiness, joined in one, are sometimes
> styled, in the inspired writings, "the kingdom of God," . . . and
> sometimes "the kingdom of heaven." It is termed "the kingdom
> of God," because it is the immediate fruit of God in the soul. So
> soon as ever he takes unto himself his mighty power, and sets up
> his throne in our hearts, they are instantly filled with this "righ-
> teousness, and peace, and joy in the Holy Ghost." It is called "the
> kingdom of heaven," because it is (in a degree) heaven opened in
> the soul. For whosoever they are that experience this, they can
> aver before angels and men, Everlasting life is won, Glory is on
> earth begun.[42]

The same wedding of soteriology and eschatology is found
in two other Pauline texts. In 2 Corinthians, the apostle speaks

41. *Sermons* 1:218-24.
42. Ibid., 224.

of "[God], who hath also sealed us, and given the earnest of the Spirit in our hearts" (1:22, KJV). To be sealed, says Wesley, is to have God stamp His image on our hearts, marking and sealing us as His property. To receive the earnest of the Spirit is to taste its firstfruits as we "wait for all the fullness" [2 Cor. 1:22]. In Ephesians we find the same imagery. The sealing implies "the full impression of the image of God on [our] souls," while the earnest is "both a pledge and a foretaste of our inheritance . . . till the Church is advanced to everlasting glory" [1:13-14].

The age to come is still ahead, but believers have "tasted . . . the powers of the world to come" [Heb. 6:5]. And they enjoy "that love to God which is both the earnest and the beginning of heaven" [Rom. 5:5].

> *Oh, what a blessed hope is ours!*
> *While here on earth we stay,*
> *We more than taste the heavenly powers,*
> *And antedate that day.*
> *We feel the resurrection near,*
> *Our life in Christ concealed,*
> *And with his glorious presence here*
> *Our earthen vessels filled.*
>
> —Charles Wesley

The kingdom of God, however, is more than "heaven already opened in the soul" of the believer; it is also "a society to be formed" where God reigns in the hearts of Christians both individually and collectively [Matt. 3:2]. As Bence says, "Wesley does not share our modern day inclination to make a distinction between the person and society. Love of God entails love of neighbor; personal holiness demands social holiness."[43] For him, as for Jesus and Paul, the salvation of the individual directly involves and reflects God's larger plan of redemption for history and the created order. The devastating ravages of sin must give way to the redemptive power of Christ. Salvation must mean "the restitution of all things" [Acts 3:21].

Wesley is fully aware of "the mystery of iniquity" at work in the Church and society. He is also cognizant of "the mystery

---

43. Bence, "Processive Eschatology," 48.

of godliness." Christ has "built His Church upon a rock, and the gates of hell [shall] not 'wholly' prevail against her." So after his painful account of "the increasing corruptions" in the Church and the world, he asks:

> But shall we not see greater things than these? Yea, greater than have been yet from the beginning of the world. Can Satan cause the truth of God to fail, or his promises to be of none effect? If not, the time will come when Christianity will prevail over all, and cover the earth. Let us stand a little, and survey this strange sight, . . . *a Christian world.*[44]

This vision he finds in "the prophets of old" who foretold: "It shall come to pass in the last days, that the mountain of the Lord's house shall be established on the top of the mountains. . . . And they shall beat their swords into ploughshares, and their spears into pruning hooks. Nation shall not lift up sword against nation, neither shall they learn war any more."[45]

This vision is not of an apocalyptic cataclysm; it is faith in the final victory of God's kingdom of grace! As those who are taught by Christ, we are to pray, "May Thy kingdom of grace come quickly, and swallow up all the kingdoms of the earth!" [Matt. 6:10]. "Such a hope for the transformation of society," Hahn says, "was built on the confidence that God was at work redeeming the world in the continuing work of Christ through the body of believers" and "set in motion the forces that would move in the direction of postmillennialism."[46]

It was in the 1780s that Wesley most confidently proclaimed the triumph of the gospel in history. Despite the dismal condition of the world and the indifference of the Church of England to Methodism, Wesley took the Methodist Revival "both as a sign of hope and a model of God's final design for the general spread of the Gospel."[47] "As God is one," he averred, "so the work of God is uniform in all ages. May we not then conceive how he *will* work in the souls of men in times to come by con-

---

44. Sermon 4, "Scriptural Christianity," *Sermons* 1:169.
45. Ibid.
46. Hahn, "Eschatology," 11.
47. Albert Outler, "Introductory Comments on Sermon 63, 'The General Spread of the Gospel,'" *Sermons* 2:485.

sidering how he does work *now?* And how he *has* worked in times past?"[48]

Noting Luther's statement that a revival never lasts more than a generation, that is, 30 years, Wesley pointed out that "the present revival has already continued above fifty."

> And is it not probable, I say, that he will carry it on in the same manner as he has begun? At the first breaking out of his work in this or that place there may be a shower, a torrent of grace, and so at some other particular seasons which "the Father has reserved in his own power." But in general it seems the kingdom of God will not "come with observation," but will silently increase wherever it is set up, and spread from heart to heart, from house to house, from town to town, from one kingdom to another.[49]

In the last sentence, Wesley was thinking of the spread of the revival over the British Isles and the American colonies. "The grand Pentecost shall 'fully come,' and 'devout men in every nation under heaven,' however distant in place from one another, shall 'all be filled with the Holy Ghost.'"[50]

This grand Pentecost will effect a total transformation of human society as God's final plan is accomplished:

> The time is coming when not only "all Israel shall be saved," but "the fullness of the Gentiles will come in." The time cometh when "violence shall no more be heard in the earth, wasting or destruction in the borders," but every city shall "call her walls salvation, and her gates praise" when the people, saith the Lord, "shall be righteous; they shall inherit the land forever, the branch of my planting, the work of my hands, that I may be glorified."[51]

For Wesley, this was more than human optimism; his hopes were based on such promises as Matt. 24:35; Ps. 2:8; Rom. 11:25-26, 32; Ezek. 36:24-28; Deut. 30:5-6. With confidence he proclaimed: "At that time shall be accomplished all those glorious promises made for the Christian church; which will not be confined to that nation, but will include all the inhabitants of the earth. 'They shall not hurt nor destroy in all my holy mountain.'"[52]

---

48. Sermon 63, "The General Spread of the Gospel," *Sermons* 2:489.
49. Ibid., 493.
50. Ibid., 494.
51. Sermon 61, "The Mystery of Iniquity," *Sermons* 2:466.
52. Sermon 63, "The General Spread of the Gospel," *Sermons* 2:498.

"The challenge of the Wesleyan revival was, then, how to turn the promises of future blessings of the eschatological reign of God into a present reality," as Tore Meistad writes, "As the movement understood the biblical gospel, the poor, the suffering, and the oppressed became participants in these promises. When they were denied the access to human and social privileges in their own society, the Wesleys felt compelled to struggle for their participation in social and economic benefits. This conclusion came out of their biblical interpretation and theology of salvation."[53]

Hahn points out that Wesley seemed to believe there were certain "critical windows in time (kairoi)" when genuine social transformation could occur. "For success to be obtained God's right time had to be matched with perfect obedience of believers and of the leaders that God had placed in strategic positions of leadership."[54] Wesley's letter to Wilberforce, written a week before his death, is an example:

> Unless God has raised you up for this very thing you will be worn out by the opposition of men and devils. But if God be for you, who can be against you? O be not weary in well doing! Go on, in the name of God and the power of his might, till even American slavery (the vilest that ever saw the sun) shall vanish away before it.[55]

The Kingdom of Glory

Wesley's grand vision is the coming of the kingdom of glory, which he believes will be the perfection and consummation of the kingdom of grace. This transformation will be preceded by the general resurrection and final judgment [1 Cor. 15:22-24].

Wesley's sermon "The Great Assize" reflects the traditional theology of the Church. "The person by whom God 'will judge the world' is his only-begotten Son" who "emptied himself" to take on the form of a man. "In his human nature . . . *as man* [he will] try the children of men."[56] Deschner suggests a possible

53. Tore Meistad, "Wesley's Theology of Salvation and Social Change" (paper presented to the Wesleyan Studies Group, The American Academy of Religion, New Orleans, November 19, 1990).

54. Hahn, "Eschatology," 10.

55. "John Wesley," ed. Albert Outler, in *A Library of Protestant Thought* (New York: Oxford University Press, 1964), 85-86.

56. Sermon 15, "The Great Assize," *Sermons* 1:359 (emphasis added).

reason for this emphasis: "Christ's human nature is thus a norm for perfect obedience, a standard which discovers and illumines human sin before the judgment seat."[57] Christ's judgment begins with the Church [1 Pet. 4:17]. It will be of "words, tempers, and works produced as evidence whether you were a true believer or not" [Matt. 12:37; 1 Pet. 1:17].[58]

After the judgment of the righteous, He will then judge the wicked by their words, intentions, and works. And they will try, even in this day, to justify themselves! [Matt. 25:44]. The essence of their punishment is being cut off from the presence of the Lord, wherein is the salvation of the righteous. Wesley shows no morbid interest in the torments of the damned. After the judgment is over, he is preoccupied with the saints in glory.[59] "Wesley's picture of hell is a literal transcription of the New Testament language," Williams points out, "but it is important that he made small use of the threat of hell." In the Minutes of the 1746 Conference he wrote:

> Q. What inconvenience is there in speaking much of the wrath of God and little of the love of God?
> A. It generally hardens them that believe not, and discourages them that do.[60]

Then, after the resurrection and judgment "cometh the end of the world," when the Son delivers up His mediatorial kingdom to the Father.

> So far as the Father gave the kingdom to the Son, the Son shall deliver it up to the Father (John 13:3). Nor does the Father cease to reign, when He gives it up to the Son; neither the Son, when He delivers it up to the Father: but the glory which He had before the world began (John 17:5; Heb. 1:8) will remain even after this is delivered up. Nor will He cease to be a king even in His human nature (Luke 1:33). [1 Cor. 15:24-25]

Christ must reign until the Father has put "all His enemies under His feet. The last enemy that is destroyed is death"—"after Satan (Heb. 2:14) and sin (1 Cor. 15:56) are destroyed. In the same order they prevailed."

---

57. Deschner, *Christology*, 132.
58. Ibid., 134.
59. Ibid., 135.
60. Williams, *Theology*, 119.

Satan brought in sin, and sin brought forth death. And Christ when He of old engaged with these enemies, first conquered Satan, then sin, in His death; and, lastly, death, in His resurrection. In the same order He delivers all the faithful from them, yea, and destroys these enemies themselves. Death He destroys that it shall be no more; sin and Satan, so that they shall no more hurt His people. [1 Cor. 15:26]

Then shall the Son himself also be subject to the Father— "shall deliver up the mediatorial kingdom" [1 Cor. 15:24].

That the three-one *God may be all in all*—All things (consequently all persons), without any interruption, without the intervention of any creature, without the opposition of any enemy, shall be subordinate to God. All shall say, "My God, and my all." This is the end. Even an inspired apostle can say nothing beyond this. [1 Cor. 15:28]

The blessedness of believers is that they are now made perfect in a higher sense than was ever possible on earth. "In a remarkable extension of the Wesleyan perfection motif," Deschner says, "they continue in 'the other world' to attain higher degrees of glory (Heb. 12:23; Rev. 7:9; Mt. 19:30). Their happiness consists in beholding the glory of God (John 17:24; Mt. 5:8). And they reign with Christ for ever and ever (Mt. 6:10)."[61] Deschner further observes:

Wesley's doctrine of the kingdom lends support to the claim that an essential motif in the Wesleyan version of the eternal decree is not a restoring, but an eternal perfecting. The goal of the Wesleyan eschatology is no church at rest, but a city in which the blessed increase in perfection, moving from one degree of glory to another! . . . It is this kingdom which is merged with the eternal rule of Christ, i.e., with providence.[62]

Blessing and honour, praise and love,
  Co-equal, co-eternal Three,
In earth below, in heaven above,
  By all thy works be paid to Thee.
Thrice holy, thine the kingdom is,
  The power omnipotent is thine;
And when created nature dies,
  Thy never-ceasing glories shine.[63]

---

61. Deschner, *Christology*, 136.
62. Ibid., 137-38.
63. *Hymns and Sacred Poems* (1742), 275-77, there titled "The Lord's Prayer Paraphrased," *Sermons* 1:591.

Conclusion

Is it possible to harmonize Wesley's various visions of the last things? In the Corinthian passage above, he elaborates a vision of the end that is consistent with his sermons, *Notes*, and the majority of his other writings. One of his most emphatic statements is his comment on Jesus' declaration in Matt. 5:17, where Wesley says unequivocally: "Christianity . . . is designed of God to be the last of all his dispensations. There is no other to come after this. This is to endure till the consummation of all things. . . . All pretense to another more perfect dispensation fall to the ground."[64]

John Wesley was no apocalypticist. His theology is that of the prophets and apostles. In his *Notes* on Daniel and Revelation, he is obliged to comment on the apocalyptic language of these books. In his *Notes* on Daniel, as we saw, he was able to harmonize his interpretation with Jesus and Paul in their "inaugurated eschatology." His *Notes* on Rev. 20 are more problematical. Yet even there, in his doctrine of a dual millennium, he leaves the way open to envision a triumph of the gospel dispensation in the first millennium. "By observing these two distinct thousand years," he says,

> many difficulties are avoided. There is room enough for the fulfilling of all the prophecies, and those which before seemed to clash are reconciled; particularly those which speak, on the one hand, of a most flourishing state of the Church as yet to come; and on the other, of the fatal security of men in the last days of the world. [Rev. 20:5]

---

64. Sermon 25, "Sermon on the Mount, V," *Sermons* 1:555.

■ **HAROLD RASER**

Views on Last Things in the American Holiness Movement

A CONCERN WITH LAST THINGS has never been too far from the center of the American Holiness Movement. However, Christians in the Holiness tradition have never achieved anything like unanimity about eschatology (nor has the whole Christian Church throughout its long history). Holiness preachers and teachers have disagreed with one another—sometimes to the point of verbal violence—about the nature of the consummation of human history on earth.

These differing views have been colored by many factors, among which are uncritical acceptance of traditional teaching; commitment to certain principles of biblical interpretation; popular ideas and movements in a particular historical period; major social, political, and intellectual upheavals; and a sense of optimism or pessimism about the direction of human history. While all Holiness writers on eschatology have no doubt sought to base their views upon Scripture and sound theological reasoning, the historian can never forget how factors like the above always help to color what one sees in the Bible and how theological reflection is carried out.

■ *Harold Raser is professor of the history of Christianity at Nazarene Theological Seminary in Kansas City.*

In this chapter we will briefly survey the history of thinking about eschatology in the American Holiness Movement. We will not only examine the views of representative writers from different periods of the movement's history, but we will also attempt to place their views in a larger historical context. This means attention will be given to developments and events in the Holiness Movement, American Christianity, American culture generally, and world affairs that appear to have a bearing on eschatological thinking.

Pre-Civil War Holiness Eschatology

The American Holiness Movement was born in a heady period of American history. The first half of the 19th century was a time of unbridled expansion. The boundaries of the United States were expanding. Population was increasing. Wealth was being generated at unprecedented levels. New inventions were revolutionizing the way people lived. A vibrant new nation was literally being created day by day.

Religiously, expansion was the order of the day as well. Beginning with the opening years of the century, a great revival swept across America, invigorating almost all the Christian churches of the country. This was the second such revival in less than 100 years. This Second Great Awakening saw thousands of persons confess faith in Christ, churches bursting at the seams, the planting of hundreds of new churches, and rekindled religious devotion channeled into scores of projects of evangelism and social reform. Newer movements like the Methodist Episcopal Church (founded in America in 1784) developed a huge popular following and soon dashed ahead of more established churches like the Presbyterians and Congregationalists, counting over 1 million members by midcentury.

The predominant mood of America during this time was one of optimism. And why not? Everything seemed to point to progress, improvement, and expanded opportunity.

Religiously, this optimism took the form of a strong millennial hope. Many Christians, excited especially by the religious revivals, growing churches, and ambitious evangelistic and reform work of the time, believed these might be a direct prelude to the millennium. Concern with eschatology swept both pulpit and pew. Some have suggested that perhaps no other time in American history has witnessed such an intense interest in the millennium.

When American Protestants of this era thought about the millennium and last things, they tended to do so by using ideas that seem to have been introduced into American Protestant theology by the great American preacher and theologian Jonathan Edwards (1703-58).[1] Influenced by English theologian and Bible commentator Daniel Whitby (1638-1726) and others, Edwards fashioned a concept of the millennium emphasizing that it was near, that it would come about through the conversion of the world to Christ through the effort of the churches, and that America would play a central role in ushering it in.

Edwards held that the millennium would come through "the preaching of the gospel and the use of the ordinary means of grace."[2] He also believed that the revivals of his day (the first Great Awakening occurred in the mid-1700s)—"this work of God's Spirit which is so extraordinary and wonderful"—were "the dawning, or at least a prelude, of that glorious work of God, so often foretold in Scripture which in the progress and issue of it, shall renew the world of mankind." He thought it likely that "this work will begin in America."[3]

Edwards' eschatology made a lot of sense to American Protestants in his day and in the century or so following him. Not one but two Great Awakenings revitalized the churches and helped shape the culture of the new nation. And a *new* nation it was. Within 25 years of Edwards' death, the American colonies had won their freedom from the "tyranny" of England

---

1. See C. C. Goen, "Jonathan Edwards: A New Departure in Eschatology," *Church History* 27 (March 1959), 25-40. Also see M. Darrol Bryant, "From Edwards to Hopkins: A Millennialist Critique of Political Culture" in M. Darrol Bryant and Donald W. Dayton, *The Coming Kingdom: Essays in American Millennialism and Eschatology* (Barrytown, N.Y.: International Religious Foundation, 1983), 45-70.

2. Jonathan Edwards, *The Works of Jonathan Edwards*, 4 vols., ed. Worcester (Boston: Leavitt and Allen, 1843), 1:481.

3. Edwards, *Works* 3:313. It should be noted that M. Darrol Bryant, "From Edwards to Hopkins," argues persuasively that Edwards eventually changed his mind about the imminence of the millennium and America's central role in its arrival. He did maintain faith, however, that the millennium would eventually be established as a result of the transformation of the world through Christian evangelism and social reform activity, and that Christ would return at the end of the millennium in judgment.

and had begun to build a democratic society that many expected to be the envy of the world. As this new society took shape, sin and injustice of every sort came under attack by organized groups of Christians at home, while eager missionaries went out to take the gospel in all its power around the world.

Who could help but be impressed by the mighty working of the Holy Spirit, and the progress of good? Surely the age of peace, justice, and righteousness foretold by biblical prophets was not far off. Thus, postmillennial eschatology came to dominate the thinking of American Protestants. They expected the world to come to Christ, ushering in a thousand years of peace and goodness, followed by the return of Christ to execute final judgment.[4]

In this exciting period of history, ripe with millennial expectation, the American Holiness Movement was born. The child of a union of Methodism and 19th-century American revivalism, the early Holiness Movement partook fully of the optimistic spirit typical of both of its parents. Methodism and revivalism seemed to many to be God's special instruments for that day. Both seemed to be at the very center of the wonderful things that God was doing. Methodism was leap-frogging the older denominations on its way toward numerical dominance. Revivals, traveling evangelists, camp meetings, protracted meetings, and invitations to the altar, or anxious bench, were re-

---

4. While postmillennialism was adopted by virtually every major American Protestant theologian and religious writer through most of the 19th century, it was not unchallenged. Two forms of premillennial eschatology had some supporters. Both tended to view American society in more negative terms than did most Americans of the day. The major impulse for these came from Europe, where there was much turmoil and anxiety associated especially with the French Revolution and its fallout. The best-known type was the "Adventist," championed in America by William Miller (1782-1849). Miller expected Christ to return to earth to personally establish His millennial kingdom, and he calculated precise dates for that event (1843-44). A lesser-known type strongly repudiated the Adventists' setting of dates but shared their expectation of Christ's imminent return to earth to usher in the millennium. Unlike Miller's version, which led to the founding of many independent churches, most of which eventually helped form the Seventh-day Adventist Church, this second type remained within the established denominations, though it was a minority view. For Miller's "Adventist" views, see William Miller, *Evidence from Scripture and History of the Second Coming of Christ, About the Year 1843* (Troy, N.Y.: E. Gates, 1838). For a discussion of the alternate view, see Robert Whalen, "Calvinism and Chiliasm: The Sociology of Nineteenth Century American Millenarianism," in *American Presbyterians* 70, no. 3 (Fall 1992), 163-72.

shaping American churches. Both Methodism and revivalism were dynamic, youthful movements.

From this parentage the American Holiness Movement sprang to life in the 1830s and 1840s. Inspired largely by John Wesley's doctrine of Christian perfection, it adopted the methods of revivalism to spread its message throughout Methodism and other American churches. In this it was highly successful in the decades leading up to the Civil War. Timothy Smith demonstrated in his classic work *Revivalism and Social Reform* how widely the doctrine of Christian perfection had pervaded American Protestantism by 1860. It had, in fact, become a powerful fuel for the great Christian social reform crusades of that day. Believers in full sanctification worked to bring the transforming grace of a Holy God to every area of social life. These were exciting times!

The only negative note in the early Holiness Movement was the concern of some Methodists that the doctrine of Christian perfection was being neglected in the rapidly expanding Methodist Church. This concern was one of the factors in the rise of the movement. However, those who guided the movement in its earliest days were fully convinced that their efforts would turn the tide of neglect and return Christian holiness to the heart of Methodist life.

Revivalistic promoters of holiness who were not Methodists, like famous Presbyterian (later Congregationalist) evangelist Charles G. Finney (1792-1875), expected the sanctifying Holy Spirit to purify and empower the American churches to live out and proclaim the whole gospel as never before in history. The end result of this would be the triumph of God's love, peace, and justice throughout the world (i.e., the millennium).[5] Finney exhorted Christians to "put away every kind of sin"

5. The best accounts of the early-19th-century Holiness Movement are as follows: Melvin E. Dieter, *The Holiness Revival of the Nineteenth Century* (Metuchen, N.J.: Scarecrow Press, 1980); John L. Peters, *Christian Perfection and American Methodism* (Nashville: Abingdon Press, 1956); and Timothy L. Smith, *Revivalism and Social Reform in Mid-Nineteenth Century America* (Nashville: Abingdon Press, 1957). A fascinating study of the millennial thrust of the early movement is Timothy L. Smith, "Righteousness and Hope: Christian Holiness and the Millennial Vision in America, 1800-1900," *American Quarterly* 31 (Spring 1979): 21-45.

and, empowered by the Holy Spirit, to "reform the world." He declared,

> The great business of the church is to reform the world—to put away every kind of sin. . . . The very profession of Christianity implies the profession and virtually an oath to do all that can be done for the universal reformation of the world. The Christian Church was designed to make aggressive movements in every direction—to lift up her voice and put forth her energies in high and low places—to reform individuals, communities, and governments, and never rest until the Kingdom and the greatness of the Kingdom under the whole heaven shall be given to the saints of the Most High God—until every form of iniquity shall be driven from the earth.[6]

If the Church would begin immediately to do its duty, Finney suggested, the millennium might arrive within three years.[7]

The Holiness paper Finney helped to found at Oberlin College in Ohio, *The Oberlin Evangelist*, reflected Finney's optimistic eschatology. In 1841 it ran a series of 23 articles on the millennium. These noted that, among other things,

> the arts and sciences—pioneers of the millennium—are making all things ready for the children of God to possess the earth. The recent improvements in the printing art are . . . miraculous. What need be more manifest than that God is preparing this instrument for his own use in converting the world, and sustaining the millennium. . . . Geographical knowledge has . . . given Christian nations remarkable access to the heathen. . . . God has secured the general peace of the civilized world.[8]

Reviewing all this, the series concluded that "We are amply justified in laying out our plans upon this basis: THE MILLENNIUM IS AT HAND."[9]

Not quite as exuberant about the millennium, perhaps, but still very much convinced that the consummation of human history was very near was Phoebe Palmer (1807-74), the most in-

6. Charles G. Finney, *Reflections on Revival*, comp. Donald W. Dayton (Minneapolis: Bethany Fellowship, 1979), 113-14. © 1979 by Bethany House Publishers. Used with permission.

7. Quoted in William G. McLaughlin, *Modern Revivalism: Charles Grandison Finney to Billy Graham* (New York: Ronald Press, 1959), 105.

8. Quoted in Donald W. Dayton, *Theological Roots of Pentecostalism* (Grand Rapids: Francis Asbury Press, 1987), 156-57.

9. Ibid., 157.

fluential Methodist Holiness leader prior to the Civil War. Palmer, whom many consider to be the founder of the American Holiness Movement, did not leave a detailed record of her views on eschatology. However, what evidence there is suggests that she probably agreed in general with the dominant outlook of her day. For example, she wrote in 1873, "For about thirty years we have unwaveringly believed that in the most emphatic sense 'the end of all things is at hand.'"[10] Also, she wrote several letters to William Miller, leader of the premillennial "Adventist" movement in the 1830s and 1840s. In these she scolded Miller for distracting Christians from the main work of the Church with his second advent preaching and criticized his date-setting as a deception of Satan. She also wrote that his charting of end-time events was mere human calculation, not supported by Scripture. "Who would ever have thought of arriving at your views from the simple word of God?" she challenged.[11]

Still, while Palmer strongly rejected Miller's eschatology, she does appear, like him, to have connected the return of Christ to earth with the ushering in of the millennium and the consummation of history, events she thought were "at hand." Palmer's 19th-century biographer said of her eschatology, "She rejected all the speculations of Pre-millenarians and Second Adventists as unwarranted by the letter of the Scriptures, and held firmly and distinctly to the duty and privilege of being fully prepared for the Lord's second coming, whenever that may be."[12] This suggests that Palmer was likely not a strict postmillennialist who expected the millennium to be followed by the return of Christ. Yet neither was she a strict premillennialist who tried to read the signs of the times and expected a rescue of Christians out of a fast distintegrating world. Like the postmil-

---

10. Richard Wheatley, *The Life and Letters of Mrs. Phoebe Palmer* (New York: Palmer and Hughes, 1876), 513. Cf. Phoebe Palmer, "The Coming One," *The Guide to Holiness*, April 1873, 122. Palmer's role in the Holiness Movement is examined in detail by Harold E. Raser, *Phoebe Palmer: Her Life and Thought* (Lewiston, N.Y.: Edwin Mellen Press, 1987), and Charles G. White, *The Beauty of Holiness: Phoebe Palmer as Theologian, Revivalist, Feminist, and Humanitarian* (Grand Rapids: Francis Asbury Press, 1986).

11. Wheatley, *Life and Letters*, 512-13; Phoebe Palmer, *Faith and Its Effects: Fragments from My Portfolio* (New York: By the author, 200 Mulberry St., 1852), 322-23.

12. Wheatley, *Life and Letters*, 511.

lennialists of her day, she sensed that the Spirit of Christ was bringing about a great transformation of the Church and world and that this was a part of last things.

So the Holiness Movement in America, as it first came to life in the 1830s and 1840s, was bathed in millennial optimism. The work of individuals like Finney and Palmer, the numerous prayer and Bible study groups, the books and magazines, the special church meetings, all emphasizing holiness of heart and life through the sanctifying grace of God, bore a strong eschatological stamp. Members of the movement believed that God was graciously and powerfully at work in the world and was quickly bringing history to a triumphant close.

Post-Civil War Holiness Eschatology

The Civil War (1861-65) was a watershed event in American history. It changed the country in more ways than it is possible here to enumerate. Certainly, it created a deep rift between North and South, which time has still not completely healed.

The war tore many American churches, flourishing in the first half of the 19th century, into weakened, warring factions. The Methodist Episcopal Church, for example, divided in two in 1845 and remained divided for nearly 100 years. American Baptists split at the same time and have never reunited.

The war badly wounded, but could not kill, the idea so widely held before the war that America was a specially chosen instrument of God to bring the millennium to the earth. Victorious Northern Christians, in fact, could see the war as just one more means God was using to purify and strengthen America for her divinely appointed destiny. By stamping out slavery and preserving the union of states, the war actually made America stronger and more "righteous." Defeated Southerners, of course, saw things in a very different light.

After the war, America rapidly underwent jarring economic, social, and intellectual revolutions. Mass production in factories replaced the handwork of individual craftsmen. Huge amounts of money were invested in, and made by, the new system. Urban manufacturing centers drew workers from the farms and small towns and from around the world. Cities exploded with new residents while the rural population declined.

Millions of immigrants from abroad crowded together with transplanted country folk in the swelling cities. Railroads snaked across the land, carrying products and people. And the theories and discoveries of modern science began to leave their mark on the intellectual landscape.

The Holiness Movement, such a vital force in American Christianity on the eve of the Civil War, suffered because of the war. For one thing, the energy and resources of all Americans were largely diverted to the war effort. War absorbed—and overshadowed—everything. Additionally, influential leaders like Phoebe Palmer and Charles Finney spent time preaching outside the United States during the war years. And their absence was felt. The *Guide to Christian Perfection*, a Holiness paper that had helped to launch the movement in 1839 and had spearheaded its spread, nearly went out of business in the early 1860s for lack of subscribers.

Then, about two years after the war's end, a group of Holiness ministers and laymen came up with an idea for reviving the work of holiness in the churches. They planned a "national" camp meeting that would be devoted entirely to preaching and teaching Christian holiness. They invited persons from all denominations to participate and solicited the support of prominent denominational leaders. The expected crowds would serve notice that the Holiness Movement was far from dead, and the event might actually help reignite widespread popular interest in the doctrine of Christian perfection.

Indeed, several thousand people responded to the invitation, and the Methodist campground at Vineland, New Jersey, became the site of the first "national Holiness camp meeting" in July 1867.

The meeting had its intended effect. It witnessed to the fact that the Holiness Movement was still very much alive. It also helped bring new vitality to the movement—Holiness camp meetings were soon springing up everywhere. It also resulted in the formation of the National Camp Meeting Association for the Promotion of Holiness (the parent of today's Christian Holiness Association). This group, formed at Vineland, brought an organizational dimension to the movement that it had not had before. In a short time, the National Camp Meeting Association was largely defining and directing the Holiness Movement. It sponsored and conducted Holiness camp meetings, certified a group of Holiness evangelists, published Holiness papers, books, and tracts, and even supported missionaries in several parts of the world.[13]

The meetings sponsored by the national association, in addition to the writings of some of its early leaders, reveal that the eschatological optimism that marked the Holiness Movement and American Protestantism as a whole before the Civil War still prevailed. Though the war had brought appalling suffering to the country, and the Holiness Movement had failed to capture the churches and transform the nation, Holiness leaders still thought that the millennium was just around the corner. The success of the early Holiness camp meetings apparently convinced them that the Holiness Movement would regain its pre-Civil War momentum and would yet help carry America and the world on into the promised kingdom of God.

Methodist Bishop Matthew Simpson (1811-84), who participated in several of the camp meetings of the national association, left no doubt about his views on last things. "Another hundred years and the earth shall stand in beauty and glory," he declared. "A hundred years and the banner of the cross shall shine triumphant over every mountain top and every valley." Another hundred years "and they will be singing . . . throughout the earth: 'Hallelujah! The Lord God omnipotent reigneth.'"[14]

Another Methodist bishop friendly to the Holiness Movement was equally outspoken about eschatology. Gilbert Haven (1821-80), who championed the abolition of slavery before the Civil War, surveyed the world four years after the war ended (and two years after the first national Holiness camp meeting) and concluded,

---

13. The story of the National Camp Meeting Association is told by Charles E. Jones, *Perfectionist Persuasion: The Holiness Movement and American Methodism, 1867-1936* (Metuchen, N.J.: Scarecrow Press, 1974). Helpful also is Kenneth Orville Brown, "Leadership in the National Holiness Association with Special Reference to Eschatology, 1867-1919" (Ph.D. diss., Drew University, 1988).

14. Quoted in Smith, *Revivalism and Social Reform*, 234.

In enterprise, the world is careening like a ship before the wind. The girdle of the nation will belt her zone before another year, and our President [U. S. Grant] enter the Pacific cities—the longest journey ever made by the head of a nation through its territory. The South will be filled with peaceful, loving, laboring populations. Emigration will set in from Africa, Asia, Europe, and the islands of the sea; and the world make gigantic strides to the glory and calm of the millennial year. To this work, and honor, and reward may all be devoted. Let Christ abolish sin from your souls, of whatever sort, by His indwelling grace. Let your heart become His peaceful realm, with its every passion, thought, and purpose subject to His sway. Labor by every word and work to make all other hearts equally perfect. Strive to bring the laws of society into subjection to His control. Root up the gnarled tusks of prejudice. Toil cheerfully, hopefully, faithfully, to bring in the Grand Sabbatic Year, the Jubilee of Heaven [i.e., the millennium].[15]

The coming millennium, said Haven, would be "a world of men, equal, brotherly, united and holy."[16]

Similar views were voiced by George Hughes (1828-1904), a close associate of Phoebe Palmer and her husband in Holiness publishing and a founder of the National Camp Meeting Association for the Promotion of Holiness. Preaching at a national association camp meeting at Cedar Rapids, Iowa, Hughes told the crowd,

To be sharers with Christ in his illustrious triumphs we need this baptism [with the Holy Spirit]. Prophecy points to glorious triumphs to be achieved by Christ on the earth. And the tokens of the period show that he is coming to claim the nations for his own. Physical progress, mental advancement, the bringing together of the nations in familiar intercourse, declare the day at hand.[17]

Hughes' close friend, John S. Inskip (1816-84), agreed. Inskip was one of the leading organizers of the first national Holiness camp meeting and was elected the first president of the National Camp Meeting Association for the Promotion of Holiness. A well-known and influential Methodist pastor, Inskip resigned his pulpit in 1871 to do full-time evangelistic work for

15. Gilbert Haven, *Sermons, Speeches and Letters on Slavery and Its War* (Boston: Lee and Shephard, 1869), 629-30.
16. Ibid., 374.
17. Quoted in Brown, "Leadership in the National Holiness Association," 251.

the national association. He eventually traveled across the United States and to several countries of the world conducting Holiness camp meetings. Inskip was convinced that the consummation of history was near and that the reviving of Holiness through the camp meeting movement was the chief means God was using to convert the world and usher in the millennium.

Inskip's biographers noted, "It very soon became impressed upon his mind that God had called him to special work, in the spread of scriptural holiness. He saw clearly that its spread in the churches meant the salvation of the world."[18] Commenting on Inskip's decision in 1871 to leave the pastorate for full-time Holiness evangelism, they explained that he had come to believe that Christian perfection was not only "the spiritual standpoint of the Methodist Church" but also "the most significant and powerful impulse leading to the speedy conversion of the world" and hence to the millennium.[19] Inskip wrote in his journal,

> It seems to me that during the remainder of my life I shall employ all my energies in endeavors to set before the people the glorious doctrine of "salvation by faith." I am persuaded that this doctrine will immensely increase the moral power of Christianity. The resources of the church of this age are very great, yet in the absence of the "gift of power" from on high, these resources are frequently unavailing. What mighty results might be achieved if believers generally were filled with the Holy Ghost! My spirit is stirred within me, and sometimes I can hardly contain myself. . . . I shall embrace every opportunity to go forth and proclaim "full redemption" through the blood of the Lamb.[20]

Such thinking was typical of Holiness postmillennial eschatology. Like all postmillennialists, Holiness postmillennialists expected the conversion of the world to inaugurate the millennium, after which Christ would return. However, Holiness postmillennialists believed in addition that their movement would provide the power the Church needed to complete its evangelistic and reforming task.

---

18. William McDonald and John E. Searles, *The Life of Rev. John S. Inskip* (Chicago: Christian Witness Co., 1885), 161.

19. Ibid., 219-20.

20. Ibid., 168-69.

The atmosphere of the early Holiness camp meetings where Inskip, Hughes, and others preached "full redemption" through the blood of Christ contributed to this conviction that the Holiness Movement had great eschatological significance. Buoyed by many testimonies to saving and sanctifying grace, a preacher at the very first national camp meeting in Vineland, New Jersey, assured his hearers,

> When the Church shall be clothed upon with the power of God we shall soon be in the neighborhood of the millennium. Did each member of the Church accomplish the salvation of only one man in each year, in one year the church members would be doubled, in two years we should stand four to one, in three years eight to one, in four years sixteen to one, in five years thirty-two to one, and in six years sixty-four to one; while in less than seven years the millennium glory would be here. [Shouts of Glory! Glory!][21]

At the third national holiness camp meeting at Round Lake, New York, in 1869, Bishop Matthew Simpson preached on Rom. 12:1, "Present your bodies a living sacrifice. . . ." Speaking of what God could do with fully consecrated Christians, he declared, "What a glorious world this would be," if the Church were filled up with such Christians. Should that happen, "I would scarcely wish then to go to heaven," he confessed, but would gladly remain on earth that "I might aid in bringing in the millennial glory."[22]

One who heard Simpson preach thought that the Round Lake camp meeting itself had brought the goal closer. "This meeting has rolled the world a hundred years toward millennium! We are coming into Isaiah's holy visions," he exulted.[23] Another listened to the preaching and witnessed lives graciously transformed, and exclaimed, "I begin to see how God is going to spread His work by the instrumentality of a holy Church. . . . . I see the morning star that will usher in the grandest day that was ever seen outside of heaven, and I expect to see that time shortly."[24]

---

21. A. McLean and J. W. Eaton, ed., *Penuel; or Face to Face with God* (1869; reprint, New York: Garland Publishing, 1984), 146-47.
22. Ibid., 458-59.
23. Ibid., 381.
24. Ibid., 316.

Similar views of last things were voiced by one of the most articulate and widely respected spokesmen for Christian holiness in the second half of the 19th century: Daniel Steele (1824-1914). Steele was a Methodist pastor and educator who served variously as professor of theology at Boston University and as president of Methodist-supported Syracuse University. Steele was also a prolific writer.

In one of his books, *A Substitute for Holiness, or Antinomianism Revived* (1887), Steele dealt extensively with eschatology. In it, he attacked some of the newer eschatological teaching gaining popularity at the time and explained and defended his own postmillennial view.

He argued that the Scriptures predict the "conversion" of the world in the "end times." This "conversion" would not be a literal conversion to Christ of every person on earth, for during the millennium the righteous and wicked would live side by side, to be separated only by final judgement at the end of the millennium. Rather, the promised "conversion" would be a "reconstruction of human society upon the Scriptural basis: 'One is your master, The Christ; and all ye are brethren [Matt. 23:8].'" The result of this conversion would be "peace and prosperity, universal and final." During this time of peace, Christ would be "Sovereign of the world," ruling through "His redemptive agencies." These would "achieve their grandest triumphs in the salvation of men from sin to holiness" at this time. This would be the millennium, "that condition of the world in which, 'All kings shall fall down before Him and all nations shall serve Him' (Ps. 72:11)."[25]

At the close of this millennial age, "the redemptive powers and agencies of Christ's kingdom cease" and Christ returns to earth and "takes the throne of eternal judgement."[26] The righteous and wicked receive their eternal rewards, and the "earth will be so dissolved by fire as to disappear forever," making way for a new earth and a new heaven.[27]

---

25. Daniel Steele, *A Substitute for Holiness, or Antinomianism Revived* (1887; reprint, New York: Garland Publishing, 1984), 327-47.

26. Ibid., 341.

27. Ibid., 342-43.

These examples demonstrate that the post-Civil War Holiness Movement, as it was guided after 1867 by the National Camp Meeting Association for the Promotion of Holiness, continued to maintain a postmillennial eschatology as it always had. Even the terrors surrounding the Civil War could not dim its faith that the work of God through His Church in the United States and around the world was moving steadily forward.

In its optimistic hopefulness, the Holiness Movement reflected the dominant mood of most of American Protestantism at that time. Though some American Protestants were beginning to feel uneasy about the many changes occurring in their society after the Civil War, thinking about last things in most of their churches for the previous 100 years assured them that the millennium was at hand.

Shifting Ground in Holiness Eschatology

As the 19th century moved toward its end, the forces of change in America grew stronger. Industrialization, urbanization, immigration, and modern science continued to profoundly alter the way Americans lived and thought. A more prosperous, diverse, urban, and secular America emerged.

Increasingly, this became a difficult time for Christians and churches. The explosive growth of cities both weakened rural churches and placed tremendous demands upon city churches. The shifting population patterns of cities due to immigration made it doubly difficult for the city churches, for the growing neighborhoods around them kept changing. Some churches tried to minister to each new immigrant group, while others despaired of doing so and moved "uptown" to more stable (and wealthier) environments.

Rapid industrialization and the production of tremendous amounts of wealth, much of it concentrated in the hands of relatively few individuals and families, forced the churches to reexamine their traditional notions about the nature of work, wealth, and economic systems. Modern science challenged many traditional ideas about the world and life in it. New theories in biology and geology appeared to contradict the teachings of Scripture concerning creation. "Scientific history" raised questions about biblical chronology. "Social sciences" like sociology and psychology threw new, sometimes troubling, light on human experience and actions.

Christians divided over how to respond. Some thought what was needed was an accommodation between modern science and Christian faith. They worked to fit the two into one harmonious system. These were labeled "modernists" or theological "liberals." Other Christians believed that modern science was a threat to Christian faith and should be opposed. The fundamental teachings of the Bible and the Christian Church needed to be protected from the assault of modern thought. These were labeled "fundamentalists."

This division of Christians into opposing theological camps further weakened churches already divided by the legacy of the Civil War. This, together with the increasing ethnic and religious diversity of America due to immigration (a growing Roman Catholic presence was the most visible evidence of this) and the other forces of change at work, resulted in the weakening of Protestant Christianity's influence over American society. Historian Mark Noll observes, "As a result of social, political, economic, and intellectual as well as religious circumstances, Protestant control over the nation's organs of communication, its centers of higher learning, and its public morality gradually receded as the nineteenth century gave way to the twentieth."[28] To American Protestants, this was perhaps the most distressing of all the post-Civil War developments.

In the midst of these circumstances a new form of eschatological thinking began to emerge among Protestant Christians in the United States. This was a unique form of premillennial eschatology known as dispensationalism.

Premillennial eschatology itself was not new to the United States. Forms of it had existed alongside the much more popular postmillennial teaching during the first half of the 19th century. However, dispensationalism was premillennialism with a difference.[29]

---

28. Mark A. Noll, *A History of Christianity in the United States and Canada* (Grand Rapids: William B. Eerdmans Publishing Co., 1992), 312.

29. See Timothy P. Weber, *Living in the Shadow of the Second Coming: American Premillennialism 1875-1982*, enl. ed. (Grand Rapids: Zondervan Corporation, 1983), for an excellent examination of dispensationalism. My discussion of dispensationalism is based largely on this work.

For one thing, early-19th-century American premillennialism was "historicist." It held that biblical prophecies concerning "end-time" events leading to the second coming of Christ and the consummation of history refer symbolically to the whole history of the Church. Some were fulfilled in the distant past, some were being fulfilled in the present, and others were yet to be fulfilled.

Dispensational premillennialism, on the other hand, is "futurist." It argues that none of the prophecies of the "last days" has been fulfilled in the history of the Church. All the prophesied events will take place in a short period of time immediately before the return of Christ. Further, early-19th-century American premillennialism had made room for several different versions of when the "rapture" or "catching away" of the Church to meet Christ in the air (1 Thess. 4:15-17) will occur in relation to the "great tribulation," or reign of terror conducted by the Antichrist. Dispensationalism insists on one version: the Church will be raptured before the tribulation (a "pretribulation rapture").

Other ideas also separated earlier American premillennialism from the new dispensationalist premillennialism. One was the concept of "dispensation," defined as "a period of time during which man is tested in respect of obedience to some specific revelation of the will of God."[30] Dispensationalists divide human history into seven such periods of "testing" (the seventh includes the rapture, tribulation, and millennium).

So, too, dispensationalists strictly separate Israel and the Church as two distinct peoples of God and believe different prophecies apply only to one or the other. "Rightly dividing the word of truth" (2 Tim. 2:15, KJV) means keeping the two properly separated.

Further, dispensationalists believe the Church occupies a "parenthesis" in history. It is a kind of afterthought God created after His chosen people, Israel, rejected His Messiah. When He is finished with it, He will "rapture" it to heaven and then take up again with Israel, resuming the "countdown," which was

---

30. Ibid., 17.

suspended during the "Church age," toward the second coming of Christ and the consummation of history.

These and other unique ideas of the "new premillennialism," which began to receive a hearing in the United States after the Civil War, are generally traced to John Nelson Darby (1800-1882), the British founder of the Plymouth Brethren movement. Along with his innovations in eschatology, Darby rejected all the churches of his day as hopelessly corrupt and called for an exodus from them into his simple fellowship of Christian "brethren." Quite successful in the British Isles, Darby made seven trips to the United States and Canada between 1859 and 1874, preaching his ideas. His call to leave the established denominations was mostly ignored, but his eschatology began to catch on. Several influential Protestant leaders like Dwight L. Moody and A. J. Gordon, a prominent Boston Baptist pastor, were converted to Darby's views and began to promote them.

The new premillennial dispensationalism seemed perfectly suited for the times. The prevailing optimism in America was beginning to weaken ever so slightly. Many American Protestants in the latter decades of the 19th century were becoming uneasy over events and were not quite certain what to make of them. Postmillennial eschatology taught them to see progress toward the millennium on every hand, but more and more, some things did not seem to fit into this pattern.

Thus, dispensationalism received a hearing and, after about 1875, began to be widely embraced by American Protestants, especially those whose sympathies were with "Fundamentalism" rather than theological "liberalism." The publication in 1909 of the Scofield Reference Bible, a study Bible with dispensationalist notes and commentary, signaled the deep inroads the "new premillennialism" had made by that time.

The Holiness Movement could not, of course, remain untouched by these developments. It was somewhat insulated from the "new premillennialism" at first by the fact that many of the most ardent Holiness promoters were Methodist, and very few Methodists were among the early converts to dispensationalism. Most dispensationalists had roots in Calvinist theology and were Presbyterian, Congregationalist, or Baptist. Many Methodists tended to view dispensationalism as a deterministic system that undercut human freedom and limited the power of divine grace. They were also wary of its extremely literalistic method of interpreting the Bible.

Even so, dispensationalism did eventually affect thinking in the Holiness Movement about last things. In fact, before the end of the 19th century it had gained so much ground that postmillennial eschatology had gone on the defensive. By 1930 or so, premillennial eschatology informed by dispensationalism had actually replaced postmillennialism in the thinking of most Christians in Holiness churches.

Daniel Steele, mentioned above, was concerned enough about the trend that he wrote *A Substitute for Holiness* in 1887, largely to "expose" dispensationalism. He saw it as part of a larger theological system that was at odds with the Wesleyan-Arminian theology of Methodism and the Holiness Movement.

In the book he quite correctly traced the "new premillennialism" back to John Nelson Darby and carefully dissected Plymouth Brethren theology. Steele objected especially to the Brethren's view of imputed righteousness, which clashed with Methodism's belief that "heart-purity is real and inwrought, and not a stainless robe, concealing unspeakable moral filthiness and leprosy."[31] He found "Darbyism" to be a form of the same antinomianism opposed by Methodism since the days of Wesley.

Taking up eschatology, Steele devoted fully half the book to it. He criticized Darby's "pessimism," charging that his views "belittle the Christian agencies now in operation by asserting that they are inadequate to the conversion of the world."[32] He found it unbelievable that dispensationalists could teach that "From the Cross to the Second Advent there is nothing but a parenthesis."[33] "I shudder," he wrote, "at the disrespect which is thus shown to the Paraclete, the personal successor to the risen Lord Jesus."[34]

Steele also charged that Darby's views were "novelties" that had never been taught by the Christian Church in its great

---

31. Steele, *A Substitute for Holiness*, 23.
32. Ibid., 168.
33. Ibid., 169.
34. Ibid.

historic creeds.[35] He also appended to the book a tract, "Was Wesley a Premillennialist?" which concluded that he was not.[36]

As vigorous as was this attack on premillennial dispensationalism by a respected Holiness leader, it was not successful. That was clear when George D. Watson (1845-1924), noted Holiness evangelist with the National Holiness Association, published his *Steps to the Throne and Holiness Manual* in 1898. In this study of the Book of Revelation, which draws heavily on dispensationalist thought, Watson recounted his "conversion" from postmillennialism to premillennialism only two years before. He testified that the Holy Spirit had led him to adopt premillennialism through a close study of the Book of Revelation.[37] He called postmillennialism an "old Roman Catholic notion" and a Catholic "sediment" contaminating Protestantism.[38]

Watson also introduced an idea in the book that would surface again and again in Holiness circles as premillennialism pushed aside postmillennial eschatology. This was the idea that the "secret rapture" prior to the tribulation (Darby's view) would involve only Christians who have been baptized with the Holy Spirit as taught by the Holiness Movement.[39]

Watson's book was prophetic of the future direction of eschatological thinking in the Holiness Movement. In 1900, Martin Wells Knapp (1835-1901), founder of God's Bible School in Cincinnati, published another study of Revelation.[40] Like Watson's book, it is strongly informed by dispensationalism. In it, Knapp repeats Watson's belief that only the entirely sanctified will be raptured. They will be those who are "promoted from

---

35. Ibid., 187-90.

36. Ibid., 271-81.

37. George D. Watson, *Steps to the Throne and Holiness Manual* (Cincinnati: God's Revivalist Office, 1898), 5-6.

38. Ibid., 61-62.

39. Ibid., 65-69. It is interesting to note that Watson's book also anticipated another important trend in the Holiness Movement, a keen interest in divine healing. Watson urged Christians to forsake doctors and medicine and exercise faith for healing. "Medicine is for those who have not faith," he writes (142). In the early years of the 20th century, the Holiness Movement would be convulsed by controversy over this teaching as well as premillennialism. Many prominent Holiness leaders considered both of these "side issues" to be avoided if possible in preaching Christian holiness.

40. Martin Wells Knapp, *Holiness Triumphant, or Pearls from Patmos, Being the Secret of Revelation Revealed* (Cincinnati: M. W. Knapp, 1900).

the holiness movement on earth to the holiness praise-service in the skies."[41] In fact, Knapp interprets the entire Book of Revelation as a story of Holiness people versus their opposers. Commenting on the terrors described in Revelation, he warns, "Listen, all ye who have refused Bible holiness, and ye who have opposed it! Yonder, in the everlasting darkness, see your final and eternal defeat blazoned in letters of fire, and hear it echoing in the moans and groans and the gnashing of teeth of your doomed associates, and then lift up your eyes and see the dazzling beauty of this celestial monument of the everlasting victory with which God has crowned the truth that you misrepresented, opposed, and even derided."[42]

Knapp's book was followed soon after by *The Blessed Hope of His Glorious Appearing*, written by L. L. Pickett (1859-1928), a southern Methodist pastor, Holiness evangelist, editor, and gospel songwriter.[43] This book is a thorough, systematic exposition of Holiness premillennialism. It is also a militant attack upon postmillennialism. Its militant tone is evidence of the strength of the "new premillennialism" in Holiness circles by this time, but also of the continuing resistance of those still holding to a postmillennial eschatology.

Pickett repeats Watson's charge that postmillennialism was invented by Roman Catholicism, which he refers to as "the baptized heathenism of the dark ages."[44] He also charges, reflecting the widening chasm between liberal and conservative, or "modernist" and "fundamentalist" Christians, that postmillennialism has become the view of theological liberals. He writes:

> Show me a one-story D. D. wearing a two-story hat, with a gold-headed cane and gold ring, and with a cigar in his mouth,

41. Ibid., 113.

42. Ibid., 238. The book reflects the increase of opposition by the older denominations to "organized holiness" as represented by the National Holiness Association and its various agencies, local and regional Holiness associations, and, by 1900, even numerous independent Holiness churches. The book identifies Holiness people with the persecuted yet finally victorious saints of Revelation. The earlier hope of winning the world through Holiness preaching has given way here to a view of Holiness people as a persecuted minority, holding on until Christ rescues and vindicates them at the end of time.

43. L. L. Pickett, *The Blessed Hope of His Glorious Appearing* (Louisville, Ky.: Pickett Publishing Co., 1901).

44. Ibid., iii.

who rides on Sunday trains, chews tobacco, buys and reads Sunday newspapers, pours forth tirades of abuse against the holiness people, sneers at the second blessing, and who has not had a dozen conversions in twelve months, perhaps not in ten years, and I will show you a man who is a strong Post-millennialist.[45]

Pickett does admit that not "all Post-millennialists are of the type we have described," but cautions, "We would advise our spiritually-minded brethren who are advocating Post-millennialism to remember poor Tray, and be careful of their company."[46] He also charges that postmillennialists "reject a large part of God's word."[47]

Pickett's book paints a dark picture of the world and the churches of the day: The churches were departing from sound doctrine, and American society was beset by a multitude of sins. Even the Holiness Movement was rent into factions over many different issues, eschatology among them. What could this mean but that the return of Christ is near, as taught by the premillennialists?[48]

Some years later, Pickett developed all these themes at greater length in a book titled *Post-Millennialism and the Higher Critics*,[49] which he coauthored with fellow southern Methodist evangelist Andrew Johnson. This book greatly expanded the

---

45. Ibid., 275.

46. Ibid., 276. Though Pickett's characterization of "Liberal postmillennialists" is a gross distortion, he is to some extent correct that theological "liberals" tended to hold to a form of postmillennial eschatology. This was, however, not the form taught by more theologically conservative Christians. Some liberal thinkers expected a millennium of peace and prosperity to result from the outworking in history of an immutable law of "progress." Theologically conservative postmillennialists expected the millennium to come by the power of Christ's Spirit transforming the world through the faithful witness of Christians and the churches.

47. Ibid., 63.

48. Ibid., 52-67. It is significant that Pickett is concerned about divisions and factions in the Holiness Movement. By 1901 there were many of these. Some Holiness leaders were still advocating the promotion of Holiness exclusively through interdenominational associations. Others, the "come-outers," were calling for separate Holiness churches in the face of widespread opposition to Holiness teaching in the major denominations. Even those who favored separate churches differed with each other over what form these should take. There was also the divisive struggle over "side issues," mainly premillennial eschatology and divine healing, together with controversial teachings about dress and behavior. The Holiness Movement hardly resembled a great united host marching victoriously forward into the millennium.

49. Andrew Johnson and L. L. Pickett, *Post-Millennialism and the Higher Critics* (Chicago: Glad Tidings Publishing Co., 1923).

case linking postmillennialism to infidelity. In doing so, it reflects the continuing battles between "modernists" and "fundamentalists," which had escalated by the time the book was written. Published just two years before the famous Scopes "Monkey Trial" in Dayton, Tennessee, which tested laws against teaching evolution in public schools, the book announces, "We have no use for a Darwinian monkey-to-man evolution."[50] It also strongly affirms certain "fundamentals" of Christian faith that were beginning to define "fundamentalist" theology. "We believe in the . . . infallibility, credibility and authority of the Holy Scriptures; the Virgin birth, the essential deity and the physical resurrection of Jesus Christ," as well as Christ's premillennial second coming, the authors declare.[51]

The book militantly announces that the time for toleration of various eschatological views in the Holiness Movement is past. Premillennialism is the only scriptural view. Postmillennialism is a "huge and unscriptural blunder."[52] Since all "destructive higher critics were postmillennialists," according to the authors' reckoning, postmillennialism is clearly in error, and to be rejected by Holiness Christians.[53]

These views typified the general trend in eschatological thinking in the Holiness Movement as the 19th century gave way to the 20th. Many more works appeared, like these endorsing a premillennial eschatology strongly colored by dispensationalism.

Especially important were theological texts like E. P. Ellyson's *Theological Compend* (1908) and W. B. Godbey's *Bible Theology* (1911), from which many Holiness preachers learned their theology.[54] Both advocated premillennialism, although Ellyson attempted to be fair toward postmillennialism and cautioned that agreement on eschatology "is not essential and should never be allowed to cause division among the saints."[55]

---

50. Ibid., vii.
51. Ibid.
52. Ibid., 331.
53. Ibid., 445.
54. Edgar P. Ellyson, *Theological Compend* (Chicago: Christian Witness Co., 1908), 58-70; W. B. Godbey, *Bible Theology* (Cincinnati: God's Revivalist Office, 1911), 221-95.
55. Ellyson, *Theological Compend*, 67.

Godbey, on the other hand, devoted a whole chapter to discrediting postmillennialism, arguing that it "contradicts the Word of God and keeps people from obeying Jesus."[56] He even engaged in speculation about the time of the Second Coming, suggesting the rapture might occur around 1924.[57]

Even though premillennialism of one sort or another clearly dominated thinking about last things in the Holiness Movement by the early 20th century, postmillennialism still retained some support. For example, for many years the National Holiness Association tried to maintain neutrality on the subject, recognizing that many Holiness believers had not "converted" to premillennialism.[58]

Also, controversy over eschatology in the founding of some Holiness churches, such as the Church of the Nazarene, reveals a continuing lack of a consensus on this point.[59] Even as late as 1931, when Nazarene theologian A. M. Hills published his *Fundamental Christian Theology*, postmillennialism was still alive in the Holiness Movement.[60]

Hills himself was a postmillennialist and expounded that view in his book. However, in a nod to the influence of premillennialism, he also included an essay by J. B. Chapman defending it, professing, "I want my readers to hear both sides and form an intelligent opinion."[61]

Shifting Again?

Most Holiness people who read Hills' text appear to have decided for Chapman's premillennialism rather than for postmillennialism. One can hardly find an open defense of postmillennialism in Holiness circles after 1931.

---

56. Godbey, *Bible Theology*, 291.

57. Ibid., 227.

58. See Brown, "Leadership," 272-83, for a discussion of the National Association's response to the shift toward premillennial eschatology.

59. See Timothy L. Smith, *Called unto Holiness; The Story of the Nazarenes: The Formative Years* (Kansas City: Nazarene Publishing House, 1962), 214-23.

60. A. M. Hills, *Fundamental Christian Theology*, 2 vols. (Pasadena, Calif.: C. J. Kinne, 1931).

61. Ibid., 2:339-60.

When Nazarene H. Orton Wiley published his *Christian Theology* just 12 years later, he was characteristically careful and evenhanded in his discussion of various eschatological views. He repeatedly urged caution and charity in dealing with such a difficult subject. However, his own view, of which he reveals only a little, seems most influenced by premillennialism. It is, to be sure, a premillennialism carefully qualified and nuanced. In fact, it is so carefully qualified, and he expresses such regard for aspects of postmillennialism, that one might argue that he is moving toward a synthesis of the two views. Still, it is premillennialism that provides the dominant framework for his thinking.[62]

Since Wiley, one can detect some tendency in the Holiness Movement to reexamine the patterns for thinking about last things established by late-19th- and early-20th-century writers like Watson, Knapp, Pickett, and the others. Certainly a spate of books with titles like *Ready for the Rapture* and *Near Midnight*, promoting premillennial and often dispensational eschatology, have continued to come off Holiness presses.[63] However, most recently *Grace, Faith, and Holiness: A Wesleyan Systematic Theology* has roundly criticized dispensational eschatology and relegated the whole matter of eschatological theories to an appendix titled "Speculative Eschatology."[64] It also urges the wisdom of avoiding dogmatism on a matter so contested throughout the history of the Holiness Movement and the whole Christian Church.

Perhaps the times are ripe once again for a rethinking of last things in the Holiness Movement.

---

62. H. Orton Wiley, *Christian Theology*, 3 vols. (Kansas City: Beacon Hill Press, 1943), 3:211 ff. See William D. Moore, "Some Distinctive Features in the Eschatological Theory of H. Orton Wiley" (M.A. thesis, Pasadena College, 1966), for a helpful analysis of Wiley's own views.

63. C. T. Corbett, *Ready for the Rapture* (Kansas City: Beacon Hill Press, 1962); Leo C. Davis, *Near Midnight: Thoughts on the Second Coming* (Kansas City: Beacon Hill Press, 1965).

64. H. Ray Dunning, *Grace, Faith, and Holiness: A Wesleyan Systematic Theology* (Kansas City: Beacon Hill Press of Kansas City, 1988), 569-89.

part **III**

THEOLOGICAL STUDIES

■ H. RAY DUNNING

Presuppositions of a Wesleyan Eschatology

W ESLEYAN THEOLOGY is totally committed to the classic Christian faith as articulated in the ecumenical creeds: the Apostles', the Nicean, and the Chalcedonian. However, it holds a unique position within the larger Christian map that differs from the Roman Catholic and classic Protestant views but retains the most biblical aspects of each. The heart of this distinctive position is its understanding of the divine-human relation, and this position has numerous ramifications, many of which impinge on the issue of eschatology. Thus, there *is* a distinctive Wesleyan approach to the subject.

Some may raise the question, "Why not simply read the Bible and take what it says at face value?" While this sounds reasonable and simple, it isn't. The fact is that where the Bible speaks plainly and straightforwardly, this might work—and does in many instances. But it is equally true that the presuppositions we bring to the text exert a formative influence on what we hear from the sacred page. No informed person will question the impossibility of presuppositionless thinking. It is important to be as aware as possible of those assumptions, but when they are unrecognized and unacknowledged, the result is usually more heat than light, especially when the topic of last things is discussed. The consequence is much acrimony and

■ *H. Ray Dunning is professor of theology at Trevecca Nazarene College in Nashville.*

dogmatism, resulting in divisions in the Body of Christ that are inconsistent with "the unity of the Spirit in the bond of peace." Meaningful and productive discussion between differing points of view must proceed at the presuppositional level.

In this chapter we propose to explore some presuppositions consistent with Wesleyan theology that bear on the doctrine of last things. The results may sound strange to some readers, since far too many who go by the name "Wesleyan" think the only difference between Wesleyan theology and other theological positions (e.g., fundamentalism, Calvinism, dispensationalism, and so on) is that Wesleyans believe in a second work of grace called entire sanctification. However, like these other positions, the Wesleyan perspective involves a whole integrated systematic theology that is unique yet unequivocally Christian and biblical. As stated at the outset, the heart of this view is a peculiar interpretation of the divine-human relation known as *synergism*.

Synergism is a term that has traditionally been used in a soteriological context, that is, having to do with salvation. It refers in this setting to the belief that in the conversion encounter there is both divine initiative and human response.[1] The alternate position is known as monergism and affirms that God's action is unilateral in the saving experience. This approach self-consciously preserves both the priority and the exclusivity of grace. God's regenerating power acts upon the human person, whose state of being is much like a stone, totally unresponsive until livened by regeneration.[2] Consequently, the monergist tends to accuse the synergist of liberalism and classifies the position as Pelagianism (Pelagius was a British monk who denied the racial consequences of original sin and taught that all persons are born into the same state as Adam, with free choice to obey or disobey the divine call).

This accusation does not understand the Wesleyan version of synergism, which is a synergism of grace. The Wesleyan fully

---

1. See John Wesley's sermon "On Working Out Your Own Salvation," in *The Works of John Wesley* (1872; reprint, Kansas City: Beacon Hill Press of Kansas City, 1978), 6:506-13. This is a sustained treatment of this point of view.

2. For a blatant expression of this position, see R. C. Sproul, *The Mystery of the Holy Spirit* (Wheaton, Ill.: Tyndale House, 1990).

concurs with the priority of grace but interprets the gracious activity of God as extended to all persons, granting a capacity not only to respond but also to reject the gospel. This is one aspect of the Wesleyan doctrine of *prevenient grace.*

Our contention here is that prevenient grace should be extended to encompass all dimensions of the divine-human relation so that man is an active partner via a capacity granted by God's grace. If this assumption is granted, a number of implications follow that bear on the question of eschatology. To these we now turn.

The first and foremost synergistic presupposition bearing on the issue of eschatology and informing many of the other presuppositions we shall examine relates to the issue of *revelation,* the divine self-disclosure. While a conservative and evangelical position, Wesleyan thought is significantly different from extreme versions of fundamentalism. The latter position is informed by two assumptions with which the consistent Wesleyan disagrees. First, fundamentalism holds that revelation is the communication of inerrant truths that transcend the normal capacity of the recipient to understand. This suggests that in the revelatory event, the reason of the "hearer" is transformed so that he hears the Word of God in abstraction from his social, cultural, and historical setting, as well as in a state of elevation above his own natural knowledge.

This view of modern fundamentalism has a long and illustrious history reaching back at least as far as Thomas Aquinas in the Middle Ages. To explain what occurs in divine revelation, Thomas borrowed a concept from Plato regarding vision and cognition. According to Plato, "seeing" and cognition have the same pattern. The possibility of vision is dependent on two conditions: (1) the object of sight must be illuminated by the sun (either directly or derivatively) and (2) the eye must become "sunlike," that is, it must be transformed so as to have the capacity to see. In like manner, the objects of cognition (universals or "forms" in Plato's system) must be illuminated (made intelligible) by the "Form of the Good" (Plato's highest reality), and the mind must also be transformed to be able to receive or apprehend the knowledge of these universals. Thomas applies this pattern to the concept of revelation, saying that when the transcendent truths are revealed, the mind of the recipient is "de-iformed," thus rendering it capable of receiving these otherwise unintelligible truths about God.

The second assumption of fundamentalism is philosophical. It operates on the basis of Scottish Common Sense Realism, a philosophy developed extensively by Scottish philosopher Thomas Reid and brought to America by John Witherspoon, where it replaced the influential philosophy of John Locke and became the dominant teaching in the universities during the 19th century. The aspect of this philosophy that bears on our topic is the belief that the structure of human understanding is the same at all times, in all places, and across cultural barriers. That is, all persons, both ancient and modern, eastern and western, oriental and Caucasian, have the same structure of intelligence. This would eliminate the need for translating a message from one culture to another, or bringing the word of an ancient text into interface with the contemporary mind. In a word, it renders the whole discipline of hermeneutics, as presently understood, irrelevant. Nowhere does the naïvete of this philosophy become more obvious than here.

These two assumptions are closely related, and authentic Wesleyan theology disagrees with both of them. The first adopts a monergistic model based on a monarchical model of the sovereignty of God; the second is based on a view of human nature contrary to all the findings of anthropology and other human sciences.

By contrast, Wesleyan theology insists that revelation has both a giving and a receiving side. The "revelatory constellation" (Tillich) is synergistic in nature. This means that the word of God (God himself) comes to humanity in the human situation. The "word" is heard within the social, cultural, historical, and cognitive limitations of the hearer. However, the word that is heard is not just a human word but is nonetheless heard by human ears. As on the Day of Pentecost, every man hears in his own native language (Acts 2:8). As contemporary Wesleyan biblical scholar Frank Carver has stated in presenting a model for biblical exegesis from the Wesleyan perspective, "The Scriptures are *incarnational*. As human documents God has given them to us through human history with its literary forms and processes.

The Scriptures are conditioned by both time and culture. Therefore, study of them begins at the literary and historical level."[3]

This understanding of revelation has important implications for interpreting prophetic scripture. When the biblical writer speaks of the future, he sees it as the future of his own day. He does not transcend his own time-conditioned situation so as to provide an "eyewitness" account of a future time unrelated to his own circumstances. That kind of "prediction" has been called "reportorial eschatology." This particular limitation to prophetic scripture is also true of apocalyptic literature even though it proposes explicitly to be peering into the future in a detailed way beyond the day of the "seer."[4]

A case in point is the message of the Old Testament prophets about the coming age of salvation. Not even the greatest of them transcended completely the nationalism that characterized Israel's faith. While the Gentiles were often included in the benefits of the new age, according to the later prophets, they were always subordinate to Israel. At best, the Gentiles received the message of the Lord from Israel, but mostly they served Yahweh *and* Israel (see Isa. 60:8-18).

Dispensational theology is thus correct in saying that the Old Testament does not envision the Church, a body of people in which the distinction between Israel and the Gentile world is both transcended and abrogated. But based on a monergistic view of revelation, they argue that the Church was not in God's plan and that the development in the New Testament period is a miscarriage of God's plan, which was revealed in inerrant detail in the prophets. In a word, they ignore the implications of a synergistic view of revelation that attributes the absence of any vision of the Church to the historically conditioned character of even the biblical writers under the "old" covenant.[5]

---

3. Frank Carver, "A Working Model for Teaching Exegesis," in *Interpreting God's Word for Today,* ed. Wayne McCown and James Earl Massey (Anderson, Ind.: Warner Press, 1982), 222.

4. See Leon Morris, *Apocalyptic* (Grand Rapids: William B. Eerdmans Publishing Co., 1972).

5. For a sustained criticism of the dispensational view of the Church as an interruption of God's primary plan, see Oswald T. Allis, *Prophecy and the Church* (Phillipsburg, N.J.: Presbyterian and Reformed Publishing Co., 1947).

The only way one can take the New Testament seriously is to recognize that the Old Testament vision of the coming age was limited by the situation and understanding of the prophets and that the fulfillment of their inspired hopes transcended the literal word. This is made possible by accepting a synergistic view of the Old Testament revelation. The Christian Church has generally adopted this position on the Old Testament from the beginning of the Christian era. Only modern dispensationalism, influenced by Calvinistic fundamentalism, has diverged from the classical Christian teaching in insisting on a literal fulfillment of all Old Testament prophecies.[6]

Another illustration of this truth pertains to a matter with which all contemporary biblical scholars are familiar. The Sinai Covenant, which is the central covenant of the Old Testament, is structured after contemporary suzerainty treaties. Many examples of Hittite covenants of this type have been discovered, and the parallels to the Sinai Covenant are remarkable. How does one explain this correlation except by the thesis that when God enters into a relation with human persons, He does so in terms of the structure of human consciousness and comprehension?

This principle relates not only to the Old Testament prophecies but also to those found in the New Testament, including those of Jesus. The best-known eschatological discourse of Jesus is the Olivet Discourse (Matt. 24; Mark 13; Luke 21). (See chapter on this discourse in this anthology.) This has been fertile ground for speculations about the end of the age, and Jesus' words have been used to attempt to set up a timetable for the end as well as to identify the course of events leading up to it.

A careful reading of Luke's account of this "sermon" makes it crystal clear that Jesus is speaking primarily about the fall of Jerusalem, which took place in A.D. 70. However, as C. E. B. Cranfield points out in his masterful treatment of the Mark 13 account, in Jesus' words the historical and the eschatological are mingled so that the final eschatological event is seen through the "transparency" of the immediate historical. If the prediction of

---

6. Oswald T. Allis demonstrates the ridiculous conclusions to which this insistence on a literal fulfillment of prophecy leads in *Prophecy and the Church*, 16ff.

the fall of Jerusalem completely exhausted the meaning of this passage, it would have only antiquarian interest to us. But on the other hand, since its contours are shaped by the historical event, it cannot be used as if it were an eyewitness account of events in the distant future unrelated to the first century. As Cranfield puts it: "In the crises of history the eschatological is foreshadowed. The divine judgments and the successive incarnations of antichrist are foreshadowings of the last supreme concentration of the rebelliousness of the devil before the end."[7]

The fact that the dynamics of the historical event foreshadow the final struggle becomes the basis for the possibility for those who do not understand the shaping forces of the prophecy to repeatedly identify situations in their own time with Jesus' descriptions. But to make a one-to-one correlation of the prophecy and any historical crisis subsequent to the original one is to miss the nature of revelation.

Walter C. Kaiser, Jr., in a small monograph that addresses the issue of interpreting prophetic scripture, makes the observation that

> the language and vocabulary of the prophetic portions of the Bible are neither as simple and straightforward as some suppose, nor as difficult and obscure as others allege. The truth of the matter is that the biblical prophecies . . . are rich in allusions to contemporary life and times. Almost always their messages are set against the backdrop of the nation's past history or its present situation. The word of God was not dropped into a cultural or historical vacuum; indeed, it was deliberately tied into the hard realities of history, geography, and the peoples of the times.[8]

The second presuppositional issue relates to the *nature of history.* Here also the difference between a Wesleyan view and many others is between a synergism and a monergism. On a monergistic interpretation, history is little more than a "prearranged puppet show" (C. H. Dodd), in which the course of events is determined as to order and time. While this sounds reverent, since it ascribes a rigid control to God and reflects a

---

7. "St. Mark 13," *Scottish Journal of Theology* 6 (1953): 297-300.
8. Walter C. Kaiser, Jr., *Back Toward the Future* (Grand Rapids: Baker Book House, 1989), 41.

strong sense of divine sovereignty, it substantially takes away human freedom.

Another way of looking at the same presupposition is to see it as holding to a chronological *(chronos)* view of time. This way of understanding history means that there is no "loose play at the joints" (William James) and can therefore be written in advance even in a detailed way by one who is privy to the script. It is easy to see how this position can be preoccupied with predictive prophecy in a wooden fashion.

Authentic Wesleyan theology holds to a significantly different interpretation of the historical process. While God is still sovereign over the total process of history, He guides the process within the context of human freedom—this is synergism. Human choices are real and actually influence the course of history. Human beings are not mere pawns being moved about the chessboard by a master chessman and having no input into the gambits in which they participate.

This is a dynamic interpretation of history and involves a "kairological" view of time in contrast to the chronological. The latter sees time as organized by a predetermined pattern so that events are synchronized with God's great "grandfather clock" and thus occur in a definite sequence and at a set point on the divine calendar. The former sees time in terms of "kairos," that is, controlled by a correlation of events. The "time" when events occur—and when the end comes—is "determined" not by the ticking off of minutes on a timepiece that moves inexorably on in measured sequence, but by the development of events that are in turn influenced by many factors—not just One.

If the monergistic view of history as described above were true, certain disturbing implications would follow: Human action would have no meaning, and redemptive efforts would be insignificant and immaterial since they cannot really make any difference. Also, petitionary prayer would be meaningless. If it is true that "more things are wrought by prayer than this world dreams of," then history is not predetermined.

These presuppositions have direct relation to eschatology. The emergence of apocalyptic literature, with its intent to speak specifically about the time of the end, was based on a view of historical determinism.[9] Modern attempts to identify patterns of history that correlate with ancient pictures of end-time events operate on the same assumption. Thus, contemporary "pop prophecy" is based on a view that is antithetical to Wesleyan theology (and, more important, biblical prophecy).

The Wesleyan presupposition of a synergistic view of history does not invalidate predictive prophecy. It does give it a dynamic character that precludes the possibility of writing history in advance in specific detail. The history of prophecy reflects this truth, since claimed fulfillments usually do not correlate literally with the "prediction" in question.[10]

John Wesley himself provides us with a principle of interpretation that correlates perfectly with the position taken here. In commenting on the discrepancy between the Old Testament passage in question and Matthew's claim to fulfillment in Matt. 2:17-18, he said: "A passage of Scripture, whether prophetic, historical, or poetical, is in the language of the New Testament fulfilled when an event happens to which it may with great propriety be accommodated."

With this principle, Wesley is simply articulating a view of prophecy that has been accepted by leading Christian scholars throughout history, namely, that the best interpreter of prophecy is history itself. Oswald Allis, in discussing this truth, quotes Patrick Fairbairn's proposed reason for this limitation. It is found "in the fact that these disclosures of things to come are made known to men by One who has made man and knows his human frailty and how much knowledge of the future is for his good."[11]

Allis's argument is directed against the view of prophecy advocated by dispensationalists, that prophecy must be taken literally and that it thus must be clear and obvious. He quotes John Nelson Darby, early leader of the Plymouth Brethren, out of which movement dispensationalism arose: "I do not admit history to be, in any sense, necessary to the understanding of prophecy."[12]

---

9. See Leon Morris, *Apocalyptic*.
10. See Gurdon Oxtoby, *Prediction and Fulfillment in the Bible* (Philadelphia: Westminster Press, 1966).
11. Quoted in Allis, *Prophecy and the Church*, 25.
12. Ibid., 26.

As early as Augustine, the principle of history as the inter-preter of prophecy was set forth. He says, "All these things, we believe, shall come to pass; but how, or in what order, human understanding cannot perfectly teach us, but only the experi-ence of the events themselves."[13] H. Orton Wiley seconds this view in his discussion of the nature of prophecy when he says, "There is enough given us in the Scriptures to furnish the Church with a glorious hope; but the events can never be un-tangled until prophecy passes into history, and we view them as standing out clearly in their historical relations."[14]

This classical view with which Wesleyan theology agrees is antithetical to the theory that prophecy is prewritten history so that we can know in advance the course of world history in de-tail or pattern. Prophecy has an altogether different function than this. (See Frank Carver's essay, "The Nature of Biblical Prophecy," in this anthology.)

Another presuppositional matter is also significant, al-though on the surface it may appear to have little to do with es-chatology: *The Wesleyan commitment to synergism rejects the idea that God enters into unconditional covenants with humankind.* God's electing love is not dependent upon any qualifying conditions in those whom He chooses, but when one responds to that call there are conditions to be met to continue the relation. At the in-dividual soteriological level, the Wesleyan rejects the idea of "once in grace, always in grace." At the corporate level, we also recognize what the Bible makes explicit, throughout the Old Testament in particular, that failure on the part of a covenant partner can and will invalidate the relation.

How does this relate to eschatology? The prevailing "pop prophecy" of our time primarily builds its construction of fu-ture events on the assumption that God has made certain un-conditional covenants with persons or people in the past that include certain promises, and this provides the grist for their es-chatological mills.

Those who insist on this point specifically have in view a

---

13. *City of God* 20.30.
14. H. Orton Wiley, *Christian Theology* (Kansas City: Beacon Hill Press, 1940-43), 3:307.

supposed unconditional covenant with Abraham, under which they claim that Israel must return to the land of Canaan and possess the whole of it. Oswald T. Allis, in a penetrating and biblically sound analysis, demonstrates that this is a misinterpretation of the so-called Abrahamic covenant for six compelling reasons: (1) a condition may be involved in a command or promise without its being specifically stated; (2) that obedience is implied in the covenant with Abraham is clearly indicated by two facts: one, that obedience is the precondition of blessing under all circumstances, and second, in the case of Abraham, the duty of obedience is particularly stressed in Gen. 18:17-18, in which God proposes to bring into being a righteous seed that will "keep the way of the Lord"; (3) obedience is connected with this covenant by the fact that there was the sign of the covenant, the observance of which was of utmost importance; (4) those who argue for the unconditional covenant do not really regard it as such, since being "in the land" is the precondition of blessing under this covenant; (5) further, they do not regard it as such, also since they never speak of the restoration of Esau to the land of Canaan and to full blessing under the Abrahamic covenant; and (6) "it is important to distinguish between the certainty of the ultimate fulfillment of the promise to the seed of Abraham and the blessedness and security of the nation or of the individual at any given time under that covenant."[15]

The fourth issue in which Wesleyan theology holds a distinctive assumption is *hermeneutical*. Most contemporary popular eschatology is based on a peculiar way of reading the Old Testament that completely ignores the coming of Christ. The true Wesleyan (and the consistent New Testament Christian, for that matter) cannot appropriately read the Old Testament as if Jesus had never come.

Paul makes this point in a graphic manner in 2 Cor. 3. Here he is describing the contrast between his ministry of the new covenant and Moses' ministry of the old. The latter is transient and temporary, and this fact was prefigured by the veil worn by Moses upon his descent from Mount Sinai. Exodus explains this

---

15. *Prophecy and the Church*, 31-36.

as being because the people could not gaze upon him due to the brightness of his countenance. Paul says Moses wore the veil so that the people could not see that the glory was fading away.

Then he compares the rabbi in the synagogue reading the Law to Moses' countenance covered with the veil. The rabbi now has a veil over his mind so that when he reads his scripture he cannot understand it. But when his heart turns to the Lord (Jesus), the veil is taken away and his own Bible now becomes illuminated.

The point is simple: anyone can capture the literal meaning, but only in the light of the transformed Word via the person of Jesus Christ can its present validity be grasped. In contemporary language, Jesus has become for Paul a "new hermeneutic." He is making the same point in chapter 5 of the same book when he declares his intent to "regard no one from a human point of view; even though we once knew Christ from a human point of view, we know him no longer in that way" (5:16). As a Jew steeped in the scripture, Paul had to begin to think in a completely new way that involved a total reorientation of his whole theological and hermeneutical perspective.

The New Testament writers speak with one voice in affirming that Jesus of Nazareth was the fulfillment of the Scriptures, that everything that happened in connection with His life and work was "according to the Scriptures." Consequently, their concept of fulfillment becomes the paradigm for biblical interpretation. To say it differently, the way the New Testament uses the Old Testament becomes the clue to properly using the Scripture as a whole.

The failure to recognize this principle of interpretation has led many conservative Christians of the 20th century into anticipating the consummation of history in Old Testament terms without realizing that the Old Testament hope has found its fulfillment in Jesus Christ. This does not lead one into a consistent "realized eschatology" but rather gives the eschaton a completely different shape than would be the case if the Old Testament hope had not been reconstructed by the coming of Jesus Christ. The future is now seen to be the future of Christ.

This statement leads to a further presupposition to which Wesleyan theology is deeply committed. This assumption can be succinctly stated as *Christological*. The previous analysis of the present situation where the Old Testament, rather than Christ, has been constitutive of eschatological expectations has led to what Adrio König has called "the eclipse of Christ in eschatology."[16]

The words of the heavenly messengers who spoke to the "sky-gazing" disciples immediately following Jesus' ascension capture the New Testament perspective. The original language emphasizes that "this same Jesus" (Acts 1:11) will return as He had gone away. The crucified Nazarene who had startled everyone who followed Him by His radical reinterpretation of the old expectations will return in terms of the same vision. The Kingdom He had come to bring transcended the narrow nationalism of His Jewish peers, and when He returns there will be no reversion to the old way of looking at things.

This principle calls into question the popular preoccupation with the restoration of the Jewish Temple, including the sacrifices by those who insist on a literal fulfillment of Old Testament prophecy. Stephen, in his apology before the Sanhedrin, saw clearly the implication of the work of Christ when he declared that "the Most High does not dwell in houses made with human hands" (Acts 7:48). In a word, he was telling his audience that God was through with the Temple in this new dispensation. They well understood what he meant and were so angered by it that they lost control and committed an illegal execution. Unfortunately that same volatile spirit is present with too many today who are addicted to this unreconstructed view of Old Testament prophecy.

In fact, one can say that in Jesus the eschaton has already occurred, or perhaps more properly, has begun to occur. His resurrection is the firstfruits of the final resurrection. The Spirit He bestows upon His disciples is a foretaste of the glory that shall follow. The salvation He provides is only the beginning of a final reversal of the consequences of the Fall, and the peace (shalom) He places in the hearts of His people foreshadows the

---

16. Adrio König, *The Eclipse of Christ in Eschatology* (Grand Rapids: William B. Eerdmans Publishing Co., 1989).

universal shalom He intends to establish at the final consummation of the Kingdom.

Furthermore, the Jesus who was the Son of God professed
ignorance regarding the time of the end and plainly told His curious disciples that such was none of their business (Acts 1:7).
How brash of us mortals to pretend to a superior knowledge to
that of our Lord!

Of one truth the follower of Christ can be sure. He who suffered on the Cross will one day be vindicated in the moment
when every knee shall bow and every tongue shall confess that
He is Lord. But when and how this universal acknowledgment
will take place is beyond the ken of humankind. It is a matter of
faith, but as John Wesley would say, the manner of the fact is
not an object of faith but of opinion, and one should hold opinion with a light grip.

One further point should be made. *Authentic Wesleyan theology has a native antipathy to speculation.* And, in general, matters
pertaining to the end of history are matters of speculation. As
Mr. Wesley said in the context of denying that he had predicted
the end of the world (also quoted earlier in this anthology), "I
have no opinion at all upon the head [subject]: I can determine
nothing at all about it. These calculations are far above, out of
my sight. I have only one thing to do,—to save my soul, and
those that hear me."[17]

Preoccupation with speculation may satisfy the curiosity,
but it is the preaching of the gospel that brings the offer of salvation to the lost and needy. And the full gospel includes the
good news that God both delivers from the guilt and power of
sin in this present age and will deliver His people from the consequences of sin in the age to come.

---

17. John Wesley, *Works* 12:319.

■ **HARVEY FINLEY** and **H. RAY DUNNING**

Apocalyptic Eschatology

*A*POCALYPSE[1] HAS BECOME a familiar term in contemporary use. It suggests a dramatic, cosmic interruption of history, bringing with it destruction and death. Novelists and moviemakers, as well as preachers, have used it to address the modern concern about the future. The development of weapons with the capacity to destroy civilization as we know it, accompanied by the many acts of personal and national violence in this century, has created expectations about the possibility of experiencing the stark reality of apocalypse.[2] What does it mean and what does an understanding of it contribute to our knowledge of the biblical view of last things? Those are the questions we propose to explore.

The Hebrew and Greek words underlying the terms "apocalypse" and/or "apocalyptic" are usually translated "to reveal"

---

1. This is a subject that is still under discussion by scholars. It is difficult to be dogmatic about a scholarly consensus. However, there is consensus that there is a definable body of literature known as "apocalyptic" with certain definable characteristics. As this essay will reflect, there are differences of opinion about its origin and its relation to the biblical materials. It appears at this stage that there may not be any future major changes in scholarly estimate of the literature and theology of apocalyptic, so we can speak with considerable certainty about the phenomenon.

2. One need only notice the numerous items of major crimes reported daily in news media to be alarmed about the future. The widespread emergence of decadent, immoral lifestyles has led some leading sociologists to give this country (the United States) perhaps 25 more years before internal collapse unless there is serious, radical change.

■ *Harvey Finley is professor emeritus of Old Testament at Nazarene Theological Seminary in Kansas City. H. Ray Dunning is professor of theology at Trevecca Nazarene College in Nashville.*

(verb) and "revelation" (noun) in most English versions of the Bible. These terms are frequently used in both the Old Testament and the New Testament. As noted, they are also being used frequently in secular as well as in religious publications in reference to any one of a number of threatening situations taking place in various areas of the world.

The word "apocalypse" (a translation of the Greek word), occurring in the New Testament passages, is used to refer to a report on a divine disclosure, that is, God revealing His will in a particular setting and in a special manner concerning earthly situations. The Book of Revelation or The Apocalypse of Jesus Christ delivered to John is a special example of the use of the word "apocalypse."

The terms relevant to this study ("apocalypse," "apocalyptic," and "apocalyptic literature") have been used to refer to (1) a particular theological understanding, (2) a type of movement, and (3) a special style of literature. Our primary concern in this chapter is with apocalyptic theology, but this cannot be considered apart from the special literature that is its vehicle.

Apocalyptic-style thought has fueled the imagination of men of faith down across the centuries from before the advent of Christ to the present time. In fact, current international uncertainties and difficult domestic problems have prompted many preachers to make end-time "apocalyptic" prognostications. In his inaugural address at Nazarene Theological Seminary, Darius Salter predicted, "Since dispensationalism marks this coming millennium as the final one, the year 2000 will be preceded by an explosion of futuristic predictions . . . a proliferation of apocalyptic literature."[3] This was also the case at the transition to the second millennium of the Christian era. (See chapter on the history of eschatology in this anthology.)

Apocalyptic as a Form of Eschatology

The Bible with its 66 books is a "library" containing many kinds of literature. There are two major literary categories: *prose* and *poetry*. Within these two categories there is a variety of liter-

---

3. Darius Salter, "The Impossibilities of Pastoral Care," *The Seminary Tower* 47, no. 1 (Fall 1992): 3.

ary types, one of which is termed apocalyptic. This is a kind of literature characterized by a unique form of expression used to convey a particular theological understanding of the *eschaton*, the consummation of history.

Some interpreters attempt to treat apocalyptic as if it were no different from regular prophetic eschatology. This confusion is widespread among radio and televangelists, as well as many popular "Bible teachers," who often recognize no difference between these two types of eschatology.[4]

Apocalyptic literature is generally identified in this approach as flourishing between about 200 B.C. and about A.D. 100. Much of this literature originated from Jewish sources in the socalled intertestamental period. Further, the Book of Daniel is the only full-fledged example from this period (see below) to find its way into the canon, but several other Old Testament prophetic books predating this period contain passages usually classified as apocalyptic. These include Isa. 24—27, portions of Joel and Amos, Zech. 9—12, Zephaniah, and elsewhere.

The ministry of Jesus and the rise of the Early Church took place within this apocalyptic period of time. Scholars have identified the presence of apocalyptic literature and theology in the New Testament writings, even occasionally in Jesus' own words to His disciples. Certain of the Epistles contain apocalyptic language and one entire book (Revelation) is commonly identified as being in this genre. We may have reason to question this identification (see below).

Because of the widespread confusion between prophecy and apocalyptic, one purpose of this study is to aid the reader in understanding the difference between the two so as to avoid this confusion and more properly interpret the canonical Scripture.

---

4. Much of this confusion results from the influence of the old Scofield Bible (1909), where the difference between Daniel and the prophetic books is recognized—but this difference is explained in terms of content rather than as a different literary genre. Daniel, it claims, deals with the future of the Gentile nations, whereas the prophets are concerned with the future of Israel. The revised Scofield Bible (Oxford NIV Scofield Study Bible, 1984) recognizes its nature as apocalyptic literature but does not materially alter the interpretation of its subject matter.

What Is Apocalyptic?

There are two major theories regarding the origin of apocalyptic literature. One view is represented by Martin Rist, who defines "apocalypticism" as "a type of religious thought which apparently originated in Zoroastrianism, the ancient Persian religion; . . . taken over by Judaism in the exilic period and post-exilic periods, and mediated by Judaism to early Christianity." He proceeds to point out that it may be defined as "the dualistic, cosmic, and eschatological belief in two opposing cosmic powers, God and Satan (or his equivalent); and in two distinct ages—the present, temporal and irretrievably evil age under Satan, who now oppresses the righteous but whose power God will soon act to overthrow; and the future, perfect and eternal age under God's own rule, when the righteous will be blessed forever."[5]

Both Rist and W. Ward Gasque[6] distinguish between major features of apocalypticism, which are normative or constitutive of the genre, and secondary characteristics, which may or may not be present. These features distinguish this type of literature from prophetic eschatology.

The two major features include its dualistic nature and its strong eschatological emphasis. Its dualism involves both a metaphysical dualism and a cosmological dualism. The first includes a belief in two "supreme," opposing beings vying with each other for control on earth, particularly over human beings. The two ruling powers are often identified as God and Satan in Jewish apocalyptic, sometimes symbolized by light and darkness.

The second form of the dualism is a dualism of two ages. Here is where the distinctively eschatological feature enters the picture. This involves a belief in two distinct periods of time: the *present*, temporal, and continuing evil age is under Satan's rule. Although Satan now harasses the righteous, God in due time will overthrow him and usher in the *future*, perfect, and

---

5. M. Rist, "Apocalyptic, Apocalypticism," in *Interpreters' Dictionary of the Bible*, ed. George Buttrick (Nashville: Abingdon Press, 1962), 1:157.
6. W. Ward Gasque, "Apocalyptic Literature," *Zondervan Pictoral Encyclopedia of the Bible* (Grand Rapids: Zondervan Publishing Co., 1975), 1:200.

eternal age for the righteous, during which they will be under God's own reign, blessed forever. The "age to come" is not an outgrowth of the first but is a new creation. God will break into history from beyond history and bring the present evil age to a close and usher in the age of salvation.

Rist lists the secondary characteristics that give vigor, interest, and mystery to the message as including a revelation received through vision. This provides one point of contrast with prophecy. Prophecy generally involves receiving a message from God that is described as auditory in nature, although not exclusively so. The prophet "hears" the word of the Lord. The list further includes pseudonymity; the presence of a messiah; angelology and demonology; animal symbolism; numerology; predicted woes; and astral influences. Gasque gives a slightly different listing that supplements the first. The chief characteristics he notes include: "esoteric, literary, symbolism, and pseudonymous [sic]."

Most studies prior to the middle of this century concurred with the analyses of Rist and Gasque. But the more recent studies of Paul D. Hanson and others following his pioneering scholarship provide a basis for proposing that *apocalyptic* became a significant *genre of eschatology* expressing a particular theology as early as the sixth century B.C., with roots even centuries earlier. These more recent studies call for revision of earlier approaches to *apocalyptic*. The primary premise of this theory is that *apocalyptic* applies to (1) a genre of literature, (2) an eschatology, and (3) a religious perspective, each of which must be considered as part of a whole.[7]

This approach moves beyond earlier studies at the points of *origin, date, relation to prophetic eschatology, and relevancy*. The characteristics such as pseudonymity, animal symbolism, vi-

---

7. Important studies for this topic are Paul D. Hanson, *Dawn of Apocalyptic* (Philadelphia: Fortress Press, 1975), esp. 1-31; Paul D. Hanson, ed., *Visionaries and Their Apocalypses, Issues in Religion and Theology 4* (Philadelphia: Fortress Press, 1983); Joel Marcus and Marion L. Soards, eds., *Apocalyptic and the New Testament: Essays in Honor of J. Louis Martyn. Journal for the Study of the New Testament Supplement Series 24* (Salem, Wis.: Sheffield Academic Press, 1989); Richard E. Sturm, "Defining the Word 'Apocalyptic': A Problem in Biblical Criticism," in Marcus and Soards, *Apocalyptic*, 17-48. John J. Collins, *The Apocalyptic Imagination—An Introduction to the Jewish Matrix of Christianity* (Crossroad, 1987), especially 1-32.

sion, and so on have been generally retained, and above all the basic pattern of dualism in both forms. There are five points emphasized by Hanson:

1. *Earlier Origin.* Certain themes of apocalyptic have a literary history much earlier than the eighth-century prophets Amos, Isaiah, et al. Some of the distinguishing themes may be traced to the time of the Exodus or even earlier.

2. *Joining of Prophecy and Apocalyptic in Exilic Period.* There is a strong case for the emergence of apocalyptic as a significant genre and theology much earlier than traditionally thought.

3. *Question of Iranian Origin.* Hanson's reconstruction also suggests a rejection concerning the Iranian roots of the apocalyptic movement. The motifs and literary features were derived from the larger ancient Near East "environment," he argued, as well as from a time considerably earlier than the Persian or Iranian times. This understanding obviously precludes an Iranian origin of *apocalyptic.* Hanson has thus shown that apocalyptic had much earlier roots than expressed in many published studies previous to his. Further, there is basis for taking the position that apocalyptic derives from a "broad social-political-economic matrix" that has to date not been adequately probed.

4. *Relation of Apocalyptic and Prophecy.* A case can be made for apocalyptic eschatology as a development out of the bitter experiences of the Exilic and post-Exilic times. Persons of visionary circles perceived that Israel's sin was so deeply ingrained in the "national psyche" as to require a radical break with the past. This suggested a need for a new beginning initiated by Yahweh. Apocalyptic eschatology thus became a developed, significant theology applicable to a genre of literature, to a particular eschatology, and to a socioreligious movement.

5. Rather than of merely antiquarian interest, apocalyptic remains a relevant genre of biblical literature for our modern "enlightened" but deeply disturbed times as much or more so as for the ancient days when first developed. One major reason for this is that apocalyptic was fostered by despair after national tragedies. Several of the earliest expressions of apocalyptic (e.g., Isa. 24—27; 56—66; and Zech. 9—14) were written against the background of two terrible national tragedies: the destruction of Samaria by the Assyrians in 722 B.C. and the two attacks on Je-

rusalem by the Babylonians, the first in 598 B.C. and the second in 587 B.C., resulting in its destruction. Similar kinds of crisic, threatening, and even death-dealing circumstances developed again for Jews in the intertestamental time under the Seleucid kings and a similar persecution of the Christians during Roman times, particularly after A.D. 70.

The mood of the times following the destruction of Jerusalem in 587 B.C. was replicated after the city's downfall in A.D. 70. There was a widespread sense of hopelessness created by the feeling that it was the end of one's culture and way of life, even one's religion. Hanson contends that a similar mood is dominant today as a result of shocking sociological and political trends that characterize our times. There is therefore considerable basis for insisting on the contemporary relevance of apocalyptic.

Early Roots of Prophetic Eschatology

Eschatology expresses the expectations that the Lord God as Creator of the world is in control of His creation, especially the history of those creatures made in His likeness. Its progress is guided toward a purposeful consummation inherent in biblical faith from Gen. 1 throughout the Scriptures. It becomes central in the context of the covenants the Lord established with His people. Covenants involve promises, and promises are future oriented. Consequently, when God makes a covenant promise, there emerges out of this relation an expectation of a future fulfillment.

Both the biblical understanding of creation and the idea of covenant promise reflect a significantly different understanding of history from that generally held in other ancient Near Eastern cultures. These cultures tend to see history as cyclical, so there is no goal, "there is nothing new under the sun."[8] By contrast, the biblical view is that history is linear and is moving toward a goal, under the guidance of the Creator.

---

8. The Book of Ecclesiastes, which contains this refrain, is an apologetic for the biblical view of history as linear against the meaninglessness of a cyclical view derived from the cycles of nature.

This understanding of divine design for and guidance of history informs the whole of Scripture and prompts not only expectations of the future but also the use of such words as "fulfillment," "in the latter days," or "the end times." It is the use of such terms that is the basis for the term "eschatology," literally the "last/final word/statement." This term is actually a translation into English of the word meaning "doctrine of last things" or "belief concerning end times."

Thus, covenant theology may be seen as the seedbed of prophetic theology. The early chapters of Genesis record covenants with persons like Abel, Enoch, Noah, and Abram/Abraham. Of these, the covenant with Abraham is the most significant for subsequent history, since the descendants of Abraham consider themselves as potential recipients of the promises made to Abraham by the Lord. This covenant with Abraham entailed specific commitments on God's part concerning His future relation with both the patriarch and his descendants. They became the basis for expectations of a glorious future for the children of Abraham. The Abrahamic, along with the Mosaic and Davidic, covenants constitute the formative covenants for the development of eschatology within the Old Testament.

The Mosaic covenant brought Israel into existence as the people of Yahweh, and this informed their self-understanding from that time forward. It manifested itself in the belief that in time to come, God would break into history, overthrow their enemies, and establish them as a great nation in the world. This day of visitation came to be referred to as the Day of the Lord. We first see it expressed—in perverted form, to be sure—in the time of Amos. His prophetic preaching was designed to correct the perversion and establish the Day of Visitation on a sound ethical basis (see Amos 5:18-24).

The Davidic covenant introduced into Israel's store of eschatological hopes the idea of a messianic king who would rule over a restored Israel and who, like David of old, would defeat their enemies and bring them to a position of prominence and prestige as in days of old. This covenant was mediated to David by Nathan the prophet and involved the promise that David's would be a perpetual dynasty (see 2 Sam. 7:16).

Perhaps arising out of the Davidic covenant, since David

had captured and established the city as his personal capital, there also arose in Israel an expectation about the perpetuity and inviolability of Jerusalem. Thus, its destruction (in 587 B.C. and A.D. 70) was a devastating blow to the faith of Israel in their God.

The major content of prophetic eschatology included the hope of a people (a new Israel), an ideal king (the Messiah), and a restored Jerusalem containing a rebuilt Temple. But the unique feature of this was that it was all to occur within history, and usually as a result of God's use of more or less natural forces such as alien armies. The goal of prophetic eschatology was not the end of the world but the end of evil.[9] These anticipated events were usually used by the prophet as the occasion for a call to repentance in the present as the human preparation for fulfillment.

The Introduction of Apocalyptic into Prophecy

The classic expression of prophetic eschatology is found in the pre-Exilic prophets Amos and Hosea, Isaiah and Micah, and Jeremiah and Ezekiel. But this chiefly involved a call to covenant faithfulness, along with a warning of dire consequences if the people persisted in unfaithfulness.

Interspersed among the oracles of these great prophets were passages that were anticipatory of apocalyptic imagery. Amos speaks of signs in the heavens as portents of judgment, such as "I will make the sun go down at noon, and darken the earth in broad daylight" (8:9).

Isa. 24—27 is considerably more advanced than the Book of Amos it its use of aspects of apocalyptic. These chapters are usually grouped together as a unit and referred to as "The Little Apocalypse." Chapters 22 and 23 have considerable similarity to this unit, also speaking about a nonearthly setting. All give evidence of a *visionary element*, one of the secondary features of apocalyptic. There seem to be elements of Isaiah's initial vision (chap. 6) present in these chapters. The central role of the vi-

---

9. See Donald E. Gowan, *Eschatology in the Old Testament* (Philadelphia: Fortress Press, 1986), 1-3.

sionary element, the introduction of themes not noticed prior to
the eighth century, such as the messages of judgment upon non-
Israelite nations and the destruction of the earth itself, and the
combination of the earthly activity/presence of the "Lord of
Hosts" with the otherworldly or heavenly abode and reign of
God are the apocalyptic aspects of these chapters.

The use of apocalyptic-type imagery increased with the fall
of Samaria in 722 B.C. and the two invasions of Jerusalem in 598
and 587 B.C. This was perhaps an inevitable development out of
the ashes of blasted hopes and disillusionment in the face of the
apparently failed promises that had been the basis for their confidence.

The prophets during this (722-587 B.C.) and later times increasingly incorporated aspects of eschatology into their messages that were new and strikingly different from normative
prophetic eschatology. This involved a tendency to shift from
the earthly scene to a cosmic or nonearthly setting.

Probably enough has been said to illustrate the thesis that
apocalyptic grew out of prophecy. One major difference is that,
for prophecy, the eschatological purposes of God will occur
within this history. Even the descriptions of the "Day of the
Lord" in Amos is a day of judgment that ushers in a new situation, but nonetheless, afterward history goes on. In apocalyptic,
history has to be transcended, a completely new beginning has
to occur. In a word, the prophet is optimistic about God's action
within history, whereas the apocalyptist is pessimistic that the
divine purposes can be fulfilled within this history. Nonetheless, it must be noted that the apocalyptist is optimistic that God
will ultimately triumph, but it is a triumph that will take place
at the close of history, or at least bring history to a finis.

H. H. Rowley has succinctly identified an important distinction between prophecy and apocalyptic: "Speaking generally, the prophets foretold the future that should arise out of the
present, while the apocalyptists foretold the future that should
break into the present."[10]

10. H. H. Rowley, *The Relevance of Apocalyptic* (New York: Association Press, 1963),
38, n. 1.

One major contrast between apocalyptic and prophecy is in the symbolism used. Apocalyptic generally uses unnatural and bizarre symbolism such as "beams dripping with blood," the moon turning to blood, and the stars falling from their courses. Prophecy, on the other hand, generally uses natural symbols, such as a plumb line, an earthquake, or a locust plague.

But there is a significant difference between apocalyptic-type literature found in the canon and the noncanonical apocalyptic literature that flourished during the 200 B.C.—A.D. 100 period. Canonical literature is thoroughly monotheistic in its theology, whereas the noncanonical type is dualistic as discussed above.

As a matter of fact, the general perspective of this theology is that God has withdrawn from an active involvement in the affairs of human history and Satan has taken complete control. "The Present Age" is dominated by demonic "powers" with Satan as the "prince of the powers of the air." Only an apocalyptist could have declared that "Satan is alive and well on planet earth." In this present darkness, the only hope is a divine inbreaking from outside history that will bring the present order to a halt. The victory of God will occur only at the consummation. As a result, there is an inordinate preoccupation with the "end," accompanied with attempts to determine precisely when that end will take place. Usually, an upsurge of apocalyptic productions occurred during times of persecution, such as the persecution of the Jews by Seleucid king Antiochus IV Epiphanes during the midsecond century B.C. Because of this, this literature has sometimes been referred to as "tracts for hard times."

This preoccupation with the time of the end reflects itself in a peculiar feature of the literature found in the Pseudepigrapha, the collection of apocalyptic writings standing alongside the Apocrypha, a collection of books quite different. This characteristic has been referred to by the term "pseudonymous," that is, written under a pseudonym. There is an interesting reason for this.

It was the Jewish belief that the spirit of prophecy was withdrawn at the time of Ezra the scribe. God had revealed His will in the Law, thus there was no need for a fresh word of prophecy. Ezra's emphasis on the Law, establishing Israel as a Law-oriented community, was identified as the terminus of the Spirit's work of revealing a direct word to the prophet. This made it theoretically impossible for anyone to claim a "word from God" subsequent to that time. Thus, if any pronouncement was to claim divine authority, it had to be attributed to some ancient worthy who lived during the "period of inspiration." The pseudonyms were taken from this period. As Leon Morris says, "No one takes seriously the idea that when an apocalyptist speaks of certain revelations as made, say to Baruch, he is describing what actually happened to Baruch, or, for that matter, what actually happened to himself. He is using a literary device to convey a message, not describing events of the past."[11]

A further feature results from this phenomenon. The structure of the literature presents the "author" as having received a divine revelation about the course of world history from his time until the end. What is involved, therefore, is a writing of history *as if* it were prophecy.

This characteristic results in an interesting phenomenon. The "supposed prediction" is actually the rewriting of history. The description of the historical events is thus quite precise since it is being described by hindsight, which, as the popular idiom says, gives "20-20 vision." It becomes even more detailed as the chronology approaches the time of the author. The purpose of this ploy is to establish faith in the "prediction" because of its accuracy in order to gain credibility for the "true" prediction that extends beyond the writer's time. Scholarship is able to date rather precisely the time of the writing, because at that point the descriptions begin to lose precision as they extend beyond the date of writing. This is now real future and thus can only be spoken about in vague, symbolic ways. But the terminus of the flow of history thus "predicted" is the consummation of history, the end of the age, and the inbreaking of the Kingdom, and this is usually depicted as imminent.

A further feature of apocalyptic emerges out of this pattern. In order to be able to predict with accuracy the actual course of

---

11. Leon Morris, *Apocalyptic* (Grand Rapids: William B. Eerdmans Publishing Co., 1972), 54.

human history, history must be deterministic. If there is any contingency involved, one cannot lay out the pattern of events or the time of the end. The assumption that informs this belief is that the course of this world's history is preordained. The end is present from the beginning and time is merely the spinning out of an eternity that exercises rigid control of every twist and turn. Persons are mere pawns in this prearranged puppet show.

If taken seriously, the practical consequence of this view of history is a pessimism about ever alleviating the ills of humankind. Such a defeatism would logically call for a retreat from engagement, a holding action accompanied with a grim determination to survive until the end. The nerve of a sense of social responsibility would effectively be cut.

This was apparently the response of the Qumran community, who produced and/or preserved the Dead Sea Scrolls. They had organized a commune of an ascetic nature awaiting the overthrow of evil. Some of their literature was clearly apocalyptic, depicting a conflict between darkness and light. This is illustrated visually by the structure in Jerusalem that houses the scrolls: a tall, jet black, rectangular tower with a pure white-tiled turret beside it in which the scrolls are actually located. Symbolically, they speak of the dualism of light and darkness in conflict.

The deterministic view of history resulted in a schematization that saw the pattern in terms of epochs or periods, often seven in number, or a multiple of seven. Naturally, when the last epoch had run its course, the end would come; and equally obvious was the fact that the writer of the literature placed himself in the last period of history, that was soon coming to a close. This concept seems to be the basis for the popular misinterpretation of the seven churches of Asia addressed in the Book of Revelation as depicting seven ages in the so-called Church age. (See below on Revelation as apocalyptic.)

Apocalypticism and the New Testament

In an oft-quoted statement, Ernst Kasemann has said that "apocalyptic is the mother of Christianity." Whether or not this is true in the sense Kasemann intended is a moot point here. It *is* the case that apocalyptic theology and language provides the background for the New Testament. But a major transformation of this theology occurs in New Testament theology.

As we noted, the dualism of apocalypticism sees the present age as evil beyond redemption, with no hope for history. The age of salvation can become a reality only through the cataclysmic intervention of God that brings the present age to an end. Into this pessimism about the present, the messages of John the Baptist and Jesus that the kingdom of God is at hand came like an unexpected bolt out of the blue.

The whole of the New Testament, most obviously in the Synoptic Gospels, is concerned to affirm that the Kingdom has broken into this present age without fanfare or cataclysmic upheaval. The social order is still intact, but the age of salvation is now here in the person and ministry of Jesus of Nazareth.

It is this transformation of the apocalyptic understanding that gives New Testament theology its central focus. What had hitherto been hoped for as an exclusively eschatological possibility was now available within the community established by Jesus. The eschatological events had already begun. The forgiveness of sins, the gift of the Spirit, and even the resurrection of the dead—all marks of the age to come—had occurred in the here and now. And these were all anticipations of a future actualization on a cosmic scale.

This New Testament emphasis has been called realized eschatology. However, it is not a complete realization but only the inauguration of an age that will be consummated at the Second Advent. The Kingdom has come, and the Kingdom will yet come in its fullness. Thus, what was postponed for another world is available in this world, especially the victory over sin, release from its binding power. It is this theme that marks all authentic New Testament theology.[12]

What About Daniel and Revelation?

It is customary in introductions to biblical literature to speak about apocalyptic literature and say that only the Books

---

12. See the chapter in this anthology on John Wesley's view of last things to see how this theme is dominant in the teachings of Wesley, leading to a reticence to engage in apocalyptic-like speculation about the end time.

of Daniel and Revelation were documents from this genre included in the canon. This raises a question. Why were they included, and are they really apocalyptic? Is there something unique in these books that sets them off from other Jewish and Christian apocalypses?

One source explains the canonicity of Daniel by the rationale that other apocalyptic writings "lack the essential marks of inspiration that Daniel possesses."[13] However, no clues are given as to the so-called marks of inspiration. This takes us nowhere. A far more feasible reason is suggested by Klaus Koch, even though he grants that it is an assumption since no reasons were actually given by the rabbis. He suggests that it was probably because the fourth monarchy of the four that appear in Daniel had come to be identified with the Roman Empire, whereas originally it referred to the Seleucid kingdom of Antiochus IV Epiphanes. This theory prevailed until the 18th and 19th centuries. Thus, the prophecies of Daniel seemed to have contemporary relevance at the time of the book's canonization.

As Koch concludes: "The perception that Daniel's prophecies were being fulfilled was strengthened by the fall of Jerusalem in A.D. 70, because along with many Christians nearly all the rabbis saw that terrible catastrophe as the fulfillment of the timetable of Dan. 9:24-27. This book was therefore the only one in the Holy Scriptures which offered a key for the second destruction of the holy city and the existence of Israel in a further exile."[14]

Daniel does share with the typical apocalyptic writing the schematization of history, depicting the process as moving to its final demise and the establishment of the kingdom of God. And in doing so it reflects the pattern of beginning the survey of history leading up to the time of the writing[15] and then passing beyond to predict the imminence of the end.

---

13. Roy E. Swim, *Beacon Bible Commentary* (Kansas City: Beacon Hill Press of Kansas City, 1966), 4:620.

14. Klaus Koch, "Is Daniel Also Among the Prophets?" *Interpretation* 39, no. 2 (April 1985): 128. It must be remembered that the final canonization of the Old Testament occurred late in the first century A.D.

15. While there are still many conservatives who argue for an earlier date to the book, the vast majority of scholars agree with the statement of Robert A. Anderson: "So compelling is the evidence in favour of placing the final promulgation within the period

W. Sibley Towner suggests that there are two pivotal points in the book where the vision divides between the rewriting of history "as if" it were prophecy and the turning of the vision to the future, where the visionary loses focus because the picture no longer corresponds to the pictures of history that actually occurred. Using the analogy of a filmmaker, Towner comments, "We can see the picture all right, but we would not be able to make out exactly what this means. Things never happened this way in the second century B.C. nor at any other time. The hindsight sequences of the film would be beautifully clear, but the foresight, brilliantly depicted as it may be and powerfully effective in its rendition of the judging power of God, nevertheless would remain disconcertingly irrelevant to the actual course of events."[16] These two pivotal points he identifies as being between Dan. 7:8 and 9 and between 11:39 and 40.

This raises some questions for us that need to be briefly addressed. How can we accept the fact of unfulfilled prophecy? The fact is that there are numerous prophecies that were never fulfilled, many of which by the nature of the case never can be and some that were fulfilled in ways other than the prophet literally described it.[17]

The Book of Daniel itself gives us two clues as to how to deal with this fact. Both are seen in connection with Daniel's discovery of Jeremiah's prophecy that the Babylonian captivity would last for 70 years. Upon finding this and checking his calendar and discovering that the time was up, Daniel began to repent for his people (9:1-19) so that they might correct their ways and make it possible for God to fulfill this prophecy. This clearly tells us that prophecy had a contingent nature and was not deterministic (see discussion in this anthology on "Presuppositions of a Wesleyan Eschatology").

---

of the persecution of the Jews under Antiochus IV Epiphanes (175-164 B.C.E.) that it is possible almost to pinpoint, not only the year, but the month when it reached its present form. It is unlikely that any other biblical book is capable of such accurate dating" ("Signs and Wonders," commentary on Daniel in *International Theological Commentary* [Grand Rapids: William B. Eerdmans Publishing Co., 1984], xiii).

16. "The Preacher in the Lion's Den," *Interpretation* 39, no. 2 (April 1985): 158.

17. See Gurdon C. Oxtoby, *Prediction and Fulfillment in the Bible* (Philadelphia: Westminster Press, 1966).

The other point is seen in the fact that Daniel reinterprets the prophecy, saying that it doesn't really mean what it says. The 70 years are really 70 *weeks* of years. This makes it possible to project the fulfillment into a yet future time so as to avoid a failure. This, according to R. H. Charles, is precisely one of the characteristics of apocalyptic.[18]

We may now see how the Book of Daniel, which clearly refers to events in the second century B.C. if taken literally, can become a paradigm through reinterpretation for a future fulfillment when the kingdom of God really does roll down the mountain, smashing the kingdoms of this earth. It becomes the paradigm for Jesus' prediction of the fall of Jerusalem in A.D. 70 as recorded in His Olivet Discourse, and doubtless also for John the Revelator in proclaiming the fall of "Babylon" (Rome) in the Apocalypse of Jesus Christ. But since it is not "reportorial eschatology," that is, describing the future as if by an eyewitness, it cannot be used in a wooden fashion to identify contemporary "persons, places, and events" as being its primary, literal point of reference.

There is, of course, another way of addressing the problem. Those like the dispensational premillenialists, who insist upon a literal fulfillment of all prophecy, do two things. First, they reject the obvious historical setting of the book, and second, they illegitimately intrude an indeterminate period of time into the picture between the sixth and seventh weeks of Daniel. The end result is much the same. We are still left with no solid clues by which to identify the specific events that will precede the consummation of history.

Through the presence of other features as well, we may say that Daniel is an apocalyptic writing. In fact, some scholars argue that Daniel becomes the paradigmatic apocalypse with all the other Jewish versions imitating it.[19] But the question of importance is "Is its *theology* apocalyptic?" It is possible to see evidence of the belief that the victory of the Kingdom will occur at the end of history. On the other hand, there is little evidence of

---

18. R. H. Charles, *Eschatology* (New York: Schocken Books, 1970), 184-89.
19. G. E. Ladd, "Apocalyptic Literature," in *Zondervan Pictoral Bible Dictionary*, ed. Merrill C. Tenney (Grand Rapids: Zondervan Publishing Co., 1967).

the cosmic dualism that is characteristic of much apocalypticism. It is true that there is a cosmic opposition to God as depicted in 10:10-14, but the tenor of the book leaves no doubt that "the Most High" is the Ultimate Reality.

When we turn to the Book of Revelation in the New Testament, we find a rather different picture. The symbolism is bizarre, the battle between evil and righteousness appears to be fierce, and the saints are (or anticipate) suffering severe persecution. All the trappings of apocalyptic are there. But there is a major difference. Unlike the typical apocalyptic, the conquest of evil has already taken place at the midpoint of history. This is the significance of the heavenly scene in chapter 5, where the seven-sealed scroll (which perhaps represents the process of world judgment consummating in the full establishment of the Kingdom) can be opened only by the "slain Lamb." The symbolism reflects the central thesis of the New Testament that in the work of Christ, focusing on the Cross, Satan was defeated and the victory over evil was won. The remainder of history will be simply the working out of this completed conquest.[20]

While Revelation is clearly apocalyptic in literary style and perhaps in other ways as well, it is not apocalyptic in its theology. In fact, it highlights a significant difference between canonical and noncanonical apocalyptic and even the Book of Daniel as a pre-Christian document. And furthermore, apocalyptic, like every other attempt to predict the future, is conditioned in its thought forms so that its conceptual boundaries are derived from its own time. Although relevant in its mood, even canonical apocalyptic cannot be used to chart the course of history and detect "signs of the time." (See the proper meaning of this term in the essay by Roger Hahn in this anthology.)

---

20. See Mathias Rissi, *The Future of the World* (Naperville, Ill.: Alec R. Allenson, n.d.), 1-17.

■ WILLIAM CHARLES MILLER

The New Apocalypticism

*A*NY MINUTE CHRIST MAY RETURN to "rapture" up believers. The true Church will be with its Lord, but the false (liberal or apostate) church will finally be exposed for what it is, having a form of godliness without power. The apostate church and other sinners will be left to face the horrors of divine wrath, Antichrist, tribulation, and final judgment.

This is the doctrine of the "secret rapture," which teaches that, without warning, Christ will rescue the Church from a pending seven-year period of tribulation. Following this tribulation will come a literal 1,000-year reign of Christ and His saints upon the earth. The millennial reign will end with a brief rebellion followed by the Judgment, and finally the new heavens and earth. Such a view of the end time (eschatology) has been the belief of many conservative Protestants during much of the 20th century.

The secret rapture is spoken of as the "blessed hope," because it is seen as the great rescue of true believers from the decay of an increasingly wicked world. Believers are to be ready at every moment for the rapture. Watchfulness, expectancy, and readiness are proclaimed repeatedly from the pulpit and printed page.[1]

---

1. For a useful bibliography of this literature, see Jon R. Stone, *A Guide to the End of the World: Popular Eschatology in America* (New York: Garland Publishing Co., 1993). Arnold D. Ehlert, *A Bibliographic History of Dispensationalism* (Grand Rapids: Baker Book House, 1965), is dated and written from the perspective of a convinced dispensationalist, but it remains an important resource.

■ *William Charles Miller is librarian at Nazarene Theological Seminary in Kansas City.*

Human society under Satan's rule is seen as rushing toward its doom. The rapture is interpreted as the first event in the final apocalyptic battle between the rule of Satan and the kingdom of God. The supposed nearness of the end, the pessimism about the present age, the total triumph of God over evil at the end, and the emphasis on being prepared for the end create an apocalyptic view of the world. This view has motivated energetic efforts at evangelism and missions.[2]

So common is this belief that few in the evangelical pew question it today. It is taught from pulpits as foundational Christian doctrine. It is presented as the apostles' view of Christ's second coming and the end time. Known as *pretribulation premillennialism*, this view of the last days has been a powerful molder of the theological and psychological ethos of conservative Protestantism in the English-speaking world. Frequently associated with Christian fundamentalism, pretribulational premillennialism has extended its influence across denominational boundaries and has been incorporated into several denominational creeds or statements of faith. It has played an instrumental role in the establishment of a number of Bible colleges and a few theological seminaries.

Dispensationalism

Pretribulational premillennialism is a special view of last things,[3] but it rests upon a larger, more comprehensive theological foundation known as dispensationalism. This theological system is essentially a way of interpreting Scripture coupled with a particular understanding of the Church and divine grace. Preference for a literal reading of prophetic passages in Scrip-

---

2. See Dana L. Robert, "'The Crisis of Mission': Premillennial Mission Theory and the Origins of Independent Evangelical Missions," in *Earthen Vessels: American Evangelicals and Foreign Missions, 1880-1980*, ed. Joel A. Carpenter and Wilbert R. Shenk (Grand Rapids: William B. Eerdmans Publishing Co., 1990), 29-46.

3. For discussions of the integral relationship between dispensationalism and the secret pretribulation rapture, see John F. Walvoord, *The Question of the Rapture*, rev. and enl. ed. (Grand Rapids: Zondervan Publishing House, 1979); and John F. Walvoord, *The Millennial Kingdom* (Finley, Ohio: Dunham Publishing, 1959; reprint, Grand Rapids: Zondervan Publishing House, 1984).

ture is a distinctive feature of this system.[4] This literal approach, combined with a futuristic interpretation of the apocalyptic books of the Bible (Daniel, Revelation), permits Israel, rather than the Church, to be the primary object of all biblical prophecies. The true Church is a spiritual fellowship of believers divorced from any particular structure or organization. There is a pessimistic perspective on the course of society, including the false churches. To understand the apocalypticism of pretribulational premillennialism, it is necessary to examine the historical development of dispensationalism.

The history of dispensationalism is difficult to discern, since its origins are widely disputed. Two basic positions concerning its origin may be identified. Popular dispensationalism assumes that its doctrines were held by the earliest Christian communities. This position holds that the Early Church lost its pure primitive eschatological hope by A.D. 400 but that this glorious hope was recovered by Bible students in the 19th century.

The other position is critical of the popular explanation. It rejects the contention of patristic (this term refers to Christian thought during the first few centuries of the Christian era) origins and holds that its so-called recovery in the 19th century was in fact the beginning of dispensationalism. Instead of being the restoration of the theology of Paul and the other apostles, dispensationalism is a recent innovation created by the cultural and spiritual needs of the modern age. Both positions agree on the importance of John Nelson Darby and the Plymouth Brethren in the spread of dispensationalism and its apocalyptic vision. Darby's major contribution to this theology was his view of the church (ecclesiology) and the secret pretribulation rapture theory that developed out of it.

---

4. Defining the essential characteristics of dispensationalism is more controversial than it may appear. Even among dispensational theologians, there are differences of opinion as to the essential characteristics. A "literal" approach to Scripture is nearly universally held to be a mark of dispensationalism, but the importance and nature of the distinction between Israel and the Church and the fulfillment of prophecy in the current and future dispensations are subject to considerable debate. See Charles C. Ryrie, *Dispensationalism Today* (Chicago: Moody Press, 1965), 22; Larry V. Crutchfield, *The Origins of Dispensationalism: The Darby Factor* (Lanham, Md.: University Press of America, 1992), 28-33; and Craig A. Blaising and Darrell L. Bock, ed., *Dispensationalism, Israel and the Church: The Search for Definition* (Grand Rapids: Zondervan Publishing House, 1992), 13-34.

John Nelson Darby and the Brethren

John Nelson Darby (1800-1882) was born in London of Irish parents and received a legal education at Trinity College, Dublin. Declining to pursue a legal career, Darby entered the ministry of the Church of Ireland (Anglican). He was ordained a deacon in 1825 and a priest the following year. His parish ministry was a success, but the interplay of civil politics and established church privilege led him to seek a fellowship expressing the purity and unity of the New Testament Church. Darby came to hold that the true Church is not an earthly institution. This true Church, the Bride of Christ, exists apart from any human organization or tradition; it is an invisible spiritual entity. Such a position led Darby to depreciate tradition, liturgy, and the role of ordained clergy.

He associated in 1827 with a small group devoted to Bible study that had been meeting for a couple of years in Dublin. This group sought to study the Bible free from what it saw as the corruption evident in the churches of the time. A slogan applicable to the group would be, "The Bible and the Bible alone." It was from this group and others like it forming a mutual fellowship that the Brethren movement began in Ireland and England.[5]

Darby, by the force of his personality and intellect, soon emerged as the leader of the movement.[6] The Brethren movement's formative years were marked by conflict within local meetings and between local assemblies. Ironically, this was due in part to the movement's efforts to reach agreement on what constituted New Testament purity and unity, but also because of Darby's inability to tolerate opinion or behavior that ran counter to his own understanding of the desired purity and unity.

---

5. The Brethren movement is frequently known as the Plymouth Brethren after Plymouth, England, the location of an important early Brethren meeting. For a history of this movement, see Napoleon Noel, *The History of the Brethren*, 2 vols. (Denver: Knapp, 1936); F. Roy Coad, *A History of the Brethren Movement: Its Origins, Its Worldwide Development and Its Significance for the Present Day* (Grand Rapids: William B. Eerdmans Publishing Co., 1968); and H. A. Ironside, *A Historical Sketch of the Brethren Movement* (Grand Rapids: Zondervan Publishing House, 1942; reprint, Neptune, N.J.: Loizeaux Brothers, 1985).

6. Darby's influence was such that in some quarters the [Plymouth] Brethren movement was known as "Darbyism."

Thus, a movement originally begun to restore the unity of Christian fellowship became known for its divisiveness. The goal of unity was subverted by the desire for purity, which led to a doctrine of separation from any form of institutional compromise or corruption. Darby was instrumental in shaping this doctrine of separation under the rubric of "the government of God."[7] Darby's understanding of the spiritual Church, as distinct from the apostate, earthly institutional church, was a major factor in moving him toward a distinctive eschatology.

Exactly when Darby began to develop his idea of a secret rapture is a mystery of history. One researcher holds that Darby came to the idea of the pretribulation rapture as early 1827.[8] Others have suggested that it was not until his participation in the Powerscourt conferences.[9] It is known for certain that by the early 1830s Darby was publicly teaching his unique view of the rapture. Before espousing the pretribulation rapture, Darby, in common with other futurists of the time, had held to the rapture of Christians at Christ's second coming following the tribulation. The secret rapture theory provided a way to understand God's faithfulness to both the Church and Israel as separate people of belief. God's offer of salvation to the Gentiles, the Church, was a great parenthesis in God's covenant with Abraham. God's promises to Israel will be fulfilled after the rapture of the Church. Rather than dealing with two chosen peoples simultaneously, God works consecutively. The true Church is united with Christ in heaven, not to an organization on earth. The secret rapture theory also provided a theological understanding for a doctrine of separation from corrupt churches. It created an expectation of any moment being caught up with the Lord. A new apocalypticism had been born.

---

7. See John Nelson Darby, "A Letter on Separation," in *The Collected Writings of J. N. Darby*, 34 vols., ed. William Kelly (Reprint, Sunbury, Pa.: Believers' Bookshelf, 1971), 1:350-52. Similar views on unity and separation are found in the same volume of his collected works: "Separation from Evil, God's Principles of Unity" (1:353-65); "On Discipline" (1:338-49); and "Grace, the Power of Unity and of Gathering" (1:367-77).

8. John L. Bray, *The Origin of the Pre-Tribulation Rapture Teaching* (Lakeland, Fla.: John L. Bray, 1983).

9. Crutchfield, *Origins of Dispensationalism*, 141.

Some Brethren leaders did not accept Darby's rapture doctrine. But faithful to his perception of biblical truth, Darby did not permit any variation from his views to go unchallenged. He defined the acceptable limits of Brethren unity as agreement with his views. Several prominent Brethren leaders left or were forced out of the movement, sometimes after bitter public controversy and condemnation.[10] Under Darby's influence, the pretribulation rapture theory rapidly became the doctrinal stance of all Brethren assemblies. In a movement that disdained Christian tradition and relied on direct Bible study for its theology, there were few barriers to accepting a doctrine so forcefully presented.

The Roots of the New Apocalypticism

Darby insisted that he had arrived at all his understandings, including the secret rapture, from personal Bible study. But his affirmation has not hindered others from looking for other sources that may have influenced his thinking. The search for the original source behind Darby has centered its attention on Edward Irving (1792-1834) and his Catholic Apostolic Church.[11]

Irving, a minister with the Church of Scotland (Presbyterian), spent his most productive years in London. His London ministry began in 1822 where his preaching and personality attracted large crowds. As his fame grew, his preaching became more critical of prevailing social conditions and included personal attacks. His popularity waned as a result. In 1830 the Scots' presbytery of London excommunicated him for having pub-

---

10. Darby's conflicts with other Brethren leaders are reviewed in Clarence B. Bass, *Backgrounds to Dispensationalism: Its Historical Genesis and Ecclesiastical Implications* (Grand Rapids: William B. Eerdmans Publishing Co., 1960), 64-99; Coad, *History of the Brethren Movement*, 105-63; Ironside, *Historical Sketch*, 30-69.

11. The most complete treatment of the church is found in Columba Graham Flegg, *"Gathered Under Apostles": A Study of the Catholic Apostolic Church* (Oxford: Clarendon Press, 1992). An older but useful study is P. E. Shaw, *The Catholic Apostolic Church; Sometimes Called Irvingite: A Historical Study* (Morningside Heights, N.Y.: King's Crown Press, 1946). A good short treatment of Irving is H. C. Whitley, *Blind Eagle: An Introduction to the Life and Teaching of Edward Irving* (London: SCM Press; Chicago: Alec R. Allenson, 1955). Flegg's volume contains an extended bibliography for both the church and Irving.

lished unorthodox views on Christ's human nature. He rejected
the presbytery's authority and withdrew from its jurisdiction.

Irving's local congregation supported him, and his pastoral
ministry continued there until 1832. In that year he was removed from his pulpit due to manifestations of "spiritual gifts"
under his ministry, including healing and speaking in tongues.[12]
Most of the membership left with him to form a new congregation, which became the Catholic Apostolic Church. Irving, de-
posed from the ministry of the Church of Scotland in 1833, was
reordained by an apostle of the new church as "Angel or Pastor
of the new congregation."[13] However, his role in the new church
was limited and secondary. He died in 1834 at Glasgow.

Irving had become interested in Bible prophecy and millennialism early in his ministry. The French Revolution's persecution of Christianity, the rise of Napoleon, and social-economic
changes within England had created a general interest in
prophetic themes and signs of the end times. Irving began to
preach on Christ's return in 1825. His understanding of eschatology was historicist with a posttribulational rapture,[14] but in
1827 he published his translation of a book—originally published in 1816—which proposed a partial rapture of selected
saints before the tribulation.[15]

The author of the translated work, Chilean Jesuit Em-
manuel Lacunza, wrote under the pseudonym Rabbi Juan Jose-
fat Ben-Ezra, a converted Jew. Some claim this book is the first
record of a pretribulation rapture (partial or full) in Christian
theology.[16] Lacunza's argument failed to convince Irving, but
Lacunza's view helped inform the context for his and others'
millennial speculations. Did Irving's translation of Lacunza in-

---

12. For a discussion of the relationship of these spiritual gifts to modern Pentecostalism, see "Introduction: Edward Irving: Reformed Pentecostal Theologian," in C.
Gordon Strachen, *The Pentecostal Theology of Edward Irving* (London: Darton, Longman,
and Todd, 1973), 13-22. For historical detail, see Flegg, *Gathered*, 51-53.

13. Strachen, *Irving*, 14. Whitley, *Blind Eagle*, 33, states that Irving was "driven to
accept reordination, or something very like it." Flegg, *Gathered*, 59-61, provides additional detail.

14. Flegg, *Gathered*, 36-41, 329-31.

15. J. J. Ben-Ezra, *The Coming of the Messiah in Glory and Majesty*, tran. E. Irving
(London: Seeley and Son, 1827).

16. Bray, *Origin*, 1-2.

fluence Darby? It is difficult to know, but as early as 1829 Darby acknowledged Irving and his translation of Lacunza. He refers to Irving's sermons and quotes, with citation, from "the translator's [Irving's] preliminary discourse to Ben-Ezra [Lacunza]."[17] He also cites from *Morning Watch,* Irving's millennial magazine.

Another suggested origin for the pretribulation rapture theory is Margaret Macdonald of Port Glasgow, Scotland.[18] Macdonald was a teenager in 1830, when she experienced a vision of the Second Coming and spoke words of prophecy. Her revelation, as preserved in print, is difficult to fully understand. Shortly after her vision, she became part of a charismatic revival that moved over western Scotland. This revival created considerable interest among those looking for the signs of the end, including those in Irving's circle. Anglican clergyman Robert Norton, who later affiliated with the Irvingite Catholic Apostolic Church, wrote an account of the revival that included Macdonald's revelation.[19] Robert Baxter, who participated in Irving's charismatic services, in 1833 published a volume in which he mentions the Scottish revival and his own conversion to a pretribulation rapture view.[20] It is interesting that the Macdonalds questioned the validity of the charismatic manifestations that later developed among Irving's followers.[21]

---

17. John Nelson Darby, "Reflections Upon the Prophetic Inquiry and the Views Advanced in It," in *Collected Writings* 2:6.

18. See Dave MacPherson, *The Unbelievable Pre-Trib Origin* (Kansas City: Heart of America Bible Society, 1973), and Dave MacPherson, *The Late Great Pre-Trib Rapture* (Kansas City: Heart of America Bible Society, 1974). These two works have been revised and combined in Dave MacPherson, *The Incredible Cover-Up* (Medford, Oreg.: Omega Publications, 1975).

19. Macdonald's revelation is reported in Robert Norton, *Memoirs of James and George Macdonald of Port Glasgow* (London: John F. Shaw, 1840), 171-76, and Robert Norton, *The Restoration of Apostles and Prophets; In the Catholic Apostolic Church* (London: Bosworth and Harrison, 1861), 15-17. It is also reprinted in MacPherson, *The Unbelievable Pre-Trib Origin,* 105-8, and MacPherson, *Incredible Cover-Up,* 151-54. The revival is recounted in Robert Norton, *Neglected and Controverted Scripture Truths; With an Historical Review of Miraculous Manifestations in the Church of Christ; And an Account of Their Late Revival in the West of Scotland* (London: John F. Shaw, 1839).

20. Reported in MacPherson, *Incredible Cover-Up,* 85-91, citing Robert Baxter, *Narrative of Facts, Characterizing the Supernatural Manifestations in Members of Mr. Irving's Congregation, and Other Individuals, in England and Scotland, and Formerly in the Writer Himself* (London: James Nisbet, 1833). Baxter eventually became disillusioned with prophetic excess and left the Catholic Apostolic Church.

21. See MacPherson, *Incredible Cover-Up,* 74-76. MacPherson quotes heavily from Norton.

Concerned with events in western Scotland, the Brethren sent their own investigator, Darby, to determine the meaning of the charismatic revival. Darby visited with the Macdonalds and later, in 1853, published his recollections.[22] He reported primarily on the Macdonalds' glossolalia. But given that Darby had already read widely in millennial literature and had written on prophecy, it would be reasonable to assume Darby heard of and would be interested in Margaret's revelation. But there is no record of Darby's response to it. To what extent her revelation influenced him is an open question. The revelation was not cast in precise theological language. It can be read as promoting a partial secret rapture,[23] a reading somewhat supported by Baxter's accepting the secret rapture doctrine, but it is also possible to read it as expounding a posttribulation partial rapture.[24] A careful reading of the revelation does not yield any unambiguous statement of a pretribulation rapture. It does contain references to a rapture that may be only spiritual (thus a secret rapture in a special sense). It is best to read Margaret's revelation as part of the general millennial fervor.

The attempts to account for the origins of the pretribulation secret rapture in Lacunza or Macdonald are informative speculations that do not fully explain Darby's espousal of a secret pretribulation rapture. They do highlight the extent of millennial interest and the willingness of some to accept novel or revolutionary apocalypticism. During the early 1800s, there were numerous conferences and public meetings devoted to prophetic issues. The Albury meetings, held annually from 1826 to 1830, and the conferences sponsored by Lady Powerscourt, 1831 to 1833, were examples of these conferences.

Lady Powerscourt is one connection between the Albury meetings and her own conferences. She attended some Albury meetings and, in the fall of 1830, Irving held public meetings and private conferences in Ireland as her guest. Darby, an ac-

---

22. John Nelson Darby, "The Irrationalism of Infidelity: Being a Reply to 'Phases of Faith,'" in *Collected Writings* 6:283-85.

23. Dave MacPherson has taken the lead in promoting this view.

24. See Thomas D. Ice, "Why the Doctrine of the Pretribulational Rapture Did Not Begin with Margaret Macdonald," *Bibliotheca Sacra* 147 (April—June 1990): 155-68.

quaintance of Lady Powerscourt, played a significant role in the Powerscourt conferences, at which "the precious truth of the rapture of the Church was brought to light."[25] Participants in the various prophetic meetings came from every social class and denominational tradition. They were bound together by their mutual prophetic expectations and interests.

Until Darby, these millennialists followed historicist views. They sought to connect historical and contemporary events with prophecy. Schemes that anticipated the Second Coming on specific dates were proposed. It would be difficult to overstate the multitude and variety of millennial expectations, some of which appear ridiculous today.[26]

Darby participated, contributed, and finally responded creatively to this millennial fever. There is ample evidence that millennial speculations were not a marginal part of Darby's theological agenda. Such speculations were a central concern. Where did the secret pretribulation rapture doctrine originate? As F. F. Bruce notes, "It was in the air in the 1820s and 1830s among eager students of unfilled prophecy, both in Darby's circle and in the following of Edward Irving."[27]

Darby's "discovery" of the doctrine arose out of discussions about the millennium and the application of a literal reading of biblical prophecy, combined with a particular understanding of the Church. In the history of Christian theology, Darby is the first to clearly articulate an eschatology containing a secret pretribulation rapture, the Church age as a parenthetical period, and the millennium as a Jewish kingdom.

Innovation or Revival?

Was Darby's discovery an innovation or a reclaiming of early Christian thought? Clearly, Christian tradition and history did not play a significant role in Darby's thought. Scripture, not

---

25. Ironside, *Historical Sketch*, 23.

26. For a discussion of millennial interest during this period, see W. H. Oliver, *Prophets and Millennialists: The Uses of Biblical Prophecy in England from the 1790s to the 1840s* (Auckland, New Zealand: Auckland University Press; Oxford: Oxford University Press, 1978). Of particular interest are the first six chapters.

27. F. F. Bruce, review of Dave MacPherson's *The Unbelievable Pre-Trib Origin*, in *The Evangelical Quarterly* 47 (January—March 1975): 58.

history, was the determining factor for him. The question of ancient precedent was not important to Darby, but early Christian precedent did become important to subsequent dispensationalists. They believed that for dispensationalism to be orthodox and part of the faith once delivered to the saints, it must have been present in the first Christian communities.

The foundation of dispensationalism, as noted above, involves the uniting of three unique elements: (1) A strict distinction between Israel (the Jewish faithful) and the Church, (2) a literal understanding of biblical prophecy and its fulfillment, and (3) a secret pretribulational, premillennial rapture. For dispensationalism and its apocalyptic vision to be a recovery of patristic faith, these essential elements need to be found in early Christian communities, especially before A.D. 350. Some dispensationalists have diligently sought to find these elements in patristic theology. While their attempts have failed to find a patristic dispensationalism, they do claim to have found partial expressions of dispensational theology.[28]

To speak of a common patristic eschatology is to oversimplify a complex and dynamic discussion extending over several centuries.[29] Surviving documents of the second through the fourth centuries show that a form of premillennialism (sometimes termed "Chiliasm") was held by some early Christians.[30] Some proponents of dispensationalism have used this to infer that early Christians held to dispensationalism.[31] But patristic premillennialism, where found, does not have dispensationalism's distinction between Israel and the Church. It saw the Church as the continuation of spiritual Israel and not as occupying a parenthetical position in God's covenant with Israel. Many Christians in the first centuries A.D. expected an immi-

---

28. Examples can be found in Ryrie, *Dispensationalism Today*, 65-85; and Ehlhert, *A Bibliographic History of Dispensationalism*, 5-30.
29. See Brian E. Daley, *The Hope of the Early Church: A Handbook of Patristic Eschatology* (Cambridge: Cambridge University Press, 1991), for an informative overview. See also the essay by George Lyons in this anthology.
30. For an introductory review of premillennialism among the Church fathers, see George Eldon Ladd, *The Blessed Hope* (Grand Rapids: William B. Eerdmans Publishing Co., 1956), 19-31.
31. For an example of this approach, see Charles Caldwell Ryrie, *The Basis of the Premillennial Faith* (Neptune, N.J.: Loizeaux Brothers, 1953).

nent second coming, but there is no trace of their anticipating a secret pretribulational rapture. For dispensationalists to claim patristic roots for their theology, they must either overlook substantial differences between patristic premillennialism and dispensationalism[32] or else hold that the Early Church "set forth principles that later evolved into dispensationalism."[33]

The developmental idea fails for two reasons. First, no one has discovered any historical continuity between patristic premillennialism and modern dispensationalism. Second, dispensationalism appeared, and has since been modified, without reference to patristic thought.

Patristic understandings of biblical prophecy and methods of reading Scripture differ from the literal approach advocated by dispensationalism. Early Christians used many methods to search and apply the teachings of Scripture. Similarly, their ecclesiology was not rigidly formulated. Nevertheless Darby's rejection of Christian tradition, an ordained clergy, and the visible Church would have been foreign to them. Dispensationalism, as understood during most of the 19th and 20th centuries, is a more structured theological system than is found in patristic theology. The differences are too great to postulate antecedents for dispensationalism in patristic thought.

---

32. Walvoord, *Millennial Kingdom*, 119-23.

33. Larry V. Crutchfield, "Israel and the Church in the Ante-Nicene Fathers," *Bibliotheca Sacra* 144 (July—September 1987): 255. In this article, Crutchfield finds four elementary features of dispensationalism present in the Early Church. The four are not unique to dispensationalism and are more representative of historic premillennialism. In footnote 7 he states, "The actual position of the earliest Fathers is what may best be described as 'imminent intratribulationism.' They generally viewed all tribulation within the context of the current persecution under Rome" (256). This "imminent intratribulationism" is not a secret pretribulation rapture view. If Crutchfield is correct here (which is open to dispute), it seems to have an affinity to the midtribulation premillennial rapture view, a view that is anathema to classical dispensationalists.

The main purpose of the article is to explore the fathers' understanding of the Church and Israel. Crutchfield presents the patristic evidence in a manner to highlight any positive relation to dispensationalism. He concludes that the views of contemporary dispensationalism are a refinement, not a contradiction, of patristic views. But he also notes, "Certain elements in their [the fathers'] thought place them close to though not altogether within the dispensational camp" (270). In order to arrive at this conclusion, he must read the fathers through a dispensational lens, and even then the evidence is not conclusive. He does prove that a selective reading of patristic sources can yield something that suggests limited similarity between patristic views and dispensationalism.

After studying the major patristic writers, Alan Boyd, himself a dispensationalist, concludes, "It would seem wise for the modern system [dispensationalism] to abandon the claim that it is the historical faith of the Church (for at least the period considered), and instead devote its efforts to establishing that it is the heir of New Testament eschatological truth in a manner in which the Fathers studied were not."[34]

Dispensationalists tend to see antecedents for their theology in any earlier Christian thought that divides God's dealings with humanity into periods. Distinctions in the history of God's dealings with humanity (dispensations) are not unique to dispensationalism. An example is the distinction between Old and New Testaments, which is accepted by all Christian denominations. Yet, modern dispensationalists tend to read anyone who holds to historical divisions in God's extending grace to humanity as a proto-dispensationalist. This tendency is especially evident in their reading of early Christian writers.[35] Such views overlook the different functions assigned to dispensations by each theological system. The dispensations of dispensationalism are not compatible with the various dispensations spoken about by patristic authors.

Attempts to assert ancient roots for dispensationalism ring hollow for lack of substantial evidence. Such attempts have the feel of after-the-fact efforts to create an orthodox heritage. A more satisfactory approach for dispensationalists would be to accept Boyd's ahistorical position, one Darby would have endorsed, to recognize dispensationalism as a modern development. Darby is the father of dispensationalism and the secret pretribulation rapture. It originated with his involvement in millennial discussions and study during the late 1820s and early

---

34. Alan Patrick Boyd, "A Dispensational Premillennial Analysis of the Eschatology of the Post-Apostolic Fathers (Until the Death of Justin Martyr)" (Th.M. thesis, Dallas Theological Seminary, 1977), 92. He maintains that dispensationalism is a "product of the post-Reformation progress of dogma," but in his view "Biblical truth and not historical precedent" establishes sound theology (91). He remains a dispensationalist based upon his understanding of Scripture.

35. For a recent example of this tendency, see Larry V. Crutchfield, "Ages and Dispensations in the Ante-Nicene Fathers," *Bibliotheca Sacra* 144 (October—December 1987): 377-99.

1830s. It was not a revival of apostolic thought but was instead
a theological innovation.[36]

The Spread of the New Apocalypticism

Darby devoted considerable time and energy promoting
his doctrinal understandings and the Brethren movement. Besides his travels within the United Kingdom, he visited the European continent, North America, and Australia. He visited
North America several times: in 1862, 1864, 1866, 1870, 1872-73,
1874, and 1876, spending approximately seven years, three and
a half of which were in the United States (no connection to the
time frame of his eschatological scheme!). Darby's major interest during these visits was to spread the Brethren message. He
attended Brethren assemblies and conferences, conducted Bible
studies, met with prominent sympathetic clergy (including
D. L. Moody), encouraged the distribution of Brethren literature, and carried on extensive personal correspondence.[37] His
success in promoting the formation of Brethren assemblies was
less than he desired. Rather, the result of his efforts consisted in
the adoption of his eschatology instead of his ecclesiology.

Darby had developed his eschatology from his ecclesiology.
In the United States his view of the Church encountered a religious culture built upon a voluntaristic principle without an established state church. Since Darby created his ecclesiology in
reaction to a national church, it had a foreign sound to American audiences. The same was not true of Darby's eschatology.
The American social and cultural climate included a strong interest in millennial speculations.[38]

At the beginning of the 19th century, postmillennialism
was the majority position among American Christians. The
American roots for the popularity of postmillennialism are

36. In addition to Boyd, this conclusion is supported, among others, by Bass, *Backgrounds to Dispensationalism*, 14, 40-41, 155; Ladd, *The Blessed Hope*, 19; and Walvoord,
The Question of the Rapture, 50.

37. Ernest R. Sandeen, *The Roots of Fundamentalism: British and American Millenarianism 1800-1930* (Chicago: University of Chicago Press, 1970), 70-80.

38. Sandeen, *Roots*, 42-46; and George M. Marsden, *Fundamentalism and American
Culture: The Shaping of Twentieth-Century Evangelicalism: 1870-1925* (New York: Oxford
University Press, 1980), 49.

found in the Great Awakening (1740s) and the thought of
Jonathan Edwards. This postmillennialism was expectant with
the hope of the glorious millennial age before Christ's second
coming. The postmillennialists saw the millennium as the triumph of the Church, empowered by the Holy Spirit, in establishing God's rule in the world. Highly optimistic and confident
of the power of redemptive grace, postmillennialism was attractive to the spirit of a people building a new society. The progressive western movement of settlement, creation of a separate nation, movement toward democratic government, and persistent
revivalism were interpreted as harbingers of the coming millennium. This optimistic vision saw the Northern victory in the
Civil War as removing a major barrier—slavery—to the millennium.

During the second half of the 1800s and into the early
1900s, social, intellectual, and economic factors called the postmillennial vision into question.[39] Industrial expansion and the
current development of urban manufacturing centers coupled
with more diversity in immigration contributed to its reinterpretation. Some saw industrial achievements, technological ad-
vances, and the pace of scientific discoveries as confirming the
approach of a golden age. Others saw the labor strife, monopo-
listic practices, profiteering, dramatic economic cycle swings,
and opulent displays of wealth associated with industrial capi-
talism as forerunners of a dark dehumanizing age. Another significant factor was the introduction to America of critical biblical scholarship, which radically altered the foundations for
biblical and theological studies and opened a division in American Christianity between those embracing its methods and conclusions (modernists) and those who rejected such scholarship
(fundamentalists).

Christians who retained their optimistic view of the future
tended to accept critical scholarship. They saw critical scholarship as part of the progress being made toward a wonderful future era. An optimistic commitment to religious, social, economic, and intellectual progress compelled them to stress human

---

39. Marsden, *Fundamentalism*, 48-51.

efforts to restructure society to overcome remaining manifestations of evil.

Other Christians were discouraged by what they saw as the decline in the social dominance of Protestantism, the rise of unbelief, the corrosive influence of critical scholarship, and the spread of urban decay. Yet they shared with their optimistic cousins a commitment to foreign missions. These Christians positioned themselves to be the advocates and defenders of traditional Protestant values.[40] Instead of seeing progress as a stimulus for social reconstruction, the defenders saw contemporary developments as a regression from realizing the millennium.[41] Increasingly they were developing a pessimistic view that undercut belief in a postmillennial reign of righteousness. It was into the early stages of this tide of pessimism that Darby appeared with his escapist premillennial teaching.

Darby found a ready hearing among those troubled by the idea that contemporary progress was a route to the millennium. As Darby's view had been formed in Irish and British millennial discussions, his views now became an ingredient in similar discussion among conservative American Christians. Darby's pretribulational premillennialism had two features that commended it to Americans. The first was its cultural pessimism. It provided a framework for understanding the events of history as a movement away from God. The world's condition would become worse until the rapture of the Church and divine judgment before the millennium. True believers would be spared God's wrath in the tribulation, but until then they should expect to experience increasing persecution.

The second feature was Darby's approach to the Bible, which was antithetical to critical scholarship. Darby's claim to have established his views upon a literal reading of the Bible strengthened its attractiveness to traditionalists. He was seen as an ally in the battle against critical scholarship, and any ally was a friend. His approach had the additional advantage of having an internal consistency; it was a systematic approach to

---

40. Ibid., 62-71.
41. Timothy P. Weber, *Living in the Shadow of the Second Coming: American Premillennialism, 1875-1982,* enl. ed. (Grand Rapids: Zondervan Publishing Co., 1983), 41-42.

the entire Bible. It could function as a defensive fortress in the battle against critical scholarship.

There is irony, however, in traditional Christians' acceptance of Darby's apocalyptic innovations as important weapons in their defense of traditional views. They were seeking an alternative to postmillennialism, which was becoming associated with modernism and liberalism, and found Darby's understanding of Scripture and eschatology a satisfactory alternative. But, as noted above, Darby's ecclesiology found little sympathy. The divisive denominational battles over modernism were still to come. Many of those seeking an alternative eschatology were pastors and evangelists who considered their denominations to be orthodox but under assault by heterodox views. Darby's extreme separatism made them uncomfortable.[42] He was too combative, and his Brethren were unable to cooperate with other Christians. The struggle with critical scholarship cut across denominational boundaries. Consequently, traditionalists formed an unstructured interdenominational fellowship bound together by their commitment to Scripture. The last thing they needed was for a separatist Brethren element to divide their ranks.[43] Yet the attractiveness of Darby's eschatology and literal Bible reading was too much to resist.

The Development of Normative Apocalypticism

Darby's apocalyptic teaching found an audience ready to adapt it to the American scene. The American adapters provided a culturally valid foundation and in doing so developed the classic 20th-century dispensationalism with a normative eschatology.[44] As Darby's eschatology had developed in the context of prophetic conferences, his American adaptation flourished in the "Bible conference" movement.

---

42. Sandeen, *Roots*, 101-2. Also see Talmage Wilson, "A History of Dispensationalism in the United States of America: The Nineteenth Century" (Th.M. thesis, Pittsburgh-Xenia Theological Seminary, 1956), 102-5.

43. As much as the 19th-century conservative resisted Darby's separatist ecclesiology, when the denominational struggles between modernists and fundamentalists were over, the 20th-century conservatives/fundamentalists had adopted a modified version of Darby's separatist doctrine.

44. The history of this adaptation is told in C. Norman Kraus, *Dispensationalism in America: Its Rise and Development* (Richmond, Va.: John Knox Press, 1958).

Bible conferences were an important feature of late 19th-century American Christianity. They developed in association with the Bible college, mass evangelism, and deeper-life movements. In the history of American Bible conferences, the Niagara Bible conference was the prototype. It began in 1868 as an informal ministerial Bible study retreat. It evolved into public meetings for Bible study and reading. Between 1883 and 1897, it met at Niagara-on-the-Lake, Ontario, therefore its popular name.

Historian Ernest Sandeen notes, "Virtually everyone of any significance in the history of the American millenarian movement during this period attended the Niagara conference."[45] There were both pretribulational and posttribulational premillennialists present at Niagara conferences, but the posttribulationalists eventually disappeared as conference speakers. Not only were the Niagara conferences concerned with prophecy and eschatology, but the focus was on "the study of the Bible, with a simple faith in its literal meaning and a desire to have its message applied."[46] Conference attenders were biblicists seeking an eschatology.

The Niagara conferences popularized a form of Bible study called Bible reading. This method of study used biblical texts to interpret other biblical texts. Study consisted of arranging selected scriptural passages in a "cut and paste" manner to highlight an understanding of the biblical message. These studies were read, or delivered, as a sermon would have been delivered. The intent was to have the Bible speak for itself. The plain, or literal, sense of Scripture was the goal. This method was similar to the practice of Brethren assemblies.

The recognized founding father of the Niagara conference was Rev. James H. Brooks. Brooks, a Princeton Theological Seminary graduate, was a pastor in St. Louis following the Civil War. Sometime before 1870 he became a convinced pretribulational premillennialist. Later in life, Brooks testified to having reached this eschatological position through personal study of

---

45. Sandeen, *Roots*, 134. For an extended discussion of the role of Bible conferences, see Sandeen's chapter, "The Prophecy and Bible Conference Movement," 132-61.

46. Larry Dean Pettegrew, "The Historical and Theological Contribution of the Niagara Bible Conference to American Fundamentalism" (Th.D. diss., Dallas Theological Seminary, 1976), 63.

the Bible.[47] As with Darby's testimony, historians have sought additional sources, especially since Brooks' views parallel those of Darby.

Several claim a definite Brethren influence in the formation of Brooks' position.[48] Darby visited St. Louis during Brooks' pastoral service in the city, but there is no firm evidence of their meeting. It has been suggested that Brooks may have become acquainted with Brethren theology as early as 1860 while seeking medical treatment in Switzerland.[49]

Many early-American pretribulational premillennialists display a fluid understanding of eschatology, but Brooks' understanding was systematically developed. His commitment to the secret rapture theory was expressed through his leadership in the Niagara conferences, many publications, his editorship of the periodical *The Truth*, and his ability to attract disciples. Brooks' most influential disciple was Cyrus Ingerson Scofield.

C. I. Scofield is famous—or infamous—for editing the notes for the study Bible that carries his name.[50] Scofield had served in the Confederate Army (awarded the Cross of Honor for bravery), practiced law, served in the Kansas Legislature, and had been appointed United States Attorney for the District of Kansas prior to his conversion in 1879 at age 36.[51] Early in his Christian

---

47. James Brooks, "How I Became a Premillennialist," *The Truth* 22 (1896), 331.

48. Sandeen, *Roots*, 139; Ironside, *Historical Sketch*, 196; and John H. Gerstner, *Wrongly Dividing the Word of Truth: A Critique of Dispensationalism* (Brentwood, Tenn.: Wolgemuth and Hyatt, 1991), 38-40.

49. Wilson, "Dispensationalism," 63-69.

50. *The Scofield Reference Bible* was published by Oxford University Press in 1907, and a slightly expanded edition ("New and Improved") with reset type appeared in 1917. A revised edition, obviously without Scofield's participation (he died in 1921) was released in 1967 as *The New Scofield Reference Bible*. The original edition used the King James Version. The revised edition contained the King James text, which had been editorially updated to remove obsolete words or English usage. The *New Scofield Reference Bible* has since been adapted to other English translations, including the *New International Version, New American Standard Bible,* and the *New King James Version*. For a highly favorable history of the study Bible's effect, consult Frank E. Gaebelein, *The Story of the Scofield Reference Bible, 1909-1959* (New York: Oxford University Press, 1959).

51. The standard favorable biography is Charles Gallaudet Trumbull, *The Life Story of C. I. Scofield* (New York: Oxford University Press, 1920). A different perspective is found in Joseph M. Canfield, *The Incredible Scofield and His Book* (Ashville, N.C.: private printed, 1984; reprint, Vallecito, Calif.: Ross House Books, 1988); a rebuttal is found in John D. Hannah, "A Review of *The Incredible Scofield and His Book*," *Bibliotheca Sacra* 147 (July—September 1990): 351-64. Much of the controversy over Scofield's life pertains to

life, Scofield was introduced to Brooks. Brooks became Scofield's spiritual father by directing him in an intensive study [reading] of the Bible. It was through this study that Scofield came to his understanding of theology and Scripture. This understanding emphasized the elements of what was to become known as dispensationalism. Scofield became a Congregational pastor, founded the Central American Mission, developed a correspondence Bible course, played an increasingly prominent role in the Bible conference movement, and was a cofounder of the Philadelphia School of the Bible. Scofield's active involvement in such a variety of activities give testimony to his stature within the circles of emerging dispensationalism. His views eventually formed the bedrock for popular fundamentalism.[52]

Scofield's contribution to the creation of a normative apocalyptic vision was through his pulpit ministry, both in his role as pastor and Bible conference speaker, and most significantly through his publications. In 1888 he published *Rightly Dividing the Word of Truth*, a concise statement of his theological position. The book rapidly became a standard work in the Bible conference movement. This was followed by the *Scofield Reference Bible* in 1907. The reference Bible presented the distinctive elements of dispensationalism as the very themes of the Bible itself.

The work was a commercial success, but more importantly, it made the new apocalypticism standard fare among many white evangelical pietistic ministers, Sunday School teachers, missionaries, and parishioners, who maintained a loyalty to a simple faith in Scripture. In reaching the popular level of American Christianity, the reference Bible represented the triumph of Darbyism in America. Sandeen notes, "It is clear that the *Scofield Reference Bible* was uncompromisingly Darbyite dispensationalist in doctrine and taught the any-moment coming and

---

his reasons for leaving Kansas and government service in 1879. Scofield had developed a problem with alcohol abuse, and there were marital difficulties. He left his wife and two daughters in Kansas. His wife obtained a divorce in 1883.

52. For the importance of Scofield and his dispensationalism, see David O. Beale, *In Pursuit of Purity: American Fundamentalism Since 1850* (Greenville, S.C.: Unusual Publications, 1986), 35-39; George W. Dollar in his *A History of Fundamentalism in America* (Greenville, S.C.: Bob Jones University Press, 1973), 111, 164, 215, 268, appears to equate use of the *Scofield Reference Bible* with commitment to fundamentalism. Beale and Dollar both write as convinced fundamentalists. Also consult Sandeen, *Roots*, 222-24.

secret rapture of the church."[53] Scofield's achievement was to "put his predecessors' work into a most ingenious and assimilable form."[54] Scofield's reference Bible with William E. Blackstone's *Jesus Is Coming* (1908) and Clarence Larkin's *Dispensational Truth: Or God's Plan and Purpose in the Ages* (1918) set the norm for the popular new apocalyptic teaching.[55]

Normative apocalypticism was highly dependent upon Darby's formula but did not reproduce it exactly.[56] There were differences in the manner of dividing history into dispensations, soteriology, and, more important, in shifting the basic concern from ecclesiology to eschatology. Darby believed that the true Church was heavenly in nature, being united with Christ, but Scofield saw the true Church as those raptured at the Second Coming.[57] In the Scofield version of dispensationalism, a trustworthy Bible, containing prophecies to be literally understood, calls for an eschatology that determines other doctrinal issues. It was intensive in its futuristic, apocalyptic orientation.

The New Apocalyptic Perspective

Normative apocalypticism creates an expectation for a dynamic, any-moment fulfillment of prophecy. There is a constant, expectant scanning of the horizon for signs of God's hand about to intervene in history. Evangelism and mission work partakes of an urgency to gather as many souls as possible before the

---

53. Sandeen, *Roots*, 224.

54. Ibid.

55. Omitted from this chapter is a discussion of what is known as "ultradispensationalism," or Bullingerism. This variant dispensationalism had its origin in the work of Ethelbert W. Bullinger (1837-1913), a Church of England clergyman. Whereas normative dispensationalism holds the Gospels were not directed to the Church, ultradispensationalism further limits the application of the New Testament to the Church. They see themselves as true "Pauline" Christians. As such, they reject water baptism. For an overview of the history and theology of ultradispensationalism from a normative dispensational perspective, see John B. Graber, "Ultra-dispensationalism" (Th.D. diss., Dallas Theological Seminary, 1949).

56. For an extensive discussion of the relationship between Darby and Scofield, see Larry Crutchfield's *The Origins of Dispensationalism*. His entire work, based on his Drew University Ph.D. dissertation, is devoted to a study of this relationship.

57. See Vern S. Poythress, *Understanding Dispensationalists* (Grand Rapids: Zondervan Publishing House, 1987), 15-16, 19. This is an excellent volume for those interested in an overview of the state of current dispensational theology and hermeneutics.

rapture. Only the watchful and working will be ready for the Second Coming.

But there is an incongruity in maintaining a constant state of watchfulness within a theological system that holds the current Church age to be a prophetic parenthetic period, the end of which may be discerned by the identifying of certain "signs of the times."[58] A more consistent position would be to view the current age as a prophetic void terminated without warning by the rapture.

Since apocalyptists believe their vision to be the vision of the Bible, they are very concerned to display the reliability of Scripture, especially in terms of the fulfillment of prophetic passages. The dual concerns of Bible reliability and expectant watchfulness have led some dispensationalists to identify many contemporary events as signs of prophetic fulfillment. Their track record in this regard is not particularly encouraging. Prophetic identifications have been made with both World Wars, Kaiser Wilhelm, Tsar Nicholas, leaders of the Russian revolution, Protocols of the Elders of Zion, the Great Depression, the New Deal, Mussolini, Hitler, Stalin, the European Common Market, and the Persian Gulf War, all without confirming evidence.[59] The effect of missed predictions by these apocalyptic authors has not been assessed, but it would be reasonable to assume readers are disillusioned with prophetic teachers and Scripture once the sensational impact is dispersed. Such authors and teachers will be held accountable for the damage done to Christ's Church by irresponsible predictions.

There is one event that has been especially interpreted as proving Bible prophecy literally true. It was the establishment of the State of Israel in 1948. As Timothy Weber writes, "The existence of Israel revitalized premillennialism and gave it, at least in its own eyes, undeniable credibility."[60] Since the restoration of Israel had long been part of the new apocalyptic vision, this

---

58. See essay by Roger Hahn in this anthology.
59. Weber, *Living in the Shadow*, 105-26. Weber provides an extended review of this phenomenon. Also see Timothy P. Weber, "Happily at the Edge of the Abyss: Popular Premillennialism in America," *Ex auditu* 6 (1990): 87-100.
60. Weber, *Living in the Shadow*, 204.

event confirmed all elements of the vision and explains the consistent support given Israel by dispensationalists. The central place of the State of Israel in the popular apocalypticism is illustrated by the sales of Hal Lindsey's predictive books.[61]

There is a complex connection between apocalypticism, with its pessimism concerning civil and religious conditions, and its enthusiasm for the State of Israel. This connection extends beyond questions of biblical authority to encompass political activity. Notable leaders in the old religious right (i.e., Carl McIntire) and the new religious right (i.e., Pat Robertson, Hal Lindsey, and Jerry Falwell) have combined an activist political agenda with a theology anticipating a continual decline in the cultural influence of Christianity.[62] This anomaly is not unique to the new apocalyptists, but it is particularly sharp among them.

Trends in the New Apocalypticism

The predictive excesses and increasing sophistication of dispensational biblical scholars have caused significant modifications in normative apocalypticism. In the 1950s a rethinking of dispensationalism began. One reason for this rethinking was a revitalized nonsecret rapture premillennial eschatology. In the early years of the Niagara conferences, several participants advocated a posttribulational premillennialism, but this position disappeared from popular view with the ascendance of normative apocalypticism.

The appearance in 1956 of George Ladd's *The Blessed Hope* helped break the hold of normative apocalypticism on evangelical thought.[63] It was Ladd's contention that the pretribulation rapture theory was "beset by certain grave dangers."[64] Charles C. Ryrie in his *Dispensationalism Today* (1965) presented a recast

---

61. The most famous is *The Late Great Planet Earth* (Grand Rapids: Zondervan Publishing Co., 1970).

62. See Weber, *Living in the Shadow*, 218-22, 235-38; and George M. Marsden, *Understanding Fundamentalism and Evangelicalism* (Grand Rapids: William. B. Eerdmans Publishing Co., 1991), 100-121.

63. Ladd's *Blessed Hope* is cited earlier. For an earlier critique of an important dispensational concept by Ladd, see his *Crucial Questions About the Kindgom of God* (Grand Rapids: William B. Eerdmans Publishing Co., 1952).

64. Ladd, *Blessed Hope*, 164.

dispensationalism in response to the criticism of Ladd and others. Ryrie felt free to modify several of normative apocalyptiticism's biblical interpretations, but he retained the basic structure of the pretribulational premillennialism. The same is true of the notations in the New Scofield Reference Bible and Ryrie's study Bible.[65]

In contemporary dispensational theology, the normative apocalypticism of Scofield is undergoing careful scrutiny. Even attempts to maintain the basic structure are open to criticism. The process of reexamination and articulation is being advanced by the Dispensational Study Group that meets annually in conjunction with the Evangelical Theological Society.[66] In these circles, hallmarks of dispensationalism such as the sharp distinction between the Church and Israel are being muted, and in the area of prophetic fulfillment the idea of multiple fulfillments is gaining ground.[67] Even more fundamental has been the reexamination of the literal interpretation of Scripture. Contemporary evangelical biblical scholarship represents a challenge "to the meaningfulness of the label 'literal.'"[68] The very foundations of the Darby/Brooks/Scofield view are being undermined by dispensationalists themselves. Apparently normative apocalypticism is neither as stable nor biblically self-evident as Brooks, Scofield, and their immediate disciples thought.

Craig Blaising, a faculty member at dispensational Dallas Theological Seminary, has noted, "Dispensationalism is undergoing the process of doctrinal development in the work of contemporary dispensational scholars."[69] He further delineates, beyond biblical interpretation, three areas of systematic theology in which this process is necessary: ecclesiology (church), soteriology (grace), and eschatology.[70] This process of the reexamina-

---

65. Charles Caldwell Ryrie, The Ryrie Study Bible (Chicago: Moody Press, 1976).

66. Some discussions of the study group have appeared in the Grace Theological Journal vol. 10, no. 2 (fall 1989); and vol. 11, no. 2 (fall 1990).

67. See Poythress, Understanding Dispensationalists, 33-38, for an overview of recent developments in dispensational thought.

68. Blaising and Bock, Dispensationalism, 31.

69. Craig A. Blaising, "Development of Dispensationalism by Contemporary Dispensationalists," Bibliotheca Sacra 145 (July—September 1988): 279. Also consult his "Doctrinal Development in Orthodoxy," Bibliotheca Sacra 145 (April—June 1988): 133-40.

70. Ibid., 279-80.

tion of dispensationalism and its apocalyptic vision makes many earlier critiques of dispensationalism outdated. It is difficult to determine the extent to which this reexamination will affect the general pattern of pretribulational premillennialism with its secret rapture teaching, but the new apocalypticism may become the "old" new apocalypticism.[71]

Conclusion

Several points are evident from this brief overview of the historical development and spread of pretribulational premillennialism (dispensational eschatology). It is not of apostolic origin, nor is it self-evident in Scripture. It arose within a specific historical context in response to environmental factors. Darby and Brooks, both of whom claimed to come to their eschatological views through direct Bible study, actually came to their ideas under the influence of the millennial/prophetic discussions of their time. Darby's views formed the background for Brooks' acceptance of the new eschatology. The normative apocalypticism became popular with a segment of Protestants because it appeared to be biblical and it provided them with a means to understand the world about them.

Changes in culture and dispensational scholarship have called normative apocalypticism into question as an adequate theological system. Above all, the dispensationalists' desire to be completely faithful to Scripture has opened doubts about the adequacy of normative dispensationalism's ability to fully reflect biblical truth. There are important questions being raised. Dispensationalists and nondispensationalists need to explore and discuss these issues under the Spirit's leading for the edification of the saints.

---

71. For current discussions of dispensational theology, see Craig A. Blaising and Darrel L. Bock, *Progressive Dispensationalism* (Wheaton, Ill.: BridgePoint, 1993); Wesley R. Willis et al., ed., *Issues in Dispensationalism* (Chicago: Moody Press, 1994); Robert L. Saucy, *The Case for Progressive Dispensationalism* (Grand Rapids: Zondervan Publishing House, 1993); and Craig A. Blaising, "Changing Patterns in American Dispensational Theology," *Wesleyan Theological Journal* 29 (Spring-Fall 1994): 149-64.

■ **ROB L. STAPLES**

The Theology of the Final Consummation

*E*SCHATOLOGY AND HISTORY belong together. Clues to the meaning of last things are best discovered by a careful reading of past things. When theology severs these two, eschatology is left without safe moorings, cast adrift on a sea of speculation. An apt illustration of this is a man in a rowboat. The rower does not face the direction in which the boat is moving, but rather faces backward—to give him better leverage on the oars. Now and then he may glance over his shoulder to catch sight of his destination, but this can easily cause an unequal pull on the oars, which will throw the boat off course. Mainly his gaze is backward—toward where he has been rather than where he is going.

It is a bit like this in eschatology. The Christian hope is best understood and appropriated by an appreciation of the history of salvation, of the acts of God in creation and redemption. Of course, one needs to be mindful of the goal. But too much "looking over the shoulder" toward the future, as it were, may result in being thrown off course. The goal, the destination, has already been defined for us "back there" in the past, particularly in the life, death, and resurrection of Jesus Christ, which has occurred in the midst of the world's history. But again, that Christ event that defines our goal can be rightly understood only by letting our vision penetrate even farther back. Christ must be seen against the backdrop of the history of Israel and God's purposes unfolded therein. This is the case because the New

■ *Rob L. Staples is professor of theology at Nazarene Theological Seminary in Kansas City.*

Testament presents Jesus as the fulfillment of the expectation and destiny of Israel. Still again, the Christian's gaze must focus all the way back past the beginnings of Israel to creation itself. This is the case because the Bible as a whole knows no revelation of God the Redeemer that is not at the same time a revelation of God the Creator. All this is what we mean when we say that history and eschatology are of one piece, that past things offer the clearest clues to last things.

History, Time, and Eternity

Because Christian faith is eschatological in nature, history has been a problem for Christians. While the Hebrew scriptures had looked for the eschaton in the future, Christian faith claims that this eschaton has been realized proleptically (i.e., ahead of time) in Jesus Christ. But if the Christian claim is correct, why does history continue on with so little apparent difference being made in the world by this eschatological event that has already taken place? Furthermore, if this eschatalogical event is the goal of history, and if this event is already realized in Jesus Christ, why should the world continue? For Christian faith, history is bounded by a mystery of ultimate origin (creation) and ultimate future (the eschaton). Do such ultimate limits mean that time will come to an end? If so, what then? Or is there any "then"?

Such questions demand a proper understanding of time. It has become customary in theology to differentiate between two concepts of time, one *cyclical*, the other *linear*. The work of Swiss theologian Oscar Cullmann has highlighted this distinction.[1] According to Cullmann, the biblical understanding of time is linear, and thus is different from the cyclical understanding that predominated in nonbiblical religions.

Emil Brunner partly disagreed with Cullmann, pointing out that all persons everywhere have always experienced time as linear.[2] That is, everyone knows that time passes away, that the present moment is soon gone, never to return. There is tran-

---

1. Cf. Oscar Cullman, *Christ and Time: The Primitive Christian Conception of Time and History*, trans. Floyd V. Filson (Philadelphia: Westminster Press, 1950).
2. Emil Brunner, *Eternal Hope*, trans. Harold Knight (Philadelphia: Westminster Press, 1954), 42 ff.

sience and irreversibility of the movement from the "not yet" to the "now" and onward to the "no longer." Time is a one-way street; we experience it in a straight line.

However Brunner suggests that time as *experienced* is different from time as *understood*, and it is here that he can agree with Cullmann that nonbiblical religions understood time as cyclical. Although human beings *experience* time as linear, they may *interpret* this experience differently. In primitive myth-religions, human beings understood themselves from the point of view of nature, saw life as part and parcel of nature, as something integral to the ever-revolving natural processes, which have neither beginning nor end. Their conception of time was circular and nonlinear. This was a specific *interpretation* of time, an interpretation that made the experience of time part of an eternal process. Individuals are mortal and transient, but "the forces manifested in the revolving course of nature's life, like the latter itself, are eternal, unchanging, abiding, immortal."[3] Thus, mortal human beings, by seeing themselves as an integral part of nature, could believe that they shared somehow in the eternity of nature.

A much more sophisticated philosophical development of this idea arose in both India and Greece. But even this shift from mythical thinking to rational thinking did not advance people's apprehension of time beyond the cyclical view of myth. Thus, in classical antiquity, time was still seen as cyclical, symbolized as a circle. This circular concept of time is an expression of the fatalism that pervaded the literature, philosophy, and religion of the ancients. Life was understood as forever moving through the inevitable cycle of seedtime and harvest, birth and rebirth, life and death. The Book of Ecclesiastes, which reflects the influence of Greek thought forms, expresses the futility of such a cyclical understanding of time and history.

According to this cyclical view of history, events can be repeated, at least in essence, in contrast to linear time, which is transient, always moving forward, never returning. That which is true is timeless. What really matters is eternity, and eternity is

---

3. Ibid., 46.

timelessness. Time as we know it in human history is just a shadow of the eternal, or a dirty mirror that occasionally reflects eternal principles. For the ancient Greeks, the future could not be important because it could not bring anything that was essentially new.

This philosophical view, since its first appearance in the Vedanta of Hinduism and in the thought of Parmenides and Plato, and later in Neoplatonism, became an integral part of the Western history of ideas. It is this philosophy of timelessness that Cullmann sets in contrast to New Testament thought. In the New Testament, time is seen as linear. The symbol is a straight line, not a circle.

With some exceptions, most scholars agree that the concept of linear time derives from the Bible, that is, from the Judeo-Christian tradition. An awareness of historical movement was awakened when people found themselves standing in the wake of a promise from God and in anticipation of a future fulfillment of that promise. From the time of Abraham, the Hebrews looked forward to the land of promise. God fulfilled this promise in the Exodus—the dramatic rescue of His chosen people from Egyptian slavery, the giving of the Law to Moses, and the entry into Canaan, a land flowing with milk and honey. The Israelites looked back on these events in a special way because they saw the Exodus as the origin of Israel. On each weekly Sabbath and annually at Passover and Pentecost, God's creation of the Hebrew people was celebrated. But in contrast to the mythical-cyclical cultures, they did not reactualize this event. They simply *remembered* it. The Exodus could not be repeated, nor made contemporary through religious rites. But it could be remembered—and remembered it was—as God's mighty act in history.

History arises because God makes promises and fulfills them. The people of Israel often perceived themselves as suspended in the tension between promise and fulfillment, and this tension gave birth to the realization that the future can be different from the past. The prophets' proclamation of judgment served to deepen this promise-fulfillment scheme and directed attention more resolutely to the future. Amos, Ezekiel, and Isaiah looked forward to the Day of the Lord, a day in the future in which God would rendezvous with His people, destroy the evil powers, and bring His people to their destiny. Amos announced that the Day of the Lord would be one of calamity, a day of "darkness, not light" (Amos 5:18). With God, things had changed; the old basis of Israel's hope was now voided; instead of peace and prosperity, and a land flowing with milk and honey, judgment would be their lot.

This aspect of prophecy is called "eschatology" by Old Testament scholar Gerhard von Rad because it pronounces a break—a break "so deep that the new state beyond it cannot be understood as the continuation of what went before."[4] Thus Israel experienced God as one who could intervene in the events of history, and such interventions brought irreversible changes.

This has implications for the *freedom* both of God and of humanity. God was seen as not tied to the rhythms of nature or cycles of history. He could react to human activity on the plane of history by changing His mind. God and human beings are thus seen as engaged in free interaction with one another. To be free means that our decisions and choices will significantly determine our future. If everything has already been decided in eternity, then our decisions have no significance. Under the cyclical understanding of time, people were not free in this sense. They simply responded to the eternal principles to which the gods themselves were subject. But with the notion of an open future, in which even God may behave differently than He did in the past, in order to carry out His unchanging redemptive purpose, the idea of freedom was born.

With the idea of freedom came the notion of change as basic. The concept of a free God introduced to Western consciousness the possibility of fundamental change. In the mythical-cyclical view, change is superficial and only the eternal rhythms are real. For the Hebrews, change was real.

The fulfillment of God's promises in the Old Testament was believed by the prophets to be a fulfillment *within* history, within the temporal succession of events. With the development of apocalyptic literature, and in the New Testament, God's ful-

---

4. Gerhard von Rad, *Old Testament Theology*, 2 vols. (Edinburgh: Oliver and Boyd; and New York: Harper and Row, 1962-65), 2:115.

fillment came to be understood as coming at the *end* of history, at the conclusion of time. In the New Testament, the Day of the Lord is understood as the Parousia, the second coming of Christ. This event will mark the end of time as we know it. "What we have here is a vision of the entire scope of human temporality. History begins at creation and proceeds in a linear fashion toward a final end and goal supplied by God. We are located somewhere along this temporal continuum with the ability to look back in memory at the promise and forward in expectation of its fulfillment."[5]

Time has a beginning. It was created by God simultaneously with His creation of the world. Or, more accurately, the creation of the world *was* the creation of time, for time as we know it is determined by the earth's rotation, its revolution around the sun, and so forth. Just as God stands above the world, although immanent within it, He also stands above time, although immanent within it. Just as time has a beginning, it will have an end. It will be gathered up and fulfilled in eternity.

Although Cullmann's insight that biblical time is linear is a healthy corrective to the Platonic view, it has a weakness. To represent eternity as an endlessly long line of time, stretching backward before creation and forward beyond the eschaton, would seem to make the difference between God's mode of existence and that of His creatures merely quantitative, in which case He would not really be the Lord of time, and a "thousand years" for Him would not really be "like a day" (2 Pet. 3:8, NIV). It is only by the clear delineation of time as having a beginning and an end that the cyclical view of time is overthrown and the straight line and not the circle becomes its proper symbol. "Beginning and end are held together by God's eternal plan, and God manifests His Lordship over time just by the fact that from the beginning He aims at the end."[6] Both humanity and the cosmos are moving toward an ultimate goal, which is eternal life in the kingdom of God, made possible through the work of Jesus Christ in our time and in our space.

---

5. Ted Peters, *Futures—Human and Divine* (Atlanta: John Knox Press, 1978), 103.
6. Brunner, *Eternal Hope*, 53.

To speak of eternity, therefore, is to speak of God, who is Lord of time just as He is Lord of the world. Eternity is neither "endless time" nor "the negation of time." God has created it just as He has created the world, and He wills that time, like the world, shall be filled with His glory. He wills that the end of time shall be the consummation of time, time that is filled with eternity.[7]

At the beginning of this chapter it was stated that eschatology can best be understood from the standpoint of history. This claim involves Christology, for Christian faith holds that Jesus Christ is the center of history. As the center, He holds together the beginning and the end of history. But for Christian faith, Christology also involves cosmology. The apostle Paul, in two majestic passages (Eph. 1:7-23 and Col. 1:13-23), proclaims that Christ is both the ground and the goal of creation; He is both the world's "whence" and its "whither": "All things were created by him and for him" (Col. 1:16, NIV). It is striking that the apostle's bold assertions that the entire cosmos holds together in Christ occur in the midst of his confession of faith in the Atonement. In Christ we have "redemption through his blood, the forgiveness of sins" (Eph. 1:7, NIV; cf. Col. 1:14).

Three realities are thus bound together—the Atonement, the Creation, and the Consummation. The reason is obvious— sin blurs our vision until we can see neither our own personal ground nor the ground of the cosmos; neither our own personal destiny nor the destiny of the cosmos. Only in Jesus Christ and the atonement He made for sin, and the forgiveness that issues from it, do we apprehend the whence (the ground of creation) as identical with the whither (the goal of creation). The world is thus understood in light of the end for which it was created, and this can be no other than the goal of human history—Christ the hope of glory.

Somewhere in his fictional writings, C. S. Lewis has one of his characters say, "Worlds are not made to last forever." This is at least a half truth, but only a half truth. This world as we know it, and this time as we know it, will have an end. But ac-

---

7. Ibid., 54.

cording to the New Testament, it is not this world, but "this world *in its present form*" (1 Cor. 7:31, NIV, emphasis added) that is passing away. Nothing that God made is purposely omitted from the possibility of redemption. Thus the "end" is not to be seen as *finis* but as *telos*. It does not mean extinction, but fulfillment. "Whatever is true, whatever is honourable, whatever is just, whatever is pure, whatever is lovely, whatever is gracious, in the whole creation, in heaven and earth, is brought together in the future City of God. But it is renewed, recreated, and developed to its greatest glory. The material for it is present in this creation."[8] This is why Christian faith speaks of the end not as cessation but as "The Final Consummation."

Images of the Final Consummation

Several years ago this writer was privileged to spend some time touring the country of Austria—fortunately with friends who had been there before and knew their way around. We visited the cities of Vienna, Salzburg, Lenz, Innsbruck, and passed through many smaller towns. Among our activities, we toured the Hapsburg palaces and other historic landmarks connected with the old Holy Roman Empire. And because my companions had musical interests, we looked up Vienna's famed Opera House, listened to the Vienna Boys' Choir, and visited the burial places of Vienna's great musicians.

We marveled at the scenery as we drove through the countryside—crystal-clear streams flowing in the valleys and quaint villages nestled between majestic snow-capped mountain peaks, each village marked by the rust-red spire of the village church. And like a typical tourist, I kept my camera clicking and collected quite an impressive set of color photographs.

Now if I were to be asked about Austria by a group of persons who knew nothing of the country but wished to go there and who desired to know what the country looks like in order to be better prepared for the visit, I could do no better than show my pictures. When they had seen all the pictures, these

---

8. H. Bavinck, *Gereformeede Dogmatiek*, quoted in Hendrikus Berkhof, *Christ the Meaning of History* (Richmond, Va.: John Knox Press, 1966), 180.

would-be travelers would have a fairly accurate, although incomplete, concept of the sights and pleasures that await them in that land to which they go. But if I showed only pictures, accompanied with no road maps or travel schedule, these viewers would have no idea of the time or distance between one Austrian city and another, how far, for example, Innsbruck is from Salzburg, and how long it took to go from one to the other. They would not know the location of all the lovely villages I had seen and would not be able to date or clock my movements through the country or to estimate their own schedule. Nevertheless—and this is the important point—by seeing my photographs, these would-be travelers to Austria would have a much better idea of what the country is like than if I merely showed them a road map and shared my travel schedule.

This is a parable about eschatology! Amazingly, many Christians desire road maps and timetables of the future. Thus, they listen eagerly to preachers on "Bible prophecy," read books about the "late great planet Earth, look for the signs of Christ's coming, and seek to 'calendarize'"[9] the last things. But the Bible does not give us explicit road maps or specific timetables. It gives us mostly "snapshots" of the future—word pictures in brilliant color! These snapshots present a much better idea of what God's future will be like than any road map or timetable human prognosticators can draw up.

Today theologians are speaking more about eschatology than they did half a century ago. It is recognized that eschatology is not peripheral but central to Christian faith. But eschatology deals less with knowledge than with hope. Knowledge is expressed in defining, articulating, deducing, and judging, but hope is expressed in pictures, symbols, and images. Therefore (with the exception of millennialists, especially the premillennialists, particularly the dispensational premillennialists) theologians have learned to speak more in terms of snapshots or portraits than of road maps and calendars. Eschatology expresses the ultimate Christian hope for struggling humanity. In describ-

---

9. I have borrowed this term from Vernard Eller, *The Most Revealing Book of the Bible: Making Sense Out of Revelation* (Grand Rapids: William B. Eerdmans Publishing Co., 1974).

ing this hope, the Scriptures use a wealth of metaphors, symbols, and images that *describe* the future more than define it. Such images are richly suggestive, but their meaning cannot be reduced to precise definitions.

Due to the very nature of its subject, eschatological language is different from ordinary language. This is because eschatological knowledge is unlike that of ordinary objects. Of all the areas of theological language, that of eschatology is, of necessity, the most symbolic and metaphorical. The necessity lies in the fact that the Christian hope points to realities that lie beyond our present world of experience, and we are therefore without adequate and precise linguistic conduits for the expression of those realities.

It cannot be denied that the Bible presents eschatological truth mostly in the language of imagery. This is especially obvious in the apocalyptic sections of Scripture, but it is also true of eschatological language as a whole. It speaks of trumpets and clouds, a banquet, a feast, a wedding, a city with streets of gold and gates of pearl. The ancient Greeks developed the language of abstract thought, and Western civilization has worked wonders with it, mastering nature and raising technology to amazing heights. But we Westerners sometimes think this is the only true language. Both fundamentalists and modernists fall into the same trap, the former saying we must take everything in the Bible literally (although the stars may be actually meteors, for otherwise they could not fall to earth!), and the latter saying that we have advanced far beyond all this primitive thinking and such expressions need to be demythologized. But, as Berkhof reminds us, only poets are prepared to understand the Bible's eschatological language because the Bible, when it speaks about the last things, can speak only poetically.[10]

The function of eschatological language is not to give us specific information about the timing of future events (such as the end of the world) or of the geography of extraterrestrial places (heaven, hell). The metaphors, symbols, pictures, and images of eschatology serve to create in us an openness to the

---

10. Cf. Hendrikus Berkhof, *Well-Founded Hope* (Richmond, Va.: John Knox Press, 1969), 25-26.

mystery that lies beyond our power to comprehend or control. Taken together, these symbols and images produce an awareness of the presence and purpose of Christ in humanity and in the cosmos as a whole, and they provide insight into the kind of future that awaits the one whose life is hidden with Christ in God. Since the Bible deals with eschatological realities, it may be compared to a picture album, with each picture shedding light on the Christian's ultimate future.

What *are* these pictures? We will examine six of the major ones. We can even give each picture a title, beginning with the words, "The Final Consummation as . . ."[11] But it should be made clear at the outset that it would be a mistake to try to "calendarize" these pictures, to fit these pictures into a precise chronological order. These are all pictures of the same future, the same consummation, each taken from a different angle, showing a different aspect of that consummation. These are not to be seen mainly as successive phases of the future, but rather as differing illustrations of that one future.

1. The Final Consummation as Resurrection

Christian faith confesses, in the words of the Apostles' Creed, "I believe in the resurrection of the body." In this confession, we acknowledge the connection between eschatology and history. Resurrection is an authentic picture of our future, because it has already happened in our history. The resurrection of Jesus Christ may be seen as the central event of the New Testament and the event that gave birth to Christian faith. For the apostle Paul, Christ's resurrection presupposes a general resurrection at the end of history (1 Cor. 15:16), of which Christ's resurrection is the "firstfruits" (vv. 20-23). The New Testament continually makes the point that in raising Jesus from the dead, God had demonstrated His intent in the future to raise others who have been united with Christ through faith. The link between His resurrection and ours is indicated in passages such as John 5:25-26; Rom. 6:5; and 1 Pet. 1:3-4.

---

11. These titles are an adaptation of those in ibid. But Berkhof uses the phrase "the Future as," which I have changed in order to indicate more precisely what future is meant. He lists only five, and I have added the one on millennium, making a total of six.

Of course, belief in resurrection had already emerged in Judaism and was widely accepted by most groups in Jesus' day, with the exception of the Sadducees. The new element was that in the person of Jesus the expectation of a future resurrection had become a reality. Paul argues in 1 Cor. 15:12-20 that Christ's resurrection means nothing if it is not a promise of a future resurrection of the dead. Christ is not the *only* one to be raised; He is the *first* one.

How much can we learn about the nature of *our* resurrection from the fact of *His?* Here it is important to claim neither too much nor too little. We know that "what we will be has not yet been made known"; nevertheless, we know that "when he appears, we shall be like him, for we shall see him as he is" (1 John 3:2, NIV) and that He "will transform our lowly bodies so that they will be like his glorious body" (Phil. 3:21, NIV).

Despite a careful reserve in the New Testament, Christian faith has steadfastly proclaimed that the *body* will be raised. The creed does not tie belief in "life everlasting" to the idea of the "immortality of the soul," but rather to faith in the resurrection of the body. Here is highlighted the great difference between Platonic philosophy and biblical thought. The former was dualistic, believing that the real essence of the person was the soul, with the body being evil (or at least not essentially good), in which the soul was imprisoned during its sojourn in this earthly life. The soul alone was immortal and untouchable by death.

In contrast to this dualism, biblical thought sees the person as a unity.[12] "A body without a soul is a corpse, but a soul without a body is a ghost."[13] Life after death means the resurrection of the whole person. In the New Testament, only God is essen-

---

12. Much discussion about the difference between these two views was provoked by Oscar Cullmann's pamphlet "Immortality of the Soul or Resurrection of the Dead?" (English translation) London, 1958. Although this publication was quite influential, the debate continues, with some scholars arguing that the difference between the two is not as sharp as Cullmann claims, and insisting that the concept of immortality still has a certain usefulness in Christian faith. Cf. Stephen H. Travis, *Christian Hope and the Future* (Downers Grove, Ill.: InterVarsity Press, 1980), chap. 6, for a concise summary of views on the subject.

13. Berkhof, *Well-Founded Hope,* 36.

tially immortal (1 Tim. 6:16). When we human beings are spoken of as having immortality, it is derivative, something with which we must be "clothed" (1 Cor. 15:53-54, NIV). It is not something we already possess by nature but is given as a gift of grace made possible by Christ's own resurrection from the dead.[14]

Paul speaks of the resurrected body as a "spiritual body" (1 Cor. 15:44, NIV). Due to the limitations of our present experience, we cannot fully know what a spiritual body is. Whatever it is, it will be that which enables us to know and communicate with one another in the future state, just as this present physical body enables us to do so in this present physical world. In modern biblical studies and also in phenomenological thought, "body" means more than simply this physical stuff that can be weighed on a scale. "Whatever makes a person available to and intendable by other people *is* that person's body. . . . Whatever makes a person available to others is *truly* that person's body if it does the same for him or her, that is, if it also lets the person see who and what he or she is."[15]

Certainly the body of the risen Jesus (whatever it was like) made Him "available to and intendable by" the disciples in the Upper Room. His risen body was different from His pre-Easter body (sometimes He was not even recognized by those who had known Him in the flesh); thus, there was discontinuity. But there was also continuity (they could see His nail prints). His resurrection is the best clue to our own. "What we will be has not yet been made known"—except for this: "We shall be like Him." Berkhof says: "From the future a double light is thrown upon our life and our world here and now. God takes this earthly existence with deadly seriousness. Redemption does not mean that this existence will be thrown off like the first stage of a rocket. We do not reach our goal by escaping vertically, nor do we reach it by running on horizontally. This existence will not be ended, nor

Quote this.

---

14. John 5:28-29 seems to teach that even the wicked will be raised from the dead in order to be condemned. Cf. Acts 24:15.

15. Carl E. Braaten and Robert W. Jenson, ed. *Christian Dogmatics*, 2 vols. (Philadelphia: Fortress Press, 1984), 2:359.

will it be continued forever. It will be renewed on the analogy of Jesus who was raised from our old existence to a new life."[16]

In discussions concerning the resurrection of the dead, the "when" question usually arises: "Do we receive our resurrected bodies immediately after death, or must we await the last day and Christ's second coming?" It is possible to find scriptural proof texts that seem to validate either position. This is the case even within the Pauline writings. For instance, 2 Cor. 5:1-7 and Phil. 1:21-24 have often been understood as teaching that dying leads immediately to full participation with Christ and life with Him. But 1 Cor. 15:23 and Phil. 3:20-21 seem to place the resurrection at the last day.

It is striking that in Philippians Paul first seems to say that, upon dying, Christians will be immediately united with Christ, and then later in the Epistle he says that Christians expect to receive a new bodily existence when the Lord comes again. The apostle apparently did not see any contradiction between these two ways of describing the future. He doubtless understood—better than we Westerners do—that the believer's future can be described only in images, or "pictures" taken from different angles, and cannot be mapped out in strict chronological detail.

Whenever the resurrection is placed at the last day, then the question arises: "*Where* are persons *between* death and resurrection?*" But all such questions are "road map and calendar" ones and are therefore ruled out of court by the nature of eschatological language, as discussed above. If our claim is correct—that biblical eschatology works mainly with imagery that presents us with word pictures rather than timetables and road maps of the future—then Christian faith need not trouble itself with such matters. In any case, it is Christ who waits for us in death and at the end of the world. Christian faith may rest content and confident that—whatever the "whenever" and the "however"—the final consummation will mean "resurrection."

2. The Final Consummation as Second Coming

The term "Second Coming" is not found in the New Testament. But expressions like "I will come back" (John 14:3, NIV;

---

16. Berkhof, *Well-Founded Hope*, 37.

cf. Acts 1:11), "I am coming soon" (Rev. 22:12, NIV), and "He will appear a second time" (Heb. 9:28, NIV) have much the same meaning.

The key term is the Greek *parousia*, which means "presence" or "arrival" and is used in Scripture to designate the presence of the coming of Christ. Scripture leaves indefinite the time of the Parousia, sometimes seemingly giving mixed signals. Matthew writes that the disciples will not have completed their mission to the cities of Israel before the Son of Man comes (Matt. 10:23). But both Matthew (24:36) and Mark (13:32) declare that the hour is known to no one, not even to the Son of Man himself, but only to the Father. Elsewhere we are warned that He will come unannounced, as a thief in the night. And yet the Synoptics describe signs of His coming that should be clear enough to alert the watchful. The images used to describe the Parousia are derived from the description of the coming of the Son of Man in the apocalyptic tradition (Dan. 7:13-14), according to which the coming of the Son of Man will be the final event in the world's history, which will bring the establishment of the kingdom of God and the defeat of all hostile powers.

In its teaching about what we call the "Second Coming," the New Testament places the emphasis not on "second" but on "coming." To do otherwise would suggest that Christ was present once and then was gone and then will be present once more. Passages such as Matt. 24 and 25 may seem to describe such a situation. But when we balance this with other words found also in Matthew, such as "I am with you always, to the very end of the age" (28:20, NIV), we must conclude that the Parousia is a coming of one who is already present—a unique and complete manifestation of a presence we now see only partially and glimpse through a glass darkly.

The Parousia is not the return at the end of history of a Christ who has been absent from the world since the Ascension. It would even be improper to say that it is the *bodily* return of one who has been absent *in body*, because the New Testament describes the Church as His Body, and through the Church Christ has been "bodily" present in the world throughout the intervening centuries. Furthermore, we receive the Lord's "body" each time we receive the bread of the Eucharist, even though we would hold that it is received in a spiritual and not a physical manner.[17]

The Parousia signals the complete working out of that which was begun in the Resurrection. It is the final stage of the one unified coming of God to the world in a history that finds its center in Jesus Christ. From the perspective of Christology, it is the universal manifestation of Christ's Lordship. From the perspective of creation, it is the world's arrival at its destiny. The Second Coming is not the return of a Lord who has been absent, but the complete and victorious breaking through of a presence that has been hitherto partially hidden by the veil of sin and evil. By divine action, the resurrected mode of Christ's existence will in this event be so thoroughly actualized in the world that it can no longer be hidden.

Since the Parousia is ultimately the free act of God, and since God has revealed little explicit information concerning its temporal or spatial details, except that which is communicated through the Bible's eschatological language of imagery, we are once more dependent on that imagery. Much of this imagery is the language of worship. The Lord's Supper is but the foretaste of the final Kingdom, an "appetizer" for the Heavenly Banquet where "people will come from east and west and north and south, and will take their places at the feast in the kingdom of God" (Luke 13:29, NIV). The Parousia is the highest realization of that which even now takes place when we celebrate the Eucharist: God's communion with His people.

But in discussions of the Second Coming, just as in discussions of resurrection, "road map and calendar" questions arise. This is especially true within fundamentalist expressions of the faith. Here the Bible is seen as a book that contains many exact, although very dispersed, details about future events. Because of the dispersal of details, they must be searched out wherever they can be found and pieced together into some kind of order or system. These orders and systems are highly arbitrary. Scripture is viewed as a puzzle, and the pieces must be sought every-

---

17. Cf. Rob L. Staples, *Outward Sign and Inward Grace: The Place of Sacraments in Wesleyan Spirituality* (Kansas City: Beacon Hill Press of Kansas City, 1991), chap. 7.

where. Ironically, fundamentalism and liberalism draw their strength from the same root in Western thought. Neither has appreciation for the poetic, nor for the fact that realities that are much removed from our normal experiences in history must be understood in figurative language. This is a language that cannot be fully translated into the concrete factual language of the Western rational mind.

The "road map and calendar" questions have called forth a confusing multiplicity of theories concerning the relation between the time of the Second Coming and the millennium. The three main theories are premillennialism (the Parousia will precede the thousand-year reign of Christ), postmillennialism (the Parousia will follow the thousand-year reign), and amillennialism (there will be no literal, earthly, thousand-year reign). Within each theory there are variations and subtheories.

Creating further complexity are the debates concerning the chronological relationship of the Second Coming to the event (or series of events) mentioned in Scripture as "the great tribulation." So we have pretribulationists, midtribulationists, and posttribulationists! Then there is the question of the "rapture," which premillennialists usually distinguish from the Second Coming itself, which supposedly comes later. A subdivision of premillennialism is dispensationalism, which outperforms them all in the vigor with which it creates its "road maps" and its "calendars."

As already indicated, it is this writer's opinion that all such "cartographical" and "calendarizing" questions are ruled invalid by the eschatological language of imagery. But in this we can be confident: The Christ who is fully manifested in the Parousia will be none other than the Christ who was incarnate, crucified, and raised, and who has remained present in His Church through the Spirit. The new element will be its worldwide manifestation and scope, and its indescribable glory. In trying to describe it now we can only stammer in verbal images, but in faith we confess that, in His second coming, Christ will be visible over the whole world as the center of the redeemed humanity of whom He is the Creator.

3. The Final Consummation as Millennium

After what has been said above concerning the millennium, only a few comments are necessary here. The idea of "millennium" is found in only one New Testament passage: Rev. 20:1-6. Millennialism is a view named from the Latin term meaning "a thousand years." It is sometimes known as *chiliasm,* meaning the same thing in Greek (*chilias* means "thousand"). Millennialism, or chiliasm, is the view that there will be a period of a thousand years' duration in which Christ will reign visibly on earth immediately before the end of the world. As indicated above, there are various and sundry theories about how this thousand-year reign relates chronologically to the Second Coming, as well as what will be taking place during such reign.

We know that the Book of Revelation is a book filled with symbols and images. This is the nature of that genre of literature known as apocalyptic. Such images (candlesticks, angels, strange beasts, numbers, geometric figures, harlots, lambs, lions, stars, and so on) are generally understood in a symbolic or metaphorical sense. That is, they are not taken in exact literalness—they are seen as pointing to something beyond themselves. But symbolic expressions are not chosen arbitrarily; there is an inherent fitness in the symbol to express the reality to which it points.

For example, Christ is described as both a "lamb" and a "lion" in chapter 5, and the Christian consciousness perceives that in some ways Christ is like a lamb and in other ways He is like a lion. But everyone knows instinctively that this is metaphorical, not literal, language. Now what immediately strikes (or should strike) the serious student of New Testament eschatology is the fact that millennialists, for the most part, take literally the "thousand years" in Rev. 20:1-6, even though they may be willing to see the symbolic nature of practically everything *else* in the Book of Revelation.

Keeping in mind our earlier assertion that biblical eschatology deals in the language of imagery, how are we to understand the "thousand years"? The answer seems simple—almost *too* simple. But such shunning of simplicity characterizes much of our theologizing, in which we "turn wine into water" by taking the simple but sparkling truths of the gospel and transforming them into ideas that are complex but bland and unexciting.

The writer of Revelation did not have at hand a numerical concept higher than "one thousand." It was a great number for him and for other people of that time. They could not have comprehended the astronomical amounts of our national debts running into the trillions (we have enough trouble comprehending them ourselves!). They could have no appreciation of the size of the universe in which the distance between galaxies must be measured in light-years. A thousand was a superlative. Even when the truth the writer wishes to express calls for a much greater number, he still is forced to write in terms of "thousands," as when he describes the angelic chorus as "numbering thousands upon thousands, and ten thousand times ten thousand" (Rev. 5:11, NIV).[18]

So what may the writer of Revelation mean by the millennium? Maybe simply this: The Final Consummation, which we cannot possibly find words to describe adequately, will at the very least be the most magnificent and glorious thing we have ever experienced—it will be superlative! It will be the greatest! To describe the future of God's faithful people as a thousand years in which they will reign with Christ is to say, "It doesn't get any better than this—ever!"

Granted, there are chronological (i.e., calendar-like) elements in the millennium passage. But can we not see in the binding of Satan for "a thousand years" an affirmation of the enemy's total defeat? So why is he described as being loosed again after the thousand years and allowed to wreak havoc a while longer? Perhaps it is to drive home the point that no matter how much leeway Satan is given (note the Book of Job), no matter how much power he may seem to wield, God is ruler yet, and Christ is Conqueror of every foe. This is certainly the message the writer of the book would know that his intended readers near the end of the first century, and the first part of the second, would need to hear in the midst of the persecutions they were to endure.

---

18. This same principle holds true of the 144,000 mentioned in Rev. 14.

These are tentative conclusions. There may be better explanations. But any explanation, we believe, must be consistent with the nature of the language of imagery that oozes from practically every verse in this strange and mysterious vision that is the Book of Revelation.

4. The Final Consummation as Judgment

We must now turn to a more somber side of the Final Consummation. The word "judgment" introduces a dark and menacing shadow into the expectation of the future that the previous images have pictured for us in such brilliant hues. The Greek words for "judge," "to judge," and "judgment" (krites, kinein, and krisis) imply a negative action of condemnation. But the equivalent Hebrew words in the Old Testament (shofet, shafat, and mishpat) are much more positive. Shafat, for example, means "to establish the right order of things." That is what God purposes to do—establish a new order in a world that is crooked and bent, an order in which the power of evil will be defeated and righteousness will reign. It is the new order Mary sang about in her hymn of praise, in which rulers are brought down from their thrones, and the humble are lifted up (Luke 1:46-55).

Christians confess their hope for this new order, promised in conjunction with the birth of Christ in Bethlehem. But because this promised work of God is not yet completed and it is obvious that oppression and injustice are still pervasive, Christians confess their faith in a Last Judgment, in which that work will be finalized in conjunction with His return at the last day.

What can we know about the nature of this judgment? In the first part of this chapter we claimed that eschatology finds its best clues in history. God's action in the future will therefore be consistent with His action in the past. There is yet little to be seen of the new order sung about in Mary's Magnificat, but faith perceives just enough of God's judging in history to take courage for the future. In the history of Israel, in the work of the incarnate Christ on earth, and in the work of the Holy Spirit in the world today, we see preambles of God's eventual liberating judgment that will forever make straight this crooked and disrupted human existence.

Central in this historical perspective is the New Testament proclamation that "God is love." Since He loves every person, He treats the actions of each person as significant. This truth is safeguarded by the idea that every person must eventually give account to God for his or her actions. Since true love never forces itself on its object, God's love means that we have freedom to accept or reject His love. To reject the idea of condemnation would mean a rejection of freedom.

By what criterion will we be judged? Surely the biblical witness is clear: We will be judged on the basis of our response to the love of God revealed to us in Christ. That response has both vertical and horizontal dimensions. The vertical has to do with whether or not we are in a trustful, responsible, loving relationship with Jesus Christ. The horizontal has to do with our works (2 Cor. 5:10; Matt. 12:36). This does not contradict the fact that we are saved by grace through faith (Eph. 2:8), for in the New Testament, works are seen not as the basis of salvation but as evidence of the reality of our relationship to God.

Matt. 25, by the use of three parables of the judgment, portrays both the vertical and horizontal dimensions of the response according to which we will be judged. In the parable of the 10 virgins, the criterion by which we are judged is pictured as the watchfulness and carefulness with which we make preparation in this life for the life beyond. In the parable of the talents, the issue is whether or not in this life we use wisely what we have been given. And in the parable of the sheep and the goats, the criterion is the degree of our compassion for our fellow human beings, even when we were not aware that we were ministering to the Lord.

The New Testament describes judgment as both a reality in this present life (John 3:18; Rom. 1:18-32) and a reality at the last day. Regarding the latter, the image of "The Great Assize" has inspired the imagination of artists, writers, and preachers. It is portrayed graphically in Rev. 20:11-15. Since the basis of judgment is the quality of our relationship with Christ, we can see the link between the present and future aspects of judgment. The Last Judgment will be the divine ratification of the relationship (either positive or negative) with Christ that we have chosen in this life. But the Last Judgment will be different from the pream-

bles of it that we see now. Judgment in this present life is not final. As long as life continues, persons created with freedom can
still change sides. The loving purpose of the present judgments
of God is to bring about just such a result. Although the Bible
says little about the matter, there is no biblical evidence that the
final choices made in this life are reversible after death.

Once again, "calendar and road map" issues arise. When
and where does the Last Judgment take place? Will all humanity be gathered together in one place and at one time to be
judged? Or does each person face his or her judgment at, or immediately after, death? Paul's declaration that "we must all appear before the judgment seat of Christ" (2 Cor. 5:10, NIV) does
not give us the "when" or tell us whether we will appear there
individually or all together in one time and place. The New Testament presents both images. As mentioned above, Rev. 20:11-
15 and other passages may seem to present the "Great Assize"
scenario. But the statement of Heb. 9:27—"Man is destined to
die once, and after that to face judgment" (NIV)—may be read
as implying that when persons die they go to their judgment,
although it is open to either interpretation. These are the kinds
of questions we have suggested that have no validity, due to the
eschatological language of imagery. We are given snapshots,
pictures, portrayals of what the Final Consummation will be
like. But we are not given schedules, timetables, or locations.

Still other issues present themselves. What about persons
who have never heard the gospel, or those who heard it inade-
quately presented? What about the mentally ill, or those who
suffer such socioeconomic deprivation that they never had
much chance to show love to neighbor or help build community? And what about the sincere and devout adherents of other
world religions? Such persons can be trusted to the God of love
who will deal with them not arbitrarily but consistent with His
nature as holy love. The parable of the sheep and the goats
(Matt. 25:31-46) seems to teach that two big surprises of the
judgment will be (1) that many who did not know it in this life
will find that they have been on God's side all along, and (2)
many who thought themselves righteous will be cast out.

This brings us to another dark and somber snapshot of the
Final Consummation:

5. The Final Consummation as Separation

Jean Paul Sartre, the French atheistic existentialist philosopher, said, "Hell is other people!" I am inclined to say just the opposite: "Hell is to be finally and utterly *alone*." Is that biblical? Well, there are no proof texts that say precisely that. But it is a truth inherent in the biblical doctrine of sin. Sin is consistently described in the Bible and in the historic Christian tradition as self-centeredness or self-rule. Sin is egocentricity rather than exocentricity—finding the meaning of life in self rather than in others and the Other. Sin is wanting to be God over one's own life, determining for oneself what is good and what is evil (Gen. 3:5, 22).

Thus the biblical understanding of sin gives us insight into the meaning of hell. God does not send men and women to hell; hell is what we choose for ourselves. God did not even create hell for humankind; it was made "for the devil and his angels" (Matt. 25:41, NIV). But God created us with freedom. When in our freedom we choose a self-centered existence, God allows us to have what we want. It is God's respect for human freedom that makes hell possible. Hell expresses the possibility that a person can reject the grace and love of God and thus choose isolation rather than communion. It is the ultimate expression of our own choice against God.

In *The Great Divorce*, C. S. Lewis describes the condemned as those to whom God, after much patience, finally says, "Your will be done."[19] Hell is not God's punishment for rejecting Christ and choosing the wrong road; it is where the road leads. Hell is the Father's heartbroken willingness to give His prodigal children what they so relentlessly demand. Hell is the expression not of God's anger but of His agony, an agony that says, "I will give you what you want; in life you wanted your own way, you lived only for self, you wanted nothing but self—now take it." It is not too far-fetched to say: "If I go to hell, I will be the only one there." For hell is utter self-chosen aloneness. Hell is having cut oneself off—from God, from fellow human beings, and from God's good creation.

---

19. C. S. Lewis, *The Great Divorce* (New York: Macmillan, 1946).

The fact of freedom is a stumbling block to some theologians. They believe that a doubt is cast on the power and persistency of God's love by the possibility that one can say an absolute "no" to God. These theologians opt for "universalism," the belief that God will have no permanent problem children, that His love will continue to pursue, even after death and through countless aeons if necessary, until the last holdout finally and freely surrenders to love. We can hope that this is the case, but there is no clear biblical evidence either (1) that we are given further chances after death to respond to God, or (2) that everyone will be saved. We are sobered by the realization that the most severe words in the Bible about the final separation of the wicked from the righteous are not found in the Old Testament (sometimes regarded as severe), but in the New Testament. And in the New Testament the most severe words come from the mouth of Jesus himself.

Whereas universalists hold that freedom casts doubt on the power of God's love, others would hold the opposite—namely, that universalism casts doubt on the reality of freedom. Wesleyan theology holds that our freedom to choose is not a natural freedom, but one which is the gift of prevenient grace. But if we are graciously given a *real* freedom, doesn't this mean that we must be given the option of finally, absolutely, and irrevocably rejecting God?

Those who are persuaded by that line of reasoning fall into two groups—those who believe that punishment for the wicked is conscious and everlasting, and those who believe in what is called "conditional immortality."[20] The latter view is sometimes called "annihilationism," indicating that only the righteous receive eternal life, the unrighteous being annihilated, that is, just ceasing to be. Within this theory, there are two further possibilities: Some would hold that the unrighteous do not exist beyond death. Others would say that existence may continue, and God may continue to pursue, even after death and through countless

---

20. "Conditional immortality" would be a misleading term if we did not keep in mind what was stated earlier—that immortality is not something we have by nature, but is given by God.

aeons if necessary, but the sinful person in a freely chosen self-rule, by turning more and more into the self, becomes a smaller and smaller bundle of ego and shrinks to nothing, resisting to the end the wooing of God, burning out like a meteor hurling through the earth's atmosphere.

Besides the reality of freedom, conditional immortality has been argued for on other grounds as well[21]: *(a)* The Bible does not teach that the soul is naturally immortal, but that resurrection is the gift of God. Therefore God raises those who love Him, and the rest are left in death. *(b)* The biblical images such as "fire" and "death" indicate destruction. *(c)* Although the state of the lost is sometimes spoken of in the Bible as "eternal punishment," the word "eternal" signifies the permanence of the *result* of judgment rather than the continuous operation of the act of punishment itself. "Eternal punishment" therefore means an act of judgment whose results are irreversible; it does not mean that the act of punishment goes on forever. *(d)* An everlasting punishment would involve an eternal cosmological dualism that is incompatible with the Christian's faith in a Final Consummation in which God is to be "all in all."

Regardless of the merits of the doctrine of conditional immortality, a growing number of evangelical scholars have sought to defend it. Among them are John R. W. Stott,[22] Philip Edgcumbe Hughes,[23] Edward Fudge,[24] and Clark Pinnock.[25] Some Wesleyans have been advocating the doctrine even longer—for example, Joseph Agar Beet at the turn of the century[26] and E. Stanley Jones in the '60s.[27] A more recent Wesleyan

---

21. Cf. Travis, *Christian Faith*, 134-35, of which these are a summary.

22. John R. W. Stott, "Judgment and Hell," in David L. Edwards and John R. W. Stott, *Evangelical Essentials: A Liberal-Evangelical Dialogue* (Downers Grove, Ill.: InterVarsity Press, 1988), 312-29.

23. Philip Edgcumbe Hughes, *The True Image: Christ as the Origin and Destiny of Man* (Grand Rapids: William B. Eerdmans Publishing Co., 1989), chap. 37.

24. Edward Fudge, *The Fire That Consumes* (Houston: Providential, 1982).

25. Clark Pinnock, "Fire, Then Nothing," *Christianity Today* 31:5 (March 20, 1987), 40-41, and "The Destruction of the Finally Impenitent," *Criswell Theological Review* 4:2 (Spring 1990), 243-59.

26. Joseph Agar Beet, *The Immortality of the Soul* (London: Hodder and Stoughton, 1901).

27. E. Stanley Jones, *In Christ* (New York: Abingdon Press, 1961), 360-66.

defense of the doctrine is by Canadian Nazarene scholar Vern A. Hannah.[28]

But such issues as these are, in a sense, calendar issues. The biblical images give us colorful snapshots of the awfulness of being separated from God. But to debate the duration of this separation (a timetable question) is almost as pointless as to debate its location (a road map question), not to mention the temperature of "unquenchable fire" and the biological makeup of "undying worms." These are not the real issues. Earlier we said that the judgment is to be decided in terms of one's relationship with God. The most significant thing about the destiny of the finally impenitent is that they will be separated from God and His Son. Could a worse hell be imagined?

6. The Final Consummation as Glorification

This perusal of biblical snapshots of the Final Consummation can be brought to a close with one that is much brighter that the previous two. Among the persistent aspirations of the human race is the vision of a time of peace and blessedness when the suffering and agony of human history will be overcome. When we confess our faith in the words of the Apostles' Creed, we conclude with the words "I believe in . . . the life everlasting. Amen." This is the summation of the Christian's hope for the future.

But we could not so confidently confess this hope were it not based on realities in the history of salvation and in our own personal history (recall the illustration of the man in a rowboat at the beginning of this chapter). The "life everlasting" has come already in the Christ who was willing to lose His life for the sake of the kingdom of God. Because of His utter self-sacrifice, God raised Him from the dead. And this life has come to all who have been "buried with him through baptism" and raised to a "new life" (Rom. 6:4, NIV), having believed in Him as "the resurrection and the life" (John 11:25, NIV). In the writings of John, eternal life is almost completely seen as a life here and now—"eternal life begun below," as an old gospel song expresses it. Yet it must be said that all these present gifts point us

---

28. Vern A. Hannah, "Death, Immortality and Resurrection: A Response to John Yates' 'The Origin of the Soul,'" *The Evangelical Quarterly* 72:3 (July 1990), 241-51.

toward the future. "If only for this life we have hope in Christ, we are to be pitied more than all men" (1 Cor. 15:19, NIV).

We have given the title "glorification" to this picture of the Final Consummation. In Scripture, the words "glory" and "glorification" are rich in meaning. In the Old Testament, "glory" belonged to God alone. When Moses prayed to be shown God's glory, God hid him in a cleft of the rock and covered him with His hand so that he could not see God's face (Exod. 33:18-23). But the New Testament proclaims the fact that the glory of God has been revealed to us in the face of Jesus Christ (2 Cor. 4:6)— and that through the Spirit we may reflect that same glory (2 Cor. 3:18). Concerning the future life, glorification stands for our participation in a renewed form of human existence that has been made known to us in the risen Christ.

In the language of worship and piety, the most common term for this expectation is "heaven." In essence, heaven is to be understood not as a freestanding, preexisting place, but as the final, fulfilling relationship between God and His creation that has been realized in Christ and remains to be realized in the rest of humanity. Just as hell was created "for the devil and his angels," heaven is that which Jesus went to prepare for us when He returned to the Father (John 14:3). Heaven, for us, is the consequence of His ascension.

The "life everlasting" has been described in different ways in the biblical and historical traditions. Roman Catholics have longed for the "beatific vision" of seeing God face-to-face. The Epistle to the Hebrews speaks of a "rest" for God's people, a meaningful metaphor for people who struggle, sorrow, and labor in this life. But rest may not be the aspiration of everyone. In a world where human labor is often an unfulfilling drudgery, many people long for creative tasks that are meaningful, where in Kipling's words,

> Each for the joy of the working,
> And each, in his separate star,
> Shall draw the Thing as he sees It
> For the God of Things as they are![29]

---

29. Rudyard Kipling, "L'Envoi."

And in a divided world, torn by strife, where there is loneliness and alienation, a more meaningful metaphor for many people today is that of community. This community or corporate image is central. Concepts of rest, creativity, and beatific vision emphasize individuality. Of course, individuality is significant. Unlike the various forms of pure mysticism, Christianity looks for a future where there is interpersonal dialogue and relationship rather than the loss of identity through being absorbed into the Absolute. But, as we already see in this present life, true individuality develops only within community. The corporate dimension is the controlling one in eschatology.

Furthermore, to the corporate must be added the *cosmic*, for the whole world shares in God's redemptive plan. For the completion of that divine plan we wait "in eager expectation" and "in hope that the creation itself will be liberated from its bondage to decay and brought into the glorious freedom of the children of God" (Rom. 8:19, 20-21, NIV). The corporate and the cosmic dimensions of the Christian hope lead us to a final brief consideration.

The Goal of History: The Kingdom of God

The Bible is rich with images depicting life everlasting as an active participation with all the redeemed in a perfect fellowship, with Christ as the center, where "people will come from east and west and north and south, and will take their places at the feast in the kingdom of God" (Luke 13:29, NIV).

The concept of the kingdom, or reign, of God was the central theme of the teaching of Jesus. This theme points us back to the claim made in the first part of this chapter, that history and eschatology belong together. The New Testament understands the kingdom of God in three tenses: The Kingdom is a *past* reality; God has established His reign on earth through the life, death, and resurrection of Jesus. To do so was His purpose in the history of Israel and in the creation of the world itself. The Kingdom is a *present* reality; God continues His activity of Kingdom-building through the work of the Holy Spirit in the Church. God's rule is therefore now within the grasp of all who will reach out and receive it. And the Kingdom is a *future* reality, for whose coming Jesus taught us to pray.

As we pray for the coming of God's kingdom, we do so in the midst of a world and in the midst of a history where evil seems not to subside. We nevertheless believe in the promise of ultimate victory. We know we have "redemption through his blood, the forgiveness of sins" (Eph. 1:7, NIV). We believe in the promise of our resurrection from the dead, and we live in hope for the fulfillment. We believe in, and hope for, the Second Coming—the triumphant worldwide manifestation of Christ's presence. We believe in, and hope for, an everlasting reign of universal peace, and the final total defeat of all the evil powers. We believe in the Final Judgment, and in the separation of those who resolutely and finally refuse the offer of salvation. We believe in the promise of glorification, a prospect that is totally indescribable from our present perspective, but for which we wait and hope with glad expectation.

And we believe the end will come, but such an end will be the *telos* of creation and the fulfillment of history. This is why we call it the Final Consummation. We believe that "this world in its present form" will pass away (1 Cor. 7:31, NIV) and that all that is good about this present existence will be incorporated into a new heaven and a new earth. This new cosmos will be free of all conflict, when Christ "hands over the kingdom to God the Father after he has destroyed all dominion, authority and power" (1 Cor. 15:24, NIV).

But for now we live between the times. God's kingdom *has come* and *is here* among us, and the whole creation is invited to share in the blessings of redemption. God's kingdom is *yet to come*, and all creation is invited to press forward toward the Final Consummation, when God's purpose will be fulfilled "according to his good pleasure, which he purposed in Christ, to be put into effect when the times will have reached their fulfillment—to bring all things in heaven and on earth together under one head, even Christ" (Eph. 1:9-10, NIV).

Printed in the United States
836400004B